CATHARINE TROTTER COCKBURN

broadview editions
series editor: L.W. Conolly

CATHARINE TROTTER COCKBURN

PHILOSOPHICAL WRITINGS

edited by Patricia Sheridan

broadview editions

©2006 Patricia Sheridan

All rights reserved. The use of any part of this publication reproduced, transmitted in any form or by any means, electronic, mechanical, photocopying, recording, or otherwise, or stored in a retrieval system, without prior written consent of the publisher—or in the case of photocopying, a licence from Access Copyright (Canadian Copyright Licensing Agency), One Yonge Street, Suite 1900, Toronto, Ontario M5E 1E5—is an infringement of the copyright law.

Library and Archives Canada Cataloguing in Publication

Trotter, Catharine, 1679-1749

    Catharine Trotter Cockburn : philosophical writings / edited by Patricia Sheridan.

Includes bibliographical references and index.
ISBN 1-55111-302-3

    1. Trotter, Catharine, 1679-1749—Philosophy. 2. Philosophy, British—18th century. I. Sheridan, Patricia, 1964- II. Title.

B1301.T76 2006   192   C2006-901197-4

Broadview Editions

The Broadview Editions series represents the ever-changing canon of literature in English by bringing together texts long regarded as classics with valuable lesser-known works.

Advisory editor for this volume: Jennie Rubio

Broadview Press is an independent, international publishing house, incorporated in 1985. Broadview believes in shared ownership, both with its employees and with the general public; since the year 2000 Broadview shares have traded publicly on the Toronto Venture Exchange under the symbol BDP.

We welcome comments and suggestions regarding any aspect of our publications—please feel free to contact us at the addresses below or at broadview@broadviewpress.com.

North America
Post Office Box 1243, Peterborough, Ontario, Canada K9J 7H5
3576 California Road, Post Office Box 1015, Orchard Park, NY, USA 14127
Tel: (705) 743-8990; Fax: (705) 743-8353;
email: customerservice@broadviewpress.com

UK, Ireland, and continental Europe
NBN International, Estover Road, Plymouth PL6 7PY UK
Tel: 44 (0) 1752 202300   Fax: 44 (0) 1752 202330
email: enquiries@nbninternational.com

Australia and New Zealand
UNIREPS, University of New South Wales
Sydney, NSW, 2052 Australia
Tel: 61 2 9664 0999; Fax: 61 2 9664 5420
email: info.press@unsw.edu.au

www.broadviewpress.com

Typesetting and assembly: True to Type Inc., Mississauga, Canada.

Broadview Press gratefully acknowledges the financial support of the Government of Canada through the Book Publishing Industry Development Program for our publishing activities.

PRINTED IN CANADA

Contents

Acknowledgements • 7
Introduction • 9
Catharine Trotter Cockburn: A Brief Chronology • 29
A Note on the Text • 31

A Defence of Mr. Locke's Essay of Human Understanding, *wherein its Principles, with reference to Morality, Revealed Religion, and the Immortality of the Soul, are considered and justified: In answer to some Remarks on that Essay* (1702) • 35

Remarks upon some Writers in the Controversy concerning the Foundation of Moral Virtue and Moral Obligation; particularly the Translator of Archbishop King's Origin of Evil, *and the author of the* Divine Legation of Moses (1743) • 87

Remarks upon the Principles and Reasonings of Dr. Rutherforth's Essay on the Nature and Obligations of Virtue: In vindication of the contrary principles and reasonings, enforced in the writings of the late Dr. Samuel Clarke (1747) • 147

Appendix: Selections from Cockburn's Correspondence • 225

Select Bibliography • 259

Index • 263

Acknowledgements

First and foremost, I wish to express my deepest appreciation to my husband Gerry for all his support and help. He has been available to listen, to read, and to advise, and for all these efforts I thank him.

I would also like to thank Tom Lennon, for originally encouraging me to pursue this project. As well, I owe a debt of gratitude to Margaret Atherton, who originally suggested that I read Cockburn's works. Her advice inspired my doctoral research and led me to my work on this edition.

I must also thank my research assistants Allen Plant, Ileana Szymanski, and Alexandra Morrison, all of whom put in many hours helping out with the more tedious aspects of this work. I would also like to thank University of Guelph Office of Research for granting me the funds to make my research assistants a real possibility.

Introduction

Catharine Trotter Cockburn (1679–1749) was one of those rare women of the early eighteenth century who wrote and published philosophical works. It was unusual enough at this time for women to engage in philosophical debate, but it was even more unusual for a woman to publish philosophical writings. There existed at this time a significant disparity between the intellectual lives of men and women—a disparity that is all the more pronounced in light of the pace of intellectual innovation in the period. The early modern period (which in philosophy generally refers to the period spanning the sixteenth through the eighteenth centuries) was a time of tremendous scientific and philosophical activity in Europe. There are different names given to intellectual movements within this period: the "Age of Reason" (so called because human reason was seen by many as an instrument for liberation from religious, scientific, and political dogmatism); the "Enlightenment" (so called because many thinkers of this period saw themselves ushering in a new phase in human history—one dominated by rational discourse and the free exchange of ideas, instead of what they saw as the brutality of the Middle Ages, and entering a period of individual self-expression, and religious and political toleration); and the "Scientific Revolution" (so called because this period saw the introduction of empirical standards of evidence, language, and theorizing, which laid the foundation for science as it is known today). This age is dominated by the philosophers and scientists of the period (although at this time there was little distinction between the two), who saw themselves as breaking free of the medieval mindset and ushering in a new "modern" way of thinking about the world. They questioned the dogmatic views of medieval and renaissance thinkers, replacing the old philosophical and scientific systems with new systems based on the ideals of objectivity and reason. In this period Francis Bacon revolutionized scientific method, René Descartes ushered in the spirit of rationalism, Isaac Newton introduced calculus and a new physics, and John Locke and Jean-Jacques Rousseau popularized the Enlightenment ideals of toleration and liberalism. In the *History of Western Philosophy*, Bertrand Russell summed up the intellectual significance of the period as follows: "The modern world, so far as mental outlook is concerned, begins in the seventeenth century."[1]

The Enlightenment spirit did not, however, extend to the situation of women. This was very much a man's world, and intellectual ambitions among women were generally discouraged. In 1583, in his pedagogical work on the education of Christian youth entitled *Dell'educazione cristiana dei figliuoli*, Silvio Antoniano recommended the following guidelines regarding women's education: "As to those of humble status, it is not necessary that they even know how to read; as to those of middle condition, do not teach them to read; as to noblewomen who must be mothers to the children of grand families, I would certainly approve their learning to read a little ... [*mediocramente*] ... and do some arithmetic."[2] In 1762 in his work *Emile*, Jean-Jacques Rousseau wrote disparagingly of the intellectual woman:

> I would a thousand times rather have a homely girl, simply brought up, than a learned lady and a wit who would make a literary circle of my house and install herself as its president. A female wit is a scourge to her husband, her children, her friends, her servants, to everybody. From the lofty height of her genius, she scorns every womanly duty.[3]

The ideal of womanhood embodied the qualities of modesty and submissiveness to husband and father. Though some women were allowed to educate themselves, they were largely discouraged from making that learning public. It was considered not only immodest to be an intellectual woman, but also detrimental to one's marriage prospects. The father of eighteenth-century philosopher Marie du Chatelet wrote that he "argued with her in vain; she would not understand that no great lord will marry a woman who is seen reading every day."[4] If a woman was taught to read, her reading was restricted to devotional books and moralistic works. Women were trained to be wives and mothers,

---

1 Bertrand Russell, *History of Western Philosophy* (London: George Allen & Unwin Ltd, 1961) 512.
2 Margaret L. King, *Women of the Renaissance* (Chicago: U of Chicago P, 1991) 186.
3 Jean-Jacques Rousseau, *Emile*, trans. Barbara Foxley (London: J.M. Dent, 1974) 371.
4 Bonnie S. Anderson and Judith P. Zinsser, *A History of Their Own*, vol. II (New York: Harper & Row, 1988) 88.

and reading, if it were to contribute to this end, had to emphasize the virtues necessary for such an occupation. The eighteenth-century political theorist Adam Smith wrote as follows of the goals of women's education: "to improve the natural attractions of their person, or to form their mind to reserve, to modesty, to chastity, and to economy; to render them both likely to become mistresses of a family, and to behave properly when they have become such."[1] For Smith, this applies only to women of the leisure classes. Women of the very lowest class were not to be educated at all. Their lives should be devoted to menial labour. For a woman to have access to education, she had to enjoy a certain number of rare privileges: she had to be of a social class that allowed the time for study; she also needed a father, brother, or husband who supported her education. Otherwise, achieving even a minimal level of education was virtually impossible.

It was in this social climate that Catharine Trotter Cockburn took up her pen to write philosophy. Cockburn, of course, was not the only woman philosopher of her day to engage in intellectual activities. A careful search through microfilm catalogues or rare manuscript collections, will unearth works by other European women. However, these are few in number and they tend to be short, single works. Few women published their own philosophical ideas (if they did write, they very often did so primarily in notebooks and personal correspondence). So Cockburn's background is not typical. She seems to have been born of fairly humble origins and we know little of her intellectual mentors. Her biographer tells us that she was both precocious and self-motivated, but we can only surmise that to the extent to which the members of her home environment were supportive of her endeavours. We also know from her biography and letters that she knew people who engaged in intellectual discussion, and who took an interest in her intellectual development.[2] However, considering her situation and the prohibitive atmosphere for women

---

1 Adam Smith, *An Inquiry into the Nature and Causes of the Wealth of Nations* (1776), Chapter 1, part 3, article II.
2 Her friend, Elizabeth Burnet, a theologian and wife of the powerful Bishop Gilbert Burnet, wrote in a letter to John Locke that Cockburn wrote plays "partly to gratify her humour, that was studious, but more I believe to help her to live ... but as you will allow by late little book [the *Defence of Mr. Locke's* Essay, included in this volume], 'tis a great pity her studies are not better directed" (John Locke, *Selected Correspondence*, ed. Mark Goldie [Oxford: Oxford UP, 2002] letter 3153, p. 305).

intellectuals, Cockburn is notable for the quality of the writings she published in her lifetime. These included, but were not limited to, philosophy. In addition to the three philosophical works included here, Cockburn was a successful playwright and also published several theological works. All the while, she kept up a voluminous intellectual correspondence.

Biographical Background[1]

Cockburn was born in London on 16 August 1679[2] to Captain David Trotter, a commander in the royal navy, and his wife Sarah, née Ballenden. Her father died of the plague while on mission in Turkey in 1683. The family had never been rich and it was this voyage (according to Cockburn's biographer Thomas Birch) that was going to make his fortune. The family suffered gravely as a result: not only did they lose all the money Trotter had himself advanced to his seamen, but soon after the tragedy, the goldsmith who held the family monies in England went bankrupt. The family was forced to live on meager pensions provided by the government in recognition of Trotter's service to the navy. There was no money for tutors, and as a result Cockburn's education was acquired through her own lively intellect and determination. According to Birch she "showed early marks of her genius."

---

1 The following biographical information is based largely on Thomas Birch, *The Life of Mrs. Cockburn*, in *The Works of Mrs. Catharine Cockburn, Theological, Moral, Dramatic and Poetical*, ed. Thomas Birch (London: J. and P. Knapton, 1751) i–xlviii. Birch's biography is currently the definitive source regarding the facts of Cockburn's life.

2 There is some debate regarding Cockburn's birth date. Margaret Connor, in her article entitled "Catharine Trotter: An Unknown Child?" (ANQ, vol. 8, #4, 1995: 11–14), notes that Cockburn makes reference to her son's approaching marriage in a letter of 13 December 1707. On the basis of this evidence, Connor suggests that Cockburn's dates would seem to have been altered by herself or Birch, as she would very likely have been older than twenty-eight in order to have a grown son. However, in response to this, Anne Kelley, in her book *Catharine Trotter*, points out that the manuscript version of this letter is a copy, not in Cockburn's handwriting. It is very possible, she writes, that there was a mistake in the transcription, rather than any of the dissembling about birth dates suggested by Connor's article (*Catharine Trotter: An Early Modern Writer in the Vanguard of Feminism* [Hampshire, England: Ashgate, 2002] p. 39). I will continue to refer to the dates provided in Birch's biography.

Growing up, she taught herself to write, became proficient in French, and studied Latin grammar and logic. In addition to her studies, she devoted time to writing plays. In 1695, at the age of 16, Cockburn's first play *Agnes de Castro* was staged, and was published the following year. Her devotion to writing is demonstrated by the fact that, three years later, in 1698, her second play, *Fatal Friendship*, was staged and printed. Both plays were very well received and she enjoyed some celebrity in theatrical circles. George Farquhar (1677–1707), a fellow playwright, sent her a copy of his 1698 play *Love in a Bottle* with a letter in which he wrote, "my passions were wrought so high by representation of *Fatal Friendship*, and since raised so high by the sight of the beautiful author, that I gladly catched this opportunity of owning myself, your most faithful and humble servant."[1] Cockburn wrote three more plays over the next three years.

While she was establishing her reputation as a playwright, Cockburn was also busy studying John Locke's seminal work, an *Essay Concerning Human Understanding* (1690). Locke's work placed him at the forefront of intellectual debate in Europe. Upon its publication he became one of the most celebrated intellectuals of his time; this brought him great fame, but it also inspired many critics. Trotter was so deeply impressed with Locke's ideas that she composed a defence against one critic in particular. Though he published anonymously, the critic in question was posthumously identified as Thomas Burnet, a theologian and philosopher.[2] He wrote three pamphlets critical of Locke's *Essay*: *Remarks upon an Essay concerning Humane Understanding* (1697), *Second Remarks upon an Essay concerning Humane Understanding* (1697), and *Third Remarks upon an Essay concerning Humane Understanding* (1699). Cockburn's first philosophical work was a response to Burnet entitled *The Defence of Mr. Locke's Essay of Human Understanding*. It was first published in 1702, when Cockburn was only 22 years old. The work was published anonymously: it is no surprise that Cockburn felt uncomfortable, as a woman, claiming authorship for a work in the traditionally male field of philosophy. As she wrote in a letter to her friend Thomas Burnet of Kenmay (a different Thomas Burnet to the Thomas Burnet who had authored the *Remarks*), "A woman's

---

1   Birch, *The Life of Mrs. Cockburn*, ix.
2   Thomas Burnet (1635–1715). Burnet was most famous in his day for his work *Sacred Theory of the Earth* (1684), which presents a diluvian account of the Earth's history.

name would give a prejudice against a work of this nature; and truth and reason have less force, when the person, who defends them, is prejudged against."[1] Both the work and the author were in time made known to Locke himself and on 30 December 1702 he wrote to Catharine Trotter (not yet Cockburn): "Give me leave ... to assure you that as the rest of the world take notice of the strength and clearness of your reasoning, so I cannot but be extremely sensible, that it was employed in my defence. You have herein not only vanquished my adversary, but reduced me also absolutely under your power."[2] He presented her with a substantial gift of money and books in appreciation of her defence.

In 1703, Cockburn returned to drama and began work on a new play *The Revolution of Sweden*. She was by now well-known as a talented dramatist (although still largely unknown as a philosopher). In the dedication of her new play to the eldest daughter of the Duke of Marlborough in 1706, Cockburn wrote of her dedicatee that

> there are so great difficulties, and such general discouragement to those of her sex who would improve their minds, and employ their time in any science or useful art, that there cannot be a more distinguishing mark of a free and beneficent spirit, than openly to condemn that ill-grounded custom, by giving countenance and protection to those who have attempted to gain it.[3]

While she felt safe enough admitting authorship for her dramatic works, Cockburn was still clearly uncomfortable being identified as an intellectual. It is hardly surprising that she retained anonymity in the publication of her philosophical works: there would have been a different stigma attached to undertaking this kind of intellectual (often seen as more "masculine") endeavour, as opposed to the artistic, more "genteel" one of playwriting.

In 1708, Cockburn married Reverend Patrick Cockburn. He took a curacy at St. Dunstan's in Fleet Street, London, and remained there until he fell out of favour with the king over his objection to the oath of abjuration (this oath would have confirmed his allegiance to the king as rightful and sole claimant to the crown). As a result, his curacy was rescinded (the exact date is unknown) and he was forced to take work instructing youth in

---

1 Letter from Mrs. Trotter to Mr. Burnet, Salisbury, 9 December 1701 (included in the selected correspondence in the present edition, p. 225).
2 John Locke, *Selected Correspondence*, letter 3234, pp. 308–09.
3 Birch, *The Life of Mrs. Cockburn*, xxvlii.

Latin and living in greatly reduced financial circumstances. In 1726, he finally agreed to take the oath and was eventually moved from London to Northumberland, with a modest income. During these years of hardship, Catharine Cockburn had been forced to put aside her own work in the interests of housekeeping and raising and educating her three children. However in 1724, Cockburn penned the first of two letters in defence of Locke's religious views, against the criticisms of an Oxford cleric, Dr. Winch Holdsworth. Her first letter, which was originally sent to Holdsworth privately, was eventually published, anonymously, in January of 1727 under the title *A Letter to Dr. Holdsworth*. Although anonymous, the letter advertised that it was written by the *"Author of a Defence of Mr. Locke's Essay of Human Understanding."* Holdsworth quickly published his response to Cockburn's letter, which had earlier been sent to Cockburn in private correspondence, in May of 1724. She followed with a second letter in response to Holdsworth, *A Vindication of Mr. Locke's Principles, from the Injurious imputations of Dr. Holdsworth*, for which she never found a publisher, and which was posthumously published as part of her collected works.

In 1739 Cockburn wrote her *Remarks upon some Writers in the Controversy concerning the Foundation of moral Duty and moral Obligation*. It was finally published, anonymously, in 1749 in the English literary journal *The History of the Works of the Learned*. In the *Remarks*, Cockburn defends the philosopher Samuel Clarke (discussed in more detail below), against critics of Clarke's moral theory. The work attracted the attention of several intellectuals, and this attention increased when it became known that the author was a woman of advanced years. Cockburn was by this time plagued with illness and failing sight, but she managed to carry on a considerable intellectual correspondence. In 1747, she published a critique of the work of a Dr. Rutherforth, whose *Essay on the Nature and Obligations of Virtue* was strongly critical of Samuel Clarke's moral theory.

Cockburn's work had attracted sufficient attention that Thomas Birch (1705–66),[1] a well-known clergyman, historian,

---

1 Thomas Birch wrote several works of biography and history, and contributed to the editing of the English translation of Pierre Bayle's famous work, *A General Dictionary, Historical and Critical*, published in ten volumes, 1734–41. Bayle's work, *Dictionnaire historique et critique*, was originally published in 1696.

and man of letters, approached her with the suggestion of publishing a volume of her collected works, including her correspondence. She aided in the editing of this work, but did not live to see its publication in 1751. She died in May 1749 at the age of 71.

Birch prefaced this collection with a biography of Cockburn. Although he praises her intellect and recounts the extent of her philosophical reputation, he nevertheless also assures us that Cockburn was a modest, "self-effacing," and unaffected woman *despite* her intellectual accomplishments: "Her conversation was always innocent, useful and agreeable, without the least affectation of being thought a wit, and attended with a remarkable modesty and diffidence of herself, and a constant endeavour to adapt to the discourse of her company."[1] It is a fitting reminder of the stigma that followed the intellectual woman in the eighteenth century that Cockburn's biographer saw the need to end his encomium by ensuring the reader that—although Cockburn may have been an intellectual—she was nonetheless a modest and self-effacing woman.

Cockburn's Philosophical Concerns in the Context of the Early Modern Period

Cockburn, as we have seen, understood that women were intellectually disadvantaged; but in spite of the many barriers to the male-dominated intellectual sphere, she entered the fray of philosophical debate. She is a remarkable figure in the context of her time: she not only produced the works that she did, but also established a reputation for herself within literary and philosophical circles. This was a time when philosophical debate was not only intense, but carried with it a sense of its own significance and consequence to the prevailing political and social order. Understanding aspects of the social and intellectual backdrop of Cockburn's writing not only provides an enhanced appreciation for her achievement; it also underlines how philosophical debate at the time concerned matters of immediate political and social importance.

Eighteenth-century philosophers were grappling with a host of problems created by the major upheavals in philosophical thought that had taken place during the seventeenth century. The scientific revolution, and the rejection of traditional metaphysical

---

1 Birch, *The Life of Mrs. Cockburn*, xlvi.

and epistemological views, led to heated debate about scientific, religious, and political systems of thought. Some of the most influential seventeenth-century philosophers had embraced new metaphysical and epistemological perspectives which rendered many traditional beliefs—e.g., spiritual causation, papal infallibility, monarchical dictatorship, and moral absolutism—difficult to justify. In the wake of this intellectual shift, fundamental intellectual questions regarding moral knowledge and practice came to have great practical import. I will briefly outline some of the ideas which influenced Cockburn's writing before discussing her work in particular.

Natural Law

The new scientific spirit affected the traditional understanding of morality. Moral theory of this period was dominated by a new understanding of *natural law*, one of the fundamental notions of traditional moral theory. While it is not a strictly defined moral position, theorists who are part of this tradition share certain assumptions about morality. One central assumption is that moral laws are based on the same fundamental laws that govern the natural world. These fundamental laws derive from God's creative will and are therefore not only natural, but also divine. Natural laws, because of their divine origin, are considered to be essentially "rational" and, as such, they are binding upon all rational creatures. Natural law theory also commonly assumes a teleological principle that arises from the observed order and regularity of the universe—i.e., that all things are created such that their natures tend towards the sustenance of the natural order and perfection of the universe. All creatures must, therefore, act according to the dictates of their natures. For many natural law theorists, this means that human beings, as rational creatures, are acting at their best, and thus morally, when acting according to the dictates of reason.

Before the philosophical "Enlightenment" of the eighteenth century, European moral philosophers had previously assumed one of two things about moral rules: either human beings were born with an innate understanding of morality; or human reason was capable of intuiting God's moral rules (and therefore of knowing them with complete certainty). The evidence for views along these lines was the apparent universality of moral beliefs—i.e., murder and theft are wrong. British philosophers of the seventeenth century saw that if morality was going to be truly scientific, and thus free of bias, the traditional assumptions had to be critically examined and the origin and nature of moral rules had to be methodically, i.e., scientifically, considered. By the late seventeenth and early eighteenth centuries, many philosophers were devoting themselves to developing a science of morality, and thereby validating Natural Law.

Two of the most influential political works of the period were Thomas Hobbes's *Leviathan* (1651) and John Locke's *Two Treatises on Government* (1690). Both of these texts, in very different ways, considered politics as if it were a kind of science. Both works sought to use objectivity and theoretical restraint demanded by the methods of the new science. Their conclusions may have differed—Hobbes proposed a totalitarian style of government, while Locke is considered one of the founders of modern liberalism—but their scientific approach was very similar and produced, in both cases, a serious reconsideration of traditional values and assumptions.

Borrowing heavily from the most abstract and meticulous of sciences, mathematics, both Hobbes and Locke sought to establish a system by which moral rules could be axiomatically deduced with the precision and certainty of mathematical theorems. This was not a new approach to moral epistemology—for a long time human reason had been called "the candle of the lord." Since the middle ages, theorists had held that moral knowledge was written into the minds of human beings—suggesting that moral truth was somehow innate in the human mind, or soul. The difference in the early modern period is that many thinkers rejected innatism as a plausible theory—the most obvious objection being the flagrant ignorance of moral duty exhibited by so many people. It seemed obvious to many theorists of the new philosophy that innatism was simply a word to describe the socially accepted rules of behaviour in a society, rather than that which was in fact obviously true and known at birth. Many theorists set out to establish morality upon a foundation that offered the certainty of innatism while resting upon a more tenable epistemological foundation. Human reason certainly seemed, to many thinkers, to be the defining feature of human nature, but it seemed more plausible to suggest that reason *discovers* moral rules, rather than that being equipped from birth with the knowledge of them. The mathematical model seemed, for many of these thinkers, a means of answering this need. Human reason, it was held, could discover moral rules with certainty and precision—thereby maintaining the certainty of moral law without appeal to unsound epistemological foundations. Moralists of this period were pressed not only to answer moral questions, but also theological ones, which, at the time, were of foundational import. The emphasis on reason as a route to moral knowledge was seen by many critics to have serious theological implications. A commonly posed question was as follows: if human reason was capable of discovering moral law, what role did God and revelation play in morality? Could human reason discover God's nature and know it to be benevolent? Could human reason know that the soul is immortal? In Cockburn, we find an attempt to grapple with these very fundamental and difficult questions.

Locke, Clarke, and Hutcheson: Some Philosophical Contexts for Cockburn's Works

Cockburn drew on many philosophical currents. Below I will discuss three thinkers, Locke, Clarke, and Hutcheson, who were important influences on Cockburn.

John Locke (1632–1704)

John Locke's moral philosophy is best characterized as a rationalistic natural law theory. Locke never wrote a work specifically devoted to moral theory, but his view is presented in several of his works, most notably in his *Essays on the Law of Nature* (1664) and *An Essay Concerning Human Understanding* (1690). Locke's theory rests upon the fundamental assumption that all true moral laws are founded upon divine natural law. According to Locke, natural law can be known with intuitive certainty by reason, and once known, all moral rules are derivable from it. For Locke, all knowledge is demonstrative, consisting either in intuitively certain principles or propositions inferable from such principles by deductive means. The demonstrative character which Locke ascribes to both moral and mathematical knowledge owes to the fact that both deal with adequate concepts, which are concepts created by reason and therefore understood with perfect clarity. But Locke's account of the adequacy of the concepts involved renders a surprising conclusion about the basis of moral knowledge. For Locke, any given concept in mathematics or morality is "referred to nothing else but it self, nor made by any other Original, but the Good-liking and Will of him, that first made this Combination."[1] Both mathematical and moral concepts are examples of what Locke calls "mixed modes." Their modal character consists in their being arbitrary human constructs—complex ideas that are unconstrained to copy any external reality. According to Locke, "[The mind] being once furnished with simple *Ideas*, it can put them together in several Compositions, and so make variety of complex *Ideas*, without examining whether they exist so together in Nature."[2] Moral terms are not, Locke suggests, attempts to describe something real and mind-independent. Rather, they are mental constructs by which our actions can be measured. Locke's account of moral concepts as human constructs introduces a tension into his broader view of morality as rationally grounded in divine natural law, since it is no longer clear how the truths reason demonstratively discovers are anything more than human constructs. This is a problem that plagued moral theories like Locke's, which tried to supply moral theory with mathematical precision.

Samuel Clarke (1675–1729)

Samuel Clarke was another eminent moral theorist of the period. He is best known for his two major works: *A Demonstration of the Being and Attributes of God* (1705), and *A Discourse concerning the Unchangeable Obligations of Natural Religion, and the Truth and Certainty of the Christian Revelation* (1706). In these works, he considers the origin of moral concepts: here, moral relations between things are immediately intuited by reason. In Clarke's view, moral reasoning does not start with arbitrarily constructed mixed modes (in the style of Locke), but rather with the observation of relations really existing between things in the world. So, moral ideas are not constructed, but reflect actual relations. In this way Clarke seeks to reify morality, while also ensuring that it has the certainty of mathematical truth. Clarke's theory is based upon a view of the universe as a harmonious structure, in which all things stand in fitting relation to all other things. Clarke's metaphysics is a teleological one, in which all things tend towards ends right and proper to their natures. As a whole, this ensures harmony and happiness for all beings. Clarke's theory of fitness describes a general cosmology that is

---

1 John Locke, *An Essay Concerning Human Understanding*, 2.31.3.
2 *Ibid.*, 2.22.2.

fundamentally reasonable and good. Reason has the special role in this system of discerning the moral import of the natural order of relations. Clarke's is a metaphysical theory of morality. The moral order detected by reason is an order that ultimately governs all created things.

For Clarke, human beings can rationally intuit moral relations. The intuition of fitness relations provides a foundation for moral knowledge that parallels the certainty of mathematical truths without sacrificing the realism of a robust conception of natural law. The problem with Clarke's position, however, is that the *natural* order of things is taken to be a *moral* order in the absence of any satisfactory account of how normativity is derived from purely natural relations. Like Locke, Clarke argues that the true rational understanding of morality reveals an inherent source of obligation attaching to moral laws—i.e., upon discovering these moral laws, any rational being will feel herself motivated to act according to their dictates. Clarke also espouses a two-tiered approach, arguing that due to the fallibility of human reason, sanctions are necessary to motivate most people. Nevertheless, for Clarke it is the rational intuition of fitness relations that provides the moral content of our ideas regarding the natural order. However, it is never entirely clear how the intuition of fitnesses (which are for Clarke a species of natural relations), can carry the force of normative rules. In effect, Clarke lacks any satisfactory account of how "is" transforms into "ought."

Frances Hutcheson (1694–1746)

Locke and Clarke are both natural law theorists who rely upon human reason as the cornerstone of moral epistemology. For Locke, a commitment to a rationalist view of moral knowledge comes at the expense of the tenability of his equally pronounced moral realism. For Clarke, reason observes the moral import of natural relations in the world, but there is no general account of how the normative differs from the merely natural. Francis Hutcheson responds to the rationalist moral systems (particularly Clarke's) with his "moral sense" theory. His two most famous works are *An Inquiry into the Original of our Ideas of Beauty and Virtue* (1725) and his *Essay on the Nature and Conduct of the Passions and Affections: with Illustrations on the Moral Sense* (1728). Hutcheson's theory departs significantly from the Locke-Clarke tradition. While Locke and Clarke both build their moral theories on the premise that reason is capable both of discerning moral truth and of motivating human action, Hutcheson's theory is founded upon the rejection of rationalism in morality. Hutcheson responds to rationalist moral systems (especially Clarke's) by arguing that morality is based on an essentially *sensory* appreciation of moral phenomena—with a special "moral sense" accounting for both our capacity to recognize moral imperatives, and for the feelings of approval that accompany our recognition of properly moral behaviour.

For Hutcheson, human beings are naturally capable of appreciating the harmony and order existing between things in the universe. We do so by means of this "internal sense." Humans are drawn to order and harmony because the internal sense appreciates order amidst complexity, whether in art, landscape, or geometry. The type of harmony found in human relations is characterized by Hutcheson as benevolence, and it is this that the *moral* sense exclusively approves. Without the moral sense, humans would see actions only in the most utilitarian terms (to borrow an anachronistic adjective), that is, by merely calculating outcomes. Hutcheson is quite clear, however, that his own moral sense theory is not meant to be taken as a form of subjectivism. Like any other sense, the moral sense is uniform in most people and correctable by the tests of reason. In Hutcheson's account, therefore, humans do not merely intellectually understand right and wrong. Humans *feel* that some acts are desirable and some are not; and we naturally approve the former and disdain the latter.

Cockburn holds a moral sense view not unlike Hutcheson's, although she is strongly critical of his view. In Cockburn we find elements of moral sense theory integrated into a rationalistic fitness theory. Her fusion of these seemingly divergent strains of thought may serve to shed some light on Hutcheson's moral sense theory with respect to rationalistic moral theories.

Cockburn's philosophical works are written in predominantly polemical form—mainly in defence of Locke and Clarke. However, in these works we actually find Cockburn grappling with the moral and theological questions that concerned these philosophers and producing quite unique answers to those questions. She does so by integrating a variety of elements. I will now turn to a consideration of Cockburn's works.

Cockburn's Works

The first work in this Broadview volume, *A Defence of Mr. Locke's Essay* (1702), is a response to one of Locke's critics, Thomas

Burnet. Burnet argues that Locke's principles are insufficient for providing the proper foundations for knowledge regarding God's veracity (i.e., God's truthfulness or sincerity), the immortality of the soul and morality. According to Locke, sensation and reflection are the two fundamental sources for all of our ideas, with sensation providing us with our ideas about the external world and reflection providing our ideas of ourselves and the operations of the mind. In his pamphlets, Burnet argues that he cannot conceive any sensory source that could provide our ideas of God, morality or the soul. In response to this perceived deficiency in Locke, Burnet proposes a brand of intuitionism, according to which humans have an innate capacity for directly perceiving the truth in these matters.

Cockburn responds to Burnet by arguing that Locke's epistemology can provide the foundations that Burnet claims are lacking. Cockburn rightly notes that Burnet focuses only on the inadequacies of sensation, ignoring any consideration of Locke's notion of *reflection*. She outlines Locke's view of "reflection" as the means by which we come to know the attributes of God. She elaborates on Locke's account in order to show that God's veracity can be adequately proven from Locke's principles. Cockburn addresses Burnet's charge that on Locke's principles the immortality of the soul cannot be known with certainty, by reiterating Locke's own position: despite the human mind's limitations on what it can know with certainty, the immortality of the soul is something that we may judge with a high degree of probability.

The third main issue Cockburn addresses is that of moral epistemology. Cockburn's main strategy for responding to Burnet on this issue involves showing that the apparent deficiencies of Locke's moral epistemology disappear once due consideration is given to Lockean reflection as an avenue for moral understanding. However, her conception of the role of reflections in establishing moral knowledge ends up being much broader than Locke's. She suggests that by reflecting on ourselves we come to understand not merely the operations of our minds, as Locke believes, but human nature in a more extended sense. Cockburn thus uses a variation of Locke's principle of reflection as a springboard for her own moral theory. This morality begins, for Cockburn, with an understanding of human nature along with an understanding of the relations that stand between human beings and their surroundings, thus anticipating the notion of "fitness relations" that animates Clarke's moral philosophy. In addition, Cockburn acknowledges that a moral sense also comes into play when we make moral decisions, which works as an intuition drawing us toward that which is right and fit and repels us from that which is wrong and unfit.

In the *Remarks upon some Writers* (1743), the second work in this volume, Cockburn's main concern is to address certain critics of Clarkean moral fitness theory.[1] The critics she addresses attack Clarke from a shared basic view of morality as a system of laws expressing God's will. These laws are enforced by rewards and punishments that obligate by appealing to the fundamental human desire for happiness and freedom from pain. Rewards and punishments are thus seen as the fundamental means of harmonizing God's will and human interest. Their main objection to fitness theory is that fitness relations are not primitive moral constructs, but actually presuppose more primitive constructs—i.e., God's will and human interest. Clarke's theory is accused of failing to provide sufficient account of these fundamental facts of divine and human nature.

Cockburn responds to this line of criticism by arguing that fitness theory in fact rests upon a more robust conception of the relationship between the will of God and human interest than do the accounts offered by Clarke's critics. According to Cockburn, fitness theory assumes that both human nature and God's creative will are fundamental for morality. Fitness theory rests upon the view that human interest is a basic expression of a human nature brought into being by divine will. Natural good and evil are thus fundamental concepts for moral fitness theory, for it is human nature and all that is associated with it that provides the basis for moral law. Cockburn understands this to be a non-hedonistic account of morality. Our natures are such that careful attention to common human experience yields the knowledge of human and divine nature that is necessary for moral knowledge. According to Cockburn, fitness theory is predicated on the idea that moral obligation arises from the demands of our natures— that is, we ought to be guided by that which is suitable and proper to our natures as rational and social beings.

---

1 While her main concern in this work is morality, Cockburn begins by briefly addressing several other philosophical issues—necessity, the infinitude of space, and the nature and existence of spirits and the notion of substance. The latter discussion revolves generally around epistemological concerns regarding the knowledge of real essences and the nature of substance, in which she argues that spirits must have extension of a sort in order to be proper substances. She makes this argument by appeal to a broadly Lockean view regarding substance.

In the *Remarks upon the Principles and Reasonings of Dr. Rutherforth's Essay on the Nature and Obligation of Virtue* (1747), the third work in this volume, Cockburn responds to Rutherforth's view that moral obligation arises solely from considerations of the pleasure or pain that might result from one's decisions—in particular, obligation arises from considerations of the sanctions laid down by a superior. He argues that this is the natural, common sense understanding of morality and moral obligation, as opposed to what he argues is the more unwieldy intellectual process suggested by people like Clarke.

Cockburn responds with her account of moral fitness by arguing that fitness relations are more consistent with common sense moral judgments than are hedonistic considerations. She argues that moral fitness relations, founded as they are in human self-knowledge, are naturally and easily knowable to all people. Even the completely uneducated person has the ability to distinguish virtuous from vicious acts, according to Cockburn. Cockburn offers as an example the labourer who works hard to feed and clothe his family. Would he do so merely because such an act is fitted to do good to others? No, she answers, because the labourer would see that, although as much good could be done by helping another family, it is right that he should take care of his own first. She explains that this labourer would not be weighing hedonistic considerations, but acting on the basis of his intuitive, or common sense, understanding of relations of fitness and his natural feelings of benevolence. Common sense judges virtuous practice according to what is fit and natural, and not merely according to the good the practice produces. In Cockburn's view, humans have a natural and innate tendency toward what is good and benevolent that transcends merely weighing the effects of one's actions. Our nature tends us towards virtue, since what it is virtuous for human beings to do corresponds, in Cockburn's account, with what it seems genuinely reasonable for them to do.

Critical Approaches to Cockburn's Work

Although Cockburn's writing gained her considerable repute when they were originally published, her work has received little critical attention since that time. Her collected works were published in 1751 but no subsequent editions were ever issued. Cockburn provides an original contribution to eighteenth-century moral theory, yet her value as a philosopher has largely been underestimated. Cockburn's philosophical works are written in predominantly polemical form—ostensibly in defence of Locke and Clarke. For this reason, she has often been characterized as a mere mouthpiece for these thinkers. Yet the interpretations she provides of Locke and Clarke are far from standard. In the *Dictionary of National Biography*, Leslie Stephen wrote of Cockburn's defence of Clarke that, "it is not much to the credit of her philosophical acuteness that she does not perceive it to be inconsistent with the theories of her old teacher Locke."[1] In fact, that the two views are not inconsistent is something Cockburn herself seems to assume rather than defend. In this sense, it is not a failing of Cockburn's that she does not see great inconsistencies between these thinkers, but rather a function of her own positive program and her particular interpretation of their views.

In recent years, there has been increasing interest in Cockburn's philosophical work. However, there remain only a small number of writings devoted exclusively to Cockburn. Mary Ellen Waithe's article "Catharine Trotter Cockburn,"[2] focuses mainly on Cockburn's *Defence*, discussing Cockburn's arguments for Locke's epistemology as a foundation for morality. Waithe also places an emphasis on Cockburn's life, effectively placing Cockburn's philosophical work into the quite remarkable context of her personal circumstances. Martha Brandt Bolton, in her article "The Philosophical Work of Catharine Trotter Cockburn,"[3] emphasizes the originality of Cockburn's contribution to the philosophical debates of the time. Bolton demonstrates how Cockburn is much more than a mere mouthpiece for Locke and Clarke, mainly by showing how her views differ from the thinkers she is defending. Jacqueline Broad, in her book *Women Philosophers of the Seventeenth Century*,[4] examines the connection between Cockburn's feminism and her philosophical views. Broad places Cockburn in the tradition of early modern women

---

1 Leslie Stephen, *Dictionary of National Biography*, Vol. IV (London: Oxford UP, 1959–60) 639.
2 Mary Ellen Waithe, "Catharine Trotter Cockburn" in *A History of Women Philosophers*, vol. 3, ed. Mary Ellen Waithe (Dordrecht: Kluwer Academic Publishers, 1991) 101–25.
3 Martha Brandt Bolton, "Some Aspects of the Philosophical Work of Catharine Trotter," in *Hypatia's Daughters: Fifteen Hundred Years of Women Philosophers*, ed. Linda Lopez McAlister (Bloomington: Indiana UP, 1996) 139–64.
4 Jacqueline Broad, *Women Philosophers of the Seventeenth Century* (Cambridge: Cambridge UP, 2002).

philosophers who oppose Cartesian dualism and the Cartesian theory of substance. In a similar vein, Anne Kelley has produced a book on Cockburn entitled *Catharine Trotter Cockburn: An Early Modern Writer in the Vanguard of Feminism*.[1] In this book, Kelley suggests that Cockburn's emphasis on reason and individual moral responsibility reflect her anti-dogmatism, a position which Kelley associates with Cockburn's general stance in respect to the persistence of socially irresponsible beliefs. Each of these works demonstrates that Cockburn is an original and important thinker who is worthy of greater critical attention than she has, up until recent years, received.

---

1 Anne Kelley, *Catharine Trotter Cockburn: An Early Modern Writer in the Vanguard of Feminism* (Hampshire, England: Ashgate, 2002).

Catharine Trotter Cockburn: A Brief Chronology

1679 Born August 16 to Captain David Trotter and his wife, Sarah
1683 David Trotter dies, leaving the family in financial hardship
1695 Catharine Trotter's first play, *Agnes de Castro*, is written and performed
1696 *Agnes de Castro* published
1697 Thomas Burnet publishes his *First* and *Second Remarks*
1698 Second play, *Fatal Friendship*, performed and published
1699 Thomas Burnet publishes his *Third Remarks*
1701 Third play, *Love at a Loss*, performed and published
      Fourth play, *The Unhappy Penitent*, performed and published
1702 *Defence* published
1704 John Locke dies October 28
1705 Samuel Clarke publishes *Demonstration of Being and Attributes of God*
1706 Fifth play, *The Revolution of Sweden*, performed and published
1707 Publication of *A Discourse Concerning a Guide in Controversies*; a theological work concerning the doctrines of the Roman Catholic Church
1708 Marries Reverend Patrick Cockburn
1720 Holdsworth publishes a critical work on Locke's religious views
1724 Cockburn writes her *Letter* to Holdsworth in defence of Locke
1727 Publishes *Letter to Dr. Holdsworth*
1740 Completes *Remarks upon some Writers*
1743 *Remarks upon some Writers* published in *The History of the Works of the Learned*
1744 Rutherforth publishes *Essay on the Nature and Obligations of Virtue*
1747 Publishes *Remarks upon the Principles and Reasonings of Dr. Rutherforth's Essay*
1749 Dies May 11 at the age of 71
1751 Publication of *The Works of Catharine Trotter Cockburn*, edited by Thomas Birch

A Note on the Text

All of the works and letters that have been included in this collection are based on the editions found in *The Works of Mrs. Catharine Cockburn* (1751), edited by Thomas Birch. Certain of the spellings have been modernized, in cases where they might otherwise be confusing to a modern reader. Apart from these and some very minor grammatical changes, the original text has been preserved.

All the original footnotes (identified by asterisk and dagger symbols) have been left intact, but some of the irregularities of Cockburn's citations have been standardized in order to make them conform more to modern styles of citation. The extent of such changes has been to insert the name or work to which the page numbers refer, in cases where they have been omitted. Where possible, referencing to modern or reprint editions has been included in square brackets following Cockburn's original page references. Any insertions made by the editor have been enclosed in square brackets, and any new footnotes that have been added into this edition are identified by superscript numbers in the usual way.

Catharine Trotter Cockburn
Philosophical Writings

A Defence of Mr. Locke's Essay of Human Understanding, *wherein its Principles, with reference to Morality, Revealed Religion, and the Immortality of the Soul, are considered and justified: In answer to some Remarks on that Essay.*

First printed in the Year 1702.

To the Excellent Mr. Locke,

Sir,
I do not presume to address these papers to you as a champion in your cause; but as an offender, to make the best apology I can for a bold unlicensed undertaking. That excellence of the *Essay of Human Understanding*, which gave me courage in encountering a caviller against it, strikes me with shame and awe, when I think of coming before you; like a rash lover, that fights in defence of a lady's honour, the juster his cause is, the more reason he has to fear her resentment, for not leaving it to assert itself by its own evidence; and the more it secures him of success against his adversary, the less pretence he has to her forgiveness. But, Sir, *The Essay of Human Understanding* is a public concern, which every one has a right and interest to defend. It came too late into the world to be received without opposition, as it might have been in the first ages of philosophy, before men's heads were prepossessed with imaginary science. At least, no doubt, if so perfect a work could have been produced so early, it would have prevented a great deal of that unintelligible jargon, and vain pretence to knowledge of things out of the reach of human understanding, which make a great part of the school learning, and disuse the mind to plain and solid truth.

But the great Mr. *Locke* was reserved for a curious and learned age, to *break in upon this sanctuary of vanity and ignorance*; and by setting men on considering first *the bounds of human understanding*, to help them in a close pursuit of true and useful knowledge. And is it possible for a lover of truth to be unmoved, or silently suffer any injurious insinuations of so excellent a design?

Your time, Sir, is too precious to be employed in taking notice of them. You still go on in farther designs for our advantage and improvement; and whilst you labour in that great end, to which you were destined, *the good of mankind*, it is every one's duty to be watchful for you, and zealous to secure the benefits you have already done us.

It is confessed, the vast disproportion between one of so mean abilities as the author of this defence, and the incomparable Mr. *Locke*, might with reason have deterred from the attempt. But I did not presume to consider myself in any kind of comparison with him. I only observed the adversary's strength, and thought (with reason and justice on my side) I need not be discouraged to enter the lists with him; and I am persuaded, what I have done will leave him no cause of triumph, how much soever it is unworthy of you. I wish, Sir, you may only find it enough worth your notice, to incite you to show the world, how far it falls short of doing justice to your principles; which you may do without interrupting the great business of your life, by a work, that will be an universal benefit, and which you have given the world some right to exact of you. Who is there so capable of pursuing to a *demonstration* those reflections on the grounds of *morality*, which you have already made? Which, on the hints you have given, is impatiently expected from you by many, who lament the great need there is of it in this age. That consideration, no doubt, will animate one, who has ever shown a careful zeal for the advancement of practical religion; and I cannot but think a man so greatly qualified for such an undertaking was given in mercy to an age, in which it is more than ever wanting; for never any age abounded like this with open advocates of irreligion, upon pretended rational grounds. To silence these unhappy reasoners, by a demonstration of the obligations their nature lays upon them, is a work worthy of the excellent Mr. *Locke*; and perhaps the weakness of this defence may show you, that those, who mean well to religion, have no little need of your instruction. In hopes of which, I have ventured to publish these papers, not without much apprehension and awe of your displeasure. But, Sir, in my offence you must perceive my zeal; and though I have not the happiness to be known to you, believe me with the profoundest respect,

Sir,
Your most humble, and most obedient Servant.

Preface

As the science of true morality is of the most universal and highest concernment to mankind, no doubt, those writers, who establish it upon the clearest, most obvious, and the most solid grounds, do the best service to religion, which has received no little prejudice, by the attempts of some well-meaning men to support it upon metaphysical notions, upon false or abstruse reasonings: And as there appears a hearty zeal for setting men right in that great concern, in all the writings of the excellent author of the *Essay of Human Understanding*, I know no philosopher before him, that has fixed morality upon so solid a foundation, as he gives many hints of in that *Essay*, wherever the subject will permit; a foundation strong enough to satisfy the wisest, and plain enough to be conceived by the weakest capacities. And yet there have not been wanting some, who have taxed that admirable *Essay* with principles prejudicial, or not sufficient to those great ends, which are evidently the main scope of all that author's works. So hard it is for men, who have been used to receive truth in a particular dress, to know her, when stripped of those false colours and borrowed ornaments, with which she is too often disguised. At least, this is the worst I would think of such cavillers. The most favourable judgment, that can be made of them, is that they have either mistaken Mr. *Locke*'s principles, or the true grounds of morality, and write out of too great a fondness of their own *hypothesis*, or ignorance of his.

But as there are no reflections so weak or ill grounded, that some or other may not be deceived by, I have met with two or three, who upon reading some remarks on the *Essay of Human Understanding* (which fell but lately into my hands)[1] concluded it contained very dangerous principles, and without farther exami-

---

1 Cockburn here refers to Thomas Burnet's series of pamphlets: *Remarks upon an Essay concerning Humane Understanding* (1697), *Second Remarks upon an Essay concerning Humane Understanding* (1697), and *Third Remarks upon an Essay concerning Humane Understanding* (1699). (In these notes I will distinguish these works, respectively, as *[First] Remarks*, *Second Remarks*, and *Third Remarks*, wherever Cockburn herself has not provided a designation.) They were originally published anonymously (Burnet was only posthumously identified as their author), which is why Cockburn refers to their author, throughout the *Defence*, simply as "The Remarker."

nation, condemned the *Essay*, having never read, or as they owned, very little considered it; on which account, several, who have a great respect for Mr. *Locke*, have wished he had leisure to answer the difficulties objected against his principles by the Remarker. But as I did not think them strong enough to need so great a hand to remove them, I persuaded myself I might do something towards it, which at first I designed only for my own satisfaction, and those few friends, who had spoke to me of them; but in examining their force, I found them so much grounded on mistakes, not only of the principles the author contends against, but of the foundation of those grand points he contends for, that it fell unavoidably in my way to make some reflections upon the *true grounds of morality*, and the danger of establishing a point of so great concern as that, and the immortality of the soul, upon false or uncertain *hypothesis*, which having been frequently attempted, and by well designing men, made me think it might not be unuseful to publish these papers. And I hope, whatever may tend to removing any prejudices against a book of so great use as the *Essay of Human Understanding*, will be thought of some consequence to the public. And though I am far from pretending to have set the principles I defend in all the lustre they are capable of, I doubt not, that I have sufficiently shown the weakness of the objections against them, and that all impartial readers will easily perceive, that whatever is defective in this defence, can only be imputed to want of judgment in the undertaker, equal to the truth and justice of the cause.

A Vindication of an Essay
Concerning Human Understanding

'Tis happy for mankind, when men of an elevated genius, and uncommon penetration, have too a truly noble and beneficent nature, above any low particular ends, and resolute enough to encounter all the oppositions they must meet in an unbiased search of truth, from those, who having with much pains imbibed the opinions of reverenced authors, are unwilling to unlearn all their former knowledge, to examine what they have been taught for first principles, not to be questioned, and lay aside their sacred *ipse dixit*.[1] He, who dares attempt against this established monarchy over men's judgments, must be looked on as a troublesome and dangerous innovator, and needs a mighty force of reason and generous courage, to break through all the prejudices of men, and free them from a willing slavery. To that united force we owe the excellent *Essay on Human Understanding*; and to these prejudices, all the cavils against it.

When the light of truth shines too clear and strong to be directly faced, the only shelter for those, who would not feel its force, is to seek for far fetched dangerous consequences, supposed inconsistencies with revealed truths, and mysteries of faith, deduced by a long train of arguments, which engaging in an intricate dispute shades them with some pretence, for not confessing the splendor of that truth, they cannot encounter; inconsistencies with revealed truths, when the real necessary consequence of any principles being sufficient proofs against them, how plausible soever they appear. But Mr. *Locke* has so well vindicated his *Essay* from those imputed to it by the most considerable of his opposers, that the rest could only hope to triumph in his neglect of their attempts, who by the help of some suppositions, and many mistakes, have endeavoured to draw an odium on that excellent *Essay*.

The Remarker, whom I have now under consideration, in his first letter,* desires to be informed how far all the principles of

---

* Page 4 [(*First*) *Remarks*. This and all subsequent of page references given by Cockburn to the series of Burnet's *Remarks* have been checked against the following modern reprint edition: Burnet, Thomas, John Locke, and Noah Porter. *Remarks upon an Essay Concerning Humane Understanding, Five Tracts* (1697–1887; 5 vols. in 1, edited by Peter A. Schouls, New York: Garland, 1984). Any discrepancies have been noted.]

---

1 *Ipse dixit* refers to a dogmatic assertion, or any statement the authority of which rests upon the authority of the speaker.

that ingenious *Essay*, taken together, will give us a sure foundation for morality, revealed religion, and a future life, which he does not find that they do. What his reasons, or rather difficulties (as he terms them) are, is my design to consider, and endeavour to satisfy. In his *Second Remarks*, he mentions an answer of Mr. *Locke*'s, which I have not read, but suppose, by what he quotes out of it, that it was rather designed to show the weakness of his objections, than to give a full answer to them, Mr. *Locke*, perhaps, thinking it sufficient to show they required none.[1] But I find they are still of weight with the Remarker, his *Second* and *Third Remarks* being only enlargements upon the same heads.

I shall therefore examine them in their order, taking on each head the substance of what I find relating to it in all the three *Remarks*, that the answer, lying together, may be the more clear, and the better considered, which, I hope, will be done by the Remarker without prejudice, as it was written, with a design to satisfy him, and in a sincere love of truth, to do justice to a book, which, I think, removes the obstacles to it, and shows the method of attaining it, clearer and more effectually, and is written in an exacter method, than any before it, to vindicate it from a defect in the foundation of certainty, in those things, which are of greatest concern to us: which I doubt not to do; it being clear to me, that whatever we can know at all, must be discoverable by Mr. *Locke*'s principles; for I cannot find any other way to knowledge, or that we have any one idea not derived from sensation and reflection. But let us see, how those points may be established on them, for which the Remarker doubts their force; and first of morality, or natural religion; of which, he thus begins:

"As to morality, we think the great foundation of it is the distinction of good and evil, virtue and vice. And I do not find, that my eyes, ears, nostrils, or any other outward senses, make any distinction of these things, as they do of colours, sounds, *&c.* Nor from any ideas taken in from them, or from their reports, am I

---

[1] Locke himself had not bothered to make any serious reply to the *Remarks*. His single response to Burnet, *An Answer to the Remarks upon an Essay Concerning Human Understanding* (which was appended to his letter *Mr. Locke's Reply to the Bishop of Worcester's Answer to his Letter*), is more an insult than a serious philosophical engagement. In his response, Locke writes that the author of the *Remarks* "shews so much Ignorance, or so much Malice, that he deserves no other Answer but Pity" (Locke, *The Works of John Locke*, 10 vols [1823; reprint, Germany: Scientia Verlag Aalen: 1963] 188).

conscious, that I do, or can conclude, that there is such a distinction in the nature of things."* In which words,† he says, he thought he had taken in enough to comprehend both Mr. *Locke*'s principles of knowledge, *sensation and reflection*, which I should not have thought; but since he owns he designed them to do so, we will suppose both expressed, and proceed with him. "I allow, that we may infer from observation and reason, that such a distinction is useful to society, but both philosophers and divines, you know, make a more immutable and intrinsic distinction, which is that I cannot make out from your principles. This I am sure of, that the distinction, suppose of gratitude and ingratitude, fidelity and infidelity, justice and injustice, and such others, is as sudden without any ratiocination, and as sensible and piercing, as the difference I feel from the scent of a rose and *assa foetida*."[1] One would think here, he were doubting, whether upon Mr. *Locke*'s principles we can distinguish *gratitude* from *ingratitude*, *fidelity* from *infidelity*, *&c*, that is, know that breaking a trust is not keeping a trust, *&c*, which (as all other moral virtues, as Mr. *Locke* has shown)‡ are a collection of simple ideas, received from sensation and reflection. But since he allowed above, that *we can from observation and reason, infer such a distinction to be useful to society*, and by consequence, that we can by them perceive such a distinction, we will guess his meaning here, to be, that the perception of the *morality* and *immorality* of these things is as sudden, *&c as the difference he feels from the scent of a rose, and assa foetida*; though I do not know what it is, to perceive the morality and immorality of these things *without any ratiocination*. *Justice and injustice*, I think, depend upon the rights of men, whether natural, or established by particular societies; and therefore to know what they are, it is necessary to know what right is, which sure requires some *reflection*. But to know, that *injustice* is *evil*, without any *reflection*, seems to me no more than to know, that the term *injustice* stands for something that we do not know, which is evil; unless it will be said, that we may know it to be a detaining any one's right, without knowing what right is, which will be a very insignificant knowledge. But if the Remarker means, that as

---

* *First Remarks*, p. 4.
† *Second Remarks*, p. 8.
‡ *Essay*, p.195, §14 [Locke, *An Essay Concerning Human Understanding* (hereafter referred to as the *Essay*), 2.28.14.]

---

1 *Assa foetida* refers to a resinous gum, with a strong odour.

soon as he knows what it is to have a right to a thing, he perceives, that to detain from a man what he has such a right to, is evil, without any farther reflection, I understand him, but see not how it can be objected against the force of Mr. *Locke*'s principles, being only a perception of the disagreement of these two ideas, of one man's having a right to a thing, and another's having a right to take it away: but this only by the way.

Let us now consider that, for which this sudden perception without ratiocination is brought as a proof, viz. that the ground of the distinction of moral good and evil is in the *nature of the things themselves*, abstract from the good of society; which is that he cannot make out from Mr. *Locke*'s principles. By which distinction in the nature of things, if he means, that without respect to men, or to society, though mankind had never been, or never been designed, justice, gratitude, fidelity, *&c* had been good, and their contraries evil; I confess myself incapable of having a notion of these virtues abstract from any subject to conceive: For example, that it would have been good to be faithful to a trust, though there had never been anyone to trust, or be trusted: nor do I find, that the assertors of this distinction in the nature of things have any real idea of them more abstracted than I have, which will appear in examining their particular instances. I will take that, which the Remarker gives,* being one of the most uncontested principles in morality, *that it is a wicked thing, for man maliciously to kill his friend, or his father, or any other innocent person. The truth of this*, he says, *seems to him as clear and eternal, as any proposition in mathematics*; and it seems to me as clear, that it cannot possibly be conceived at all, either *true* or *false*, in itself, i.e. without any relation to man. I desire any one, to try, whether he can conceive it to be an eternal truth, that it is a wicked thing, for a man to kill his father, or his friend, though there had never been, or designed to be such a thing as friend, father, or man. But whether he can or not, it will still be a truth as *certain and immutable*, as any proposition in mathematics. No mathematician, that I know of, thinks it necessary to establish the immutability of this truth, that the three angles of a triangle are equal to two right ones; to affirm, that it is true, without any relation to angles or triangles. Either of these propositions are sufficiently established, if it is, and always must be true, supposing those things, to which it relates, to exist.†

---

* *Second Remarks*, p. 26.
† This whole paragraph is a partial and temporary consideration of moral truths (as the opposers of Dr. *Clarke* do now consider them) with rela-

But here the Remarker's* question will be made, upon what grounds must it be so? If *good* and *evil*, virtue and vice, are not such in their own nature, *they must be so from the arbitrary will of God; and all things are indifferent, till he declare this, or that, to be sin, according to his pleasure*: that is, he might, if he had so pleased, have made *virtue, vice*; and *vice, virtue*: To which, I answer, that God having made man such a creature as he is, it is as impossible, that good and evil should change their respects to him, as that *pleasure* can be *pain*, and *pain pleasure*, which no one in his senses will affirm; and yet, I think, nobody has supposed them to be real existences, independent of any subject. And if the relation, which moral good and evil has to natural good and evil, were sufficiently observed, there would be as little dispute about the nature and reality of *virtue* and *vice*. Those, who think they are only notions in the mind, would be convinced they are as real as natural good and evil; all *moral good* consisting in doing, willing, or choosing, for oneself or others, whatever is a *natural good*; and all moral evil, in doing, willing, or choosing whatever is a *natural evil*, to oneself or others. This, I doubt not, will appear a full definition, when tried by every instance of *moral good* and *evil*, to all, who reflect on it; unless there are any, who do not place the perfection and imperfection, the advantages and disadvantages of the *mind*, in their account of *natural good* or *evil*; which I believe no rational man will own.

And as this unalterable relation makes the real and immutable nature of virtue and vice undeniable; so also from thence it is plain, *that nature of man is the ground or reason of the law of nature*; *i.e.* of moral good and evil. But if the Remarker will rather have it, that the nature of these things is the reason of the nature of man, that they are essentially in the nature of God, which is the rule of his will, and according to which he formed man; let it be so, as it is unquestionable, that he cannot will any thing contrary to his nature. But however the moral attributes of God, goodness,

---

tion only to the present constitution of things, not to their original ground, as they exist eternally in the divine mind. An error, the author is now sensible of, and that there was no need of this for the defence of Mr. *Locke*'s principles. If his plan led him only to speak of the immediate origin of our ideas, or how we come by our ideas of moral relations, his principles are sufficient by the reflections we make on the operations of our own minds, to lead us to the supreme mind, where all truth, and the abstract nature of all possible things, must eternally and immutably exist.

* *Second Remarks*, p. 22. [Burnet's discussion of this point begins on page 21 of the *Second Remarks*.]

justice, &c are in him (who is infinitely beyond the reach of our narrow capacities) this I say (which Mr. *Locke* has observed of our idea of their infinity) that we have no idea of them, but what carries with it a respect to their objects, *the natural good or evil of his creatures*; and we could have no idea of them at all without reflection upon ourselves; for whatever is the original standard of good and evil, it is plain, we have no notion of them but by their conformity, or repugnancy to our reason, and with relation to our nature; and that what according to it we perceive to be good, we ascribe to the Supreme Being; for we cannot know, that the nature of God is good, before we have a notion of good. It must be then by reflecting upon our own nature, and the operations of our minds, that we come to know the nature of God; which therefore cannot *be to us* the rule of good and evil; unless we will argue in a circle, that by our notion of good, we know the nature of God, and by the nature of God, we know what is good.

From whence it will follow, that the nature of man, and the good of society, are *to us* the reason and rule of moral good and evil; and there is no danger of their being less immutable on this foundation than any other, whilst man continues a rational and sociable creature. If the law of nature is the product of human nature itself (as the great *Grotius* speaks)[1] it must subsist as long as human nature; nor will this foundation make it the less sacred, since it cannot be doubted, that it is originally the will of God, whilst we own him the author of that nature, of which this law is a consequence.

If then, in Mr. *Locke*'s way, we can perceive what is comformable, or not, to our own nature, which cannot be doubted; if by reflecting on ourselves, we can come to know there must be a Supreme Being, the source of all others, which he has admirably shown;* we have a sacred and immutable foundation for natural religion, on his principles; this being a plain and infallible inference, that the Author of our being does require those things of us, to which he has suited our nature, and visibly annexed our happiness, which he has made the necessary motive of all our actions. For it is inconsistent with that divine wisdom, which we see has

---

* *Essay*, B. iv. c. x.

---

1 Hugo Grotius (1583–1645), a legal and moral theorist most famous for his work *The Law of War and Peace* (1625). He developed a view of natural law which was adopted by many of the moralists of the seventeenth century.

fitted all other things to their proper and certain end, to have formed us after such a manner, that if we employ those faculties, which he has given us, we cannot but judge, that such things are fit to be done, and others to be avoided, and this to no end at all. Much less can we suppose he has designed us to act contrary to the necessary motives of our actions, and judgment of our minds; it being a flat contradiction, that infinite wisdom and power should form any of his works so disproportionate to their end.

It will not be much from the purpose here, to take notice of the folly of those men, who think to weaken the authority of religion, by calling it a politic contrivance, established for the good of government or society; which is as much as to say, it is the less obligatory, because it is necessary. Whereas that very thing shows it to be our indispensable duty, and of divine authority, without any revelation; since the divine workmanship, *human nature*, could not subsist without it. If they could prove it unpolitic or destructive to society, it would be much more for their purpose; for such a religion must necessarily be false; nothing can be a *law to nature*, which of direct consequence would *destroy nature*.

But if any one thinks it better established on the nature of God, I have shown how we come to the knowledge of it in Mr. *Locke*'s way, by ascribing to him whatever by its conformity to our nature we perceive to be good; because we see, that we cannot admit any imperfection in the Supreme Being, without a contradiction (which I shall show in Mr. *Locke*'s way, when I come to the next head) and having by the *effect* found out the *cause*, we may then conclude the nature of God to be the archetype of ours, because we cannot suppose the most perfect Being can will any thing contrary to his own nature; for if he could, the rule of that will must be something less perfect than himself, (for whatever is most perfect is God) and therefore to will any thing contrary to his own nature, would be an imperfection in him, which to admit in the most perfect being, is a contradiction. Thus (when I have more fully shown, how we come by the idea of perfection in the Supreme Being) the Remarker may perceive, that we can, in Mr. *Locke*'s way, arrive to the original notion of intrinsic holiness,* into which 'tis ultimately resolved, which he is so much concerned to find; and that I hope will reconcile him to Mr. *Locke*'s principles.

And if he will attentively examine his own without prepossession, if he will trace his idea of God, and of moral good and evil, to their first source, I believe he will find he has no other princi-

---

* *Second Remarks*, p. 2. [This is found on page 23 of the *Second Remarks*.]

ple of knowledge than Mr. *Locke*; and that the mistake lies, in that being taught truths after they are discovered, and finding them agreeable to our reason, we immediately assent to them, without reflecting how they were first found out, and are apt to conclude those things, which we find first in our knowledge, to be the first principles of knowledge; though they were proceeded to by many steps and degrees, and were the last established in the discovery.

But the Remarker will object, that Mr. *Locke* does not establish morality upon the nature of man, and the nature of God,* but *seems to ground his demonstration upon future punishments and rewards, and upon the arbitrary will of the law-giver; and he does not think these the first grounds of good and evil.* To which I answer, first, supposing it were so, the question is not what Mr. *Locke* thinks, but what may be proved from his principles.† But secondly, I say, that Mr. *Locke* does ground his demonstration upon the *nature of God and man*, as will plainly appear by his express words, which are these.‡ "The idea of a Supreme Being, infinite in power, goodness, and wisdom, whose workmanship we are, and on whom we depend, and the idea of ourselves, as understanding rational creatures, being such, as are clear in us, would, I suppose, if duly considered and pursued, afford such foundations of our duty and rules of action, as might place morality among the sciences capable of demonstration." Nothing can be clearer than this; and in all those places, which the Remarker quotes out of Mr. *Locke*, where he seems to establish morality upon *the will of God, and rewards and punishments*, he is speaking of it, as it has the force of a law; and the Remarker cannot deny, whatever he thinks, *the first grounds of good and evil*; or however clearly we may see the *nature of these things,* we may approve or condemn them; but they can only have the force of a *law* to us, considered as *the will of the Supreme Being*, who can, and certainly will, reward the compliance with, and punish the deviation from that rule, which he has made knowable to us by the light of nature.§

---

* *Second Remarks*, p. 2. [This is found on page 21 of the *Second Remarks*.]
† *Second Remarks*, p. 4.
‡ *Essay*, B. iv. c. 3. §.18.
§ Some, who had lately read this defence, have thought that the author's sentiments, on *the grounds of moral obligation*, were different when this was written, from what they now appear to be in some late pieces. But the author thinks there is no real difference: the grounds of moral obligation are not here discussed at all; the notion of founding morality upon on arbitrary will is carefully rejected; and the nature of God, or

But that we can only know these things to be his will by their conformity to our nature, and that therefore they cannot be arbitrary, I have before shown; and that he will punish or reward us according to our obedience or disobedience to it, is a consequence of his nature. So that, though Mr. *Locke* says, that the will of God, rewards and punishments, can only give morality the force of a law; that does not make them the *first grounds* of good and evil, since by his principles, to know what the will of God is (antecedently to revelation) we must know what is good by the conformity it has to our nature, by which we come to know the nature of God, which therefore may be to him the first ground or rule of good; though *the will of God, &c* can only enforce it as a *law*.

I cannot here omit to take notice of a question the Remarker asks on this subject: How, pray you upon these principles, do you preserve the distinction (that good old distinction, which it may be you despise) of *Bonum Utile*, and *Honestum*? In your way, either the parts are coincident, or *Bonum Utile* is superior to *Bonum Honestum*.* I'm afraid the Remarker will have hard thoughts of me, if I should say I do not like his good old distinction, and that I think the parts are coincident. I know not whether he will have a better opinion of me, when I tell him, I do not

---

the divine understanding, and the nature of man, all along supposed to be the true grounds of it. New terms have been since introduced into these subjects; we talk now of essential differences, nature, relation, truth, and fitness of things: but the meaning is the very same; for all these are to be sought for in the nature of God, or of man. But Mr. *Locke* is here defended in establishing morality on *the will of God, and rewards and punishments considered, as it has the force of a law*; there I suppose lies the *apparent* difference, tho' there is none in reality. The author still agrees to that proposition; for strictly and properly speaking a law implies authority and sanctions; and though we say the *law of reason*, and *the law of nature*, this is in a less proper sense, importing, that they are as effectual grounds of obligation, as if they were real laws, but they oblige us not as *dependent*, but as *reasonable* beings; in the same manner as the Supreme Being, who is subject to no laws, and accountable to none, obliges himself to do always what he perceives to be right and fit to be done. In this light the author has all along considered the grounds of moral obligation; and this I presume is not inconsistent with allowing, that the will of God, rewards and punishments, can only give morality the force of a law.

* *Second Remarks*, p. 25. [*Bonum utile* refers to a good that we seek as a means to a further end. *Bonum honestum* refers to a good that we seek as an end in itself.]

mean it in the way, which he injuriously insinuates to be Mr. *Locke*'s; but that nothing can be truly profitable, that is not honest. However, not to cavil about words, this am I sure of, that there is no ground for the Remarker's reflection on those principles, which he is dissatisfied with, *viz.* "That morally good and evil is the conformity or disagreement of our actions to the divine law; which* Mr. *Locke* says is the only true touch-stone of moral rectitude; and that by comparing them to this law, men judge of the most considerable moral good or evil of their actions, that is, whether as duties or sins, they are like to procure them happiness or misery from the hands of the Almighty." Upon these principles *Bonum Utile* can never be superior to *Bonum Honestum*, in Mr. *Locke*'s way, till the Remarker can show him some moral evil, that is not contrary to the divine law; or a way to escape the hands of the Almighty, when we disobey him.

What has been said, will be sufficient to answer, all that the Remarker has said directly on this point: but what further concerns it, *of natural conscience,* and the proofs of *the moral attributes of God,* will be considered in their order; which leads us to the second head, of which the Remarker.

As to revealed religion, my difficulty is only this, how it can be proved from your principles, that the author of the revelation is veracious; and p. 7. *to establish the certainty of revealed religion, we must know the moral attributes of the divine nature, such as goodness, justice, holiness, and particularly veracity. Now these I am not able to deduce from your principles. You have proved very well an eternal all-powerful and all-knowing being: but, &c.*† The Remarker, it seems, does not find what Mr. *Locke* says, after he has very well proved an eternal, most powerful, and most knowing being;‡ That *from this idea, duly considered, will easily be deduced all those other attributes we ought to ascribe to this eternal Being.* The Remarker is *not able to do it,* though, to help him, Mr. *Locke* says, *he may be ashamed to have raised such a doubt as this,* viz. *whether an infinitely powerful and wise being be veracious, or no, unless he concludes lying to be no mark of weakness, and folly.*§ As I find in his words repeated by the Remarker, which he complains of, *as misrepresenting, and perverting his sense; the question is not,* (says he) *whether God be veracious, but whether, according to your principles, he can be proved to be so.* Answ. But the question is, *whether an infinitely pow-*

---

* *Essay*, B. ii. c. 28. [From the *Essay*, 2.28.5.]
† *First Remarks*, p. 6.
‡ *Essay*, B. iv. c.10. §6.
§ *Second Remarks*, p. 3.

erful and wise being is *veracious or no*; for such a being Mr. *Locke* has *very well proved*, as the Remarker owns: so that the doubt must be, whether, as such, he must be veracious; for the Remarker allows *veracity* to be a consequence of *infinite power and wisdom*. The veracity of God is proved by Mr. *Locke*'s principles; and this is an absurd question, whether the veracity of God can be proved from his principles, if *falsehood* is allowed to be *a mark of weakness and folly*; for then it cannot possibly be admitted in a being, which he has proved of *infinite wisdom and power*; and I know no better way of proving anything, than by proving principles, upon which it cannot be denied without a contradiction; so that Mr. *Locke* has not *perverted* the Remarker's sense; for he cannot avoid this dilemma, either he concludes falsehood to be *a mark of weakness and folly*, or he does not: if not, then Mr. *Locke* has rightly represented his sense; if he does, then this is an absurd question, whether one, who has proved an infinitely powerful and wise Being, can prove he is not false.

But this is not sufficient for the Remarker: he is *not able to deduce* one attribute from another. Let us see then what is his way to know the moral attributes of God, which, he tells us, is this, he *ascribes veracity to God, because it is a perfection*. But from what grounds does he conclude, that whatever is a perfection must be in God? Will he say, that it is a principle imprinted on the mind, without any reflection; that is, we clearly see, that God must be perfect, we don't know why: or will he not rather say, that the want of any perfection would imply either that he does not know what is best, or cannot attain it, and therefore is inconsistent with infinite wisdom and power? Or that to suppose there may be a being of greater perfection than the supreme source of all being, is a gross contradiction? I believe, if he reflects attentively on the progress of the mind in the knowledge of God, he will find perfection is not first in our notion of him, (as an ingenious author has shown)* but that having discovered a first being, the source of all others, and what attributes we must necessarily ascribe to him, as such, we perceive, that to admit any imperfection in him would be a contradiction to our first necessary conceptions of him; which Mr.

---

* Norris, *Reason and Religion.* [John Norris, *Reason and Religion; or The grounds and measures of devotion consider'd from the nature of God and the nature of man* (London, 1689). Norris's main theory consists in the belief that the proper object of human knowledge is God, in whom all necessary truths are known. For Norris, the knowledge of God brings us to the knowledge of necessary truths, and vice versa.]

Locke has established in his way, and tells us, that from them all his other attributes will easily be deduced.

But this will not satisfy the Remarker, unless Mr. *Locke* tells us, *what is to be understood by perfection in his way; how it is derived from the* senses; *and how it includes veracity.** The Remarker is very apt to forget, that Mr. *Locke* has another principle of knowledge, which he calls *reflection*; or he thinks it insignificant. Perhaps it may be so as to his purpose; but happening to be serviceable in the present enquiry, I take leave to remind him of it, that we may consider how far it will help us to the idea of perfection.

But first, I observe, that we have no adequate idea of perfection; but perceiving in ourselves some *powers and faculties*, as of *knowing, willing, moving*, &c and of particular actions, and general abstract ideas; that some are congruous, and others repugnant to each other, and to our reason; we know, that some things are better than others; and from every thing about us, and within us, we may learn, that the vastly greater part of them escape the extent of our power, knowledge, and goodness; from whence we conclude, these things may be far more extensive, even to all that can exist. And the highest possible degree of these, which we find it better to have, than to be without, that we call perfection; which to have an adequate idea of, we must comprehend the existence of an infinite spirit. But we cannot add any thing to make up this idea, which we do not find in ourselves; only the degrees, which we perceive must be ascribed, far beyond our measures, to that Being, from which we received all our powers and faculties, and by whose wisdom, power, and goodness, all things exist; for perfection is only the highest degree, or the best manner of possible existence; and that the eternal source of all being must exist in the most perfect manner possible, cannot be doubted; for there cannot be a greater absurdity, than to suppose there may be a more perfect being, than the eternal source of all Being. Thus we see how the idea of perfection, such as we have, may be derived from *sensation and reflection*; and any one, who considers it, will find, that he has no positive idea of it, and that there is nothing in that idea, which he has, but what the objects without him, or the faculties he perceives in himself, have furnished him with; and that therefore it is needless to seek for any other original of it.

Having now got the idea of perfection, in Mr. *Locke*'s way, and found, that it must necessarily be ascribed to the eternal source of all being, we must next consider the other part of the

---

* *First Remarks*, p. 8.

Remarker's question, *how it includes veracity*, which he is the more concerned to know, because he says, *not only the truth of revelation, but also of our faculties in other things, depends upon the veracity of their author.** And here he must give me leave to ask him, upon what grounds veracity is to him a perfection? He will not say, because God is veracious (though the nature of God is to him the rule of good) for he ascribes veracity to God, because it is a perfection, and he does not approve of arguing in a circle. He must then know, that veracity is a perfection from some other rule; and here I am afraid he will be involved in a great difficulty; *for the truth of our faculties*, he says, *depends upon the veracity of their author*: but before he can know the veracity of their author, he must be sure, that veracity is a perfection, since it is only as such he does, or it can be ascribed to him. Now by whatsoever means he perceives it to be so, how can he be certain, that the faculty, by which he receives that information, does not deceive him? for unless he is certain, that veracity is a perfection, he cannot be certain, that God is veracious, nor therefore of the truth of his faculties. He must then remain in doubt, whether God is veracious, unless he can know it without the help of his faculties, that is, without the power or capacity of knowing it; or he must suppose the truth of his faculties without any proof. If that is not a first principle not to be doubted of, I see no defence against an incurable scepticism: we cannot argue for, or against anything, and the Remarker cannot know, that his position is true, *viz.* That the truth of our faculties depends upon the veracity of their author, since he must take it upon the credit of those faculties. Let him doubt the truth of his faculties as much as he will, if he affirms any one thing, in that one he must believe them upon their own evidence; and since he could not trust them in other things, till he was certain of the veracity of their author; whatever principle he establishes that certainty upon, he must rely upon the evidence of his faculties for the truth of that principle, which he tells us is this, *that veracity is a perfection, and consequently must belong to the nature of God.*† For which propositions we may therefore conclude, he was contented to suppose the truth of his faculties; and he cannot deny Mr. *Locke* the same privilege, till he can show him some way to knowledge without their help.

In the meantime there can be but two ways of knowing, that veracity is a perfection: either it is an innate principle, originally imprinted on the mind; (which I shall not endeavour to confute,

---

* *First Remarks*, p. 8.

† *First Remarks*, p. 7. *Second Remarks*, p. 18.

Mr. *Locke* having done it sufficiently, nor is it needful to my purpose.) Let that be the Remarker's way of knowledge, if he pleases, since he must no less rely upon the truth of his faculties in that way than any other, it being impossible for God himself to make any impression on us, without giving us a faculty whereby to receive it. But let us see, whether it is discoverable in the other way, which must be Mr. *Locke*'s of *sensation and reflection*. I suppose the Remarker does not doubt, that in this way we can distinguish truth from falsehood, *i.e.* know, that things are as they are; appear, as they appear; and that doing a thing differs from not doing it; that an apple, for example, is not a horse; that pain is not pleasure; and that performing our promise is not breaking it; or that representing things as they are, or as they appear to us, and performing our promise, *i.e.* veracity, is more agreeable to our nature, and beneficial to mankind, than the contrary; which how far *to us* the rule of good and evil, I have before shown, and shall only add here, that if in Mr. *Locke*'s way we can know, that what is beneficial to mankind, is better than what is destructive to it; that happiness is better than misery, that power and knowledge is better than impotence and ignorance; if we may trust our faculties in discerning truths, as sensible to us as our own existence; it cannot be doubted, that in his way we can be assured, that veracity is a perfection, till some other reason of falsehood can be imagined, than ignorance, impotence, or willing evil for its own sake, which cannot be conceived possible; to choose or prefer evil, as evil, being no less a contradiction, than to judge that to be the best, which we know to be worst.

And the Remarker could not have been at a loss how to deduce this, and all the other moral attributes of God, from Mr. *Locke*'s principles, if he had carefully considered his discourse of our idea of God, where he shows, that it is *made up of the simple idea we have received from sensation and reflection, by putting together all the qualities and powers, which we experiment in ourselves, and find it better to have, than to be without, and enlarging every one of them with our idea of infinity;** to which place I refer the Remarker. And if he can by *reflection* find veracity, justice, and goodness, among the things, that *it is better to have than to be without,* I hope (with what I have said) it will help him to deduce those attributes of God from Mr. *Locke*'s principles; which will satisfy him, that they give us a sure foundation for *natural and revealed religion*; by which we have a full assurance of a future state; the Remarker's third head of enquiries, which we are next to consider.

---

* [*Essay*], B. ii. c. 23. § 33, 34.

That the immortality of the soul is only highly probable by the light of nature, none can deny, who believes that Apostle, by whom we are told, *that life and immortality is brought to light be Jesus Christ through the gospel.* Why then is it objected against Mr. *Locke*'s principles, that they give us no certainty of the immortality of the soul without revelation? By what other way can we be certain of anything, that is only highly probable by the light of nature? Which is all that can be proved by any principles; and so far Mr. *Locke*'s will go, as I doubt not to make appear. But farther I shall show, that there is nothing in his principles, which at all weakens the main proofs of a future state; so that if they are thought to amount to a demonstration, they have no less force and evidence, upon his principles, which will leave no pretence on this account against them; as will plainly appear in examining the Remarker's objections.

You suppose, (says he) *that the soul may be sometimes absolutely without thoughts, of one kind or other; and also, that God may, if he pleases (for any thing we know by the light of nature) give, or have given, to some systems of matter a power to conceive and think. Upon these two suppositions, I could not make out any certain proof of the immortality of the soul, and am apt to think it cannot be done.**

As to the first of these objections, I confess I do not see of what consequence it is at all to the proofs of the immortality of the soul. Do they depend upon the contrary supposition, that the soul *always thinks?* If they do, proofs upon a supposition have a very unsure foundation. But let it be granted, that it is ever so clearly proved, that thinking is necessary to the soul's existence, that can no more prove, that it shall always exist, than it proves, that it has always existed; it being as possible for that omnipotence, which from nothing gave the soul a *being,* to deprive it of that *being* in the midst of its most vigorous reflections, as in an utter suspension of all thought. If then this proposition, *that the soul always thinks,* does not prove, that it is immortal, the contrary supposition takes not away any proof of it; for it is no less easy to conceive, that a being, which has the power of thinking with some intervals of cessation from thought, that has existed here for some time in a capacity of happiness or misery, may be continued in, or restored to the same state, in a future life, than that a *being,* which always thinks, may be continued in the same state. But to do the Remarker all the justice, and give him all the satisfaction I can, I shall examine the substance of what he objected against Mr. *Locke*'s assertion, without entering farther into the dispute,

---

* *First Remarks,* p. 8.

than may serve to show, whether it is of any consequence for, or against, the immortality of the soul.

Mr. *Locke* says, *men do not think in sound sleep*; and his reason is, because they are not *conscious* of it, and it is a contradiction to say a man thinks, but is not *conscious* of it; thinking consisting in that very thing of our being conscious of it. Upon which supposition, the Remarker *cannot make out any certain proof of the immortality of the soul.*

I suppose Mr. *Locke* did not design it as a proof of the immortality of the soul; but let us see, whether it weakens any proof of it, which the Remarker should have shown, but instead of that proposes difficulties, which that supposition involves him in, and begins with this notable one, *I wonder how you can observe, that your soul sometimes does not think; for when you do observe it, you think: if a man could think, and not think, at the same time, he might be able to make this observation.** This reversed may be an argument of some force indeed; but to conclude, that my soul does not always think, 'tis sufficient to know, that there has some time past, in which I was not conscious, that I thought; unless we will allow, that the *soul* may think, when the *man* does not, which is plainly to make them two *persons*, as Mr. *Locke* has shown† on p. 44, and 45, in which the Remarker says he does *not understand what that discourse about the identity or non-identity of the same man sleeping and waking, and about* Castor *and* Pollux,[1] *aims at, and tends to*.‡ A discourse about the *non-identity of the same man* would, I confess, be very hard to understand; but I find no such in that place, or any other of Mr. *Locke*'s *Essay*: he does not trifle at that rate, as to talk of the *same man's* not being the *same man*. He says indeed, that *if the* soul *can, whilst the body is sleeping, have its thinking and enjoyments apart, which* the man *is not at all conscious of; his* soul, *when he sleeps, and the* man *consisting of body and soul, when he is waking, are two* persons. And he further illustrates the same thing in his discourse

---

* [*First*] *Remarks*, p. 8.
† *Essay of Human Understanding.* [2.1.12.]
‡ [*First*] *Remarks*, p. 12.

---

1 Castor and Pollux were the twin children of Leda and Jupiter according to ancient Greek mythology. Their sister was Helen, the famous beauty who was the cause of the Trojan war. Castor and Pollux were famously close siblings who showed great affection for one another, and were supposedly rewarded for this affection by being immortalized in the constellation Gemini.

of *Castor* and *Pollux*, which, if it be thought absurd to assert, 'tis not hard to find what that discourse aims at, *v.g.* to show, that such an absurdity will follow from this supposition, that the soul thinks, when the man is not conscious of it. But whatever that discourse aims at, of what consequence can it be to the immortality of the soul, supposing it *does not* always think? That the Remarker says nothing of. But it will not be improper here to take notice of an inference he draws from it in his second Remarks; that Mr. *Locke* does not think the soul a *permanent substance* distinct from the body. *This* (says he) *seems to be the supposition you go upon, when you question, whether a man waking and sleeping* without *thoughts be the same* man. *If there be still the same soul, the same permanent substance, I see no room for that question, or doubt, which you make.** Here the question is again turned, not only from the same *person* to the same *man*, but to sleeping *without* thoughts, from sleeping *with* thoughts, that he is *not conscious of*; which are very different cases as to this question, though much the same indeed, as to the thing itself; but that the Remarker won't allow. But perhaps he takes the *soul, man* and *person*, to signify the same thing, and so they may to him: every man has the liberty to make his own words stand for what idea he pleases; but when he argues against the opinion of another, he must consider in what sense those terms are used by that other, and in that sense oppose him; otherwise he fights with his own notions, and not his, whom he seems to dispute with. And 'tis impossible to read Mr. *Locke*'s *Essay* with the least attention, and not know, that he does not use those three terms in one and the same signification; which if the Remarker had considered, he could not have so much mistaken Mr. *Locke*, or found such difficulties in his discourse. If Mr. *Locke* had understood by the *soul, man*, and *person*, the same thing, he would never have made such a question, whether the *soul* thinking apart, what the *man* is not at all conscious of, were not a *distinct person*, from the *man*; which would be just the same thing, as to ask, whether the soul thinking apart, what the soul is not conscious of, be not a distinct soul from the soul: But understanding by *person*, as he does, *self consciousness*, and by *man* the *soul and body united*, he may question, whether the *same soul*, the *same permanent substance*, thinking *apart from the body* in sound sleep, what the waking *man* is not conscious of, whether that *incommunicable consciousness* does not make the *soul*, and the *man* consisting of body and soul, two distinct persons; *personal identity*, according to him, consisting in the *same consciousness*, and not in the same *substance*: for whatever substance there is, without con-

---

* *Second Remarks*, p. 14–15.

sciousness there is no *person*. *Consciousness* therefore, and not *substance*, making a *person*, the same consciousness must make the same person, whether in the same, or in different substances; and no farther than the same consciousness extends, can there be the same person: but wherever there are *two distinct incommunicable consciousnesses*, there are two distinct *persons*, though in the same substance.

But farther, not only Mr. *Locke*'s question may be made, supposing the soul a *distinct permanent substance*, but he could not make it upon any other supposition with the least sense, to his purpose, which is to confute this opinion, that the *soul* thinks, in sound sleep, when the *man* is not conscious of it. Now what manner of argument, I pray, would this make?

If the soul thinks, when the man is not conscious of it, the *soul* and the *man* are two *persons*.

But the soul not being a permanent substance, *may* make two persons. *Ergo*, the soul *cannot* think when the man does not, because that makes them two persons; the sum of which is, the soul *cannot* think apart, because it *can*.

But if this assertion, that the soul and the man are two persons, implies, that it is not a permanent substance, let those look to it, who say, that the *soul* thinks, when the *man* is not conscious of it, since it is only a consequence of that supposition; but can no way concern Mr. *Locke*, who denies that supposition. But the Remarker is to be excused for making an inference so inconsistent with the design of that discourse, since he confesses he does not understand what it tends to, and perhaps only ventured at a shrewd guess to provoke a clearer account. And indeed, the best construction I can make of the Remarker's writing against Mr. *Locke*'s *Essay*, is, that he understands very little of it; so groundless are the difficulties he makes, and his consequences so wrong. This I am sure, no man that means well, if he understands any thing of what Mr. *Locke* says upon this subject, *that men think not always*, can from thence infer, that he does not think the soul a permanent substance; for it is plain, all the difficulties he finds in supposing the soul does not always think, arise only from its being in a sleeping, and waking man, the same permanent substance. Why else does he find it *so very hard to be conceived, that the soul in a sleeping man should this moment be busy a thinking; and the next moment in a waking man, not remember, nor be able to recollect one jot of all those thoughts?** Why, does he think it strange, *if the soul has ideas of its own, that it derived not from sensation or reflec-*

---

* *Essay*, p. 45. [*Essay*, 2.1.14.]

tion, that it should never, in its private thinking, retain any of them, the very moment it wakes out of them; and then make the man glad with new discoveries?* Or why does he call it an *absurdity*, to make the *soul* and the *man* two *persons*?† There is nothing strange or absurd in all this, if the soul in a sleeping and *waking* man be not the same permanent substance.

I hope what has been said, is sufficient to help the Remarker's understanding in that discourse of Mr. *Locke*'s, which so much puzzled him; and then I am certain he cannot apprehend it of any consequence to the immortality of the soul, supposing *it does not think, when the man is not conscious of it*. I now proceed to his second difficulty.

I do not understand (says he) *how the soul, if she be at any time utterly without thoughts, what it is, that produces the first thought again, at the end of that unthinking interval.*‡ And what then? Must we therefore conclude it cannot be done? If that be a good argument, we must deny the most common and visible operations in nature. Do you understand *how* your soul thinks at all? *How* it passes from one thought to another? *How* it preserves its treasure of ideas, to produce them at pleasure on occasions? And recollects those it had not in a long time reflected on? *How* it moves your body, or is affected by it? These are operations, which I suppose you are not so sceptical as to doubt of; nor yet pretend to understand how they are done: and since we are certain, that the soul is affected with all the considerable changes of the body, that it is sick, and in pain, and unable to perform its functions, according as the body is disordered; since we so sensibly perceive it to become drowsy, when the body is so; so many degrees abated of its action, even to very near not thinking at all, from that intenseness and vigour of thought it had, and recovers, when the body is refreshed with sleep; whatever is the cause of these effects, whether some immediate connection between them, or an arbitrary law of their union; where is the difficulty to conceive, that the same cause, which lulls it almost, should lay it quite to rest, and awaken it again with the body?

But *upon this supposition* (says the Remarker) *that all our thoughts perish in sound sleep, we seem to have a new soul every morning*.§ That is a pretty conceit indeed, but how does this seem? Thus, as he explains himself; *if a body cease to move, and*

---

* [*Essay*], p. 47. [2.1.17.]
† [*Essay*], p. 46. [2.1.15.]
‡ *First Remarks*, p. 9.
§ *Second Remarks*, p. 17.

come to perfect rest, the motion it had cannot be restored, but a new motion *may be produced. If all cogitation be extinct, all our ideas are extinct, so far as they are cogitations, and seated in the soul: so we must have them new impressed, we are, as it were, new born, and begin the world again.** The force of which argument lies thus: *cogitation* in the soul answering to *motion* in the body; as the same motion cannot be restored, but a new *motion* may be produced; so the same *cogitations* cannot be restored, but new *cogitations* must be produced. *Ergo*, we seem to have a new *soul* every morning. This may be a good consequence, when the Remarker has proved, that every *new motion* makes, or seems to make a *new body*. In the mean time, all I can infer from this parallel, is, that my thoughts today are not the same numerical thoughts I had yesterday; which, I believe, nobody supposes they are, though they did not suspect they had a *new soul* with every *new thought*.

But if the Remarker thinks, that if all our thoughts cease in sound sleep, all our ideas are extinct, and must be new impressed; I desire him to consider, when a sleeping or waking man thinks, what becomes of all those ideas, which he does not actually perceive in his own mind; for the mind is capable of taking notice but of very few at once: must not all the rest by this argument be extinct? And so we must have them new impressed; and are, as it were, new born, whenever we have any ideas, which we have not always actually perceived, *i.e.* every time we pass from one thought to another. This is a sure consequence, if, when all our thoughts cease, all our ideas must be new impressed, unless a man could actually perceive all the ideas he ever had at once; for his having only one thought in his mind can no more keep any other there, or excite any other, that it has no connexion with, than if he had not thought at all. I am thinking, for example, in my sleep, of a horse; his beauty, strength, and usefulness: does this thought preserve in my mind the idea of a church, of happiness or misery? Or can it help me to any of them, when I have occasion for them? If not, then these ideas must be new impressed, when I awake; but if they remain in the soul, when I was only thinking of a horse, wherever they are bestowed, it may be presumed, there is room for that one idea more without thrusting out another to give it place; and when that one is among them, I see no more reason, why they must be all new impressed, than that the others must have been new impressed, when I only thought of that one; unless it be supposed, that the soul has always just one idea more than there is place for in the

---

* *Ibid.*

repository of its ideas; and if that happen to crowd in, before another has got out, they will all be stifled together, or fly away for air.

But here the Remarker interposes, *If you say the ideas remain in the soul, and need only a new excitation; why then, say I, may not infants have* innate ideas *(which you so much oppose) that want only objects and occasions to excite and actuate them, with a fit disposition of the brain?** By what hath been said, it will appear, that this argument gains no force from Mr. *Locke*'s opinion, that *the soul does not always think*; since if the soul does always think, it can perceive but very few ideas at once; so that the same consequence will follow from a man's having only one thought, as from his having no thought at all; whether all his other ideas must be new impressed, or remain in the soul, and need only a new excitation. This objection therefore would have been as much to the purpose in any other place: the Remarker might have asked, if when a man thinks only upon one object, there remain ideas in the soul, which he does not perceive to be there; why may not infants have *innate ideas*, that want only occasions to excite them? This then, having no particular relation to the question in dispute, requires no answer here: but that the Remarker may not think he has entangled Mr. *Locke* with his own principles, I desire him to consider, if these are parallel cases, how comes it, that when objects or occasions excite these ideas in children, they do not perceive, that they were in their minds before; but consider them as things new, and till then absolutely unknown to them? But when ideas are excited in a man, which he has before received by sensation or reflection, he considers them as things he is acquainted with, and clearly perceives they have been in his mind before. Why does not every thing appear equally new to a man, which he has, or has not known before, as every idea does, the first time it is excited in him? But since it is certain, that the mind does perceive when any ideas are excited in it, that were there before; and that every idea appears new to it the first time it is excited; this can be no argument, that because the soul is capable of retaining the ideas it has received by sensation or reflection; that it can record them for its use, and recollect them at pleasure; therefore, it may have innate ideas, though it never perceives, that it had them, not even when they are excited in it; for this makes the cases so far from being the same, that it is one of the greatest arguments against *innate ideas*, that the mind does always perceive, when the ideas, which are excited in it, were there before. Besides, how can it be con-

---

* *Second Remarks*, p. 17.

ceived, that innate ideas should need any objects to excite them; and that the mind should never excite any of them in itself without those objects; as it often does excite in itself the ideas it received by sensation, or reflection, without the presence of those objects, by which it first received them. Why then are such objects necessary to excite *innate ideas,* since the mind has a power of exciting ideas in itself, without the presence of any object? When the Remarker has shown the reason of this considerable difference, and proved, that it does not hinder them from being parallel cases; then we may conclude against Mr. *Locke,* that since the soul can retain the ideas it has received, and excite them at pleasure, though it do not always perceive them, therefore it may have ideas, which it never did perceive, nor can excite in itself, nor, when they are excited, perceive, that it ever had them before; and then he can have nothing to say for himself, but must let us enjoy our *unperceivable ideas,* and be as much the better, and wiser for them, as we can.

But still the soul may be sometimes without any thought, and yet (for any thing we have heard) not endanger its immortality. Let us consider the Remarker's next difficulty.

Besides (says he) *I am utterly at a loss, how to frame any idea of a* dead soul, *or of a spirit without life or thoughts.** How a dead soul comes in here, I do not know. Can there be no life, where there is no thought? I confess, that I have hitherto thought, that insects and plants have life, though I did not suppose, that they do always think. He goes on: *What is the soul, when she does not think? She must be actually something, if she exist. She must then have some properties, whereby she is distinguished from nothing, and from matter.*[1] And again, in the second Remark, *You say the soul has no extension, nor at certain fits any cogitation. What can the soul be then but a certain power acting in the body, when the body is prepared for the exercise of it; and ceasing to act, when the body is indisposed?*† To which I answer, that it is true, we have no idea of the soul but by her operations; but that is no more a reason to conclude, that she is nothing when she does not operate, than when she does, since we are equally ignorant what the soul is, when we do think, as when we do not. I ask what is the soul when she does think? Is she a real permanent substance? What then are her peculiar prop-

---

* *First Remarks,* p. 9. *Second Remarks,* p. 16.
† [*Second Remarks*], p. 14.

---

1 [*First*] *Remarks,* p. 9.

erties, whereby she is distinguished from other substances? If it be said the power of thinking; I ask, whether she has any other properties to distinguish her from nothing, and from matter? If not, then nothing, or matter, may have the power of thinking. This is plain, if the soul has no essential properties distinct from matter, whereby she alone is capable of the power of thinking, there can be no reason, why matter may not have that power. If it be said she has other essential properties, without which she could not have the power of thinking, when the Remarker has found out what those properties are, he will then know what the soul is, when she does not think; for whatever that substance is, that has the power of thinking, there is no reason to doubt, that it remains the same, when it ceases from that action, any more than there is to doubt, that a body in motion, and at rest, is the same substance; for we have no clearer idea of the substance of body, than we have of the substance of spirit, as Mr. *Locke* has shown:* which excellent discourse alone one would have thought sufficient to prevent the least insinuation, that he does not think the soul a real permanent substance.

There is much more reason to conclude, that those do not think the soul a real permanent substance, who make this question, If the soul has no extension, nor at certain fits any cogitation, what can the soul be then, but a certain power acting in the body, when the body is prepared, *&c.* For from what other reason can they make it? If the soul be really something else than a certain power acting in the body, what can hinder it from being the same thing, when it does not act? But if it must be nothing, when it is not in action, *What then can the soul be, but a certain power acting in the body, when the body is prepared for the exercise of it and ceasing to Be when the body is indisposed?* But (to retort the Remarker's words) *whether that be a superior divine power distinct from matter, as a* vis movens,[1] *or a power fastened, I know not how, to the body, or upon such and such systems of matter; whether I say of these two suppositions better agrees with this doctrine, I cannot certainly tell; but either of them destroys the immortality of the soul, upon the dissolution of the body.*[2] I leave the reader to judge, which is most concerned in this consequence, Mr. *Locke*, who says, that it is not necessary to the existence of the soul, that it should be

---

* *Essay* B. ii. c. 23. [This discussion starts at 2.23.15.]

---

1 *Vis movens* means "moving force."
2 *Second Remarks*, p.14.

always in action; which would be absurd to say, if it be not a *distinct permanent substance*; or the Remarker, who thinks the soul cannot exist, when it is not in action; which there is no ground to think, if it be a *real permanent substance*.

The vanity of men seems to be the great reason, why they have so readily supposed, without any proof, that the soul does always think; for having no idea of it, but by its operations, we are unwilling to perceive our own ignorance, and loath to part with the only idea we have of that dear thing which we call self. On this account the Remarker seems offended with Mr. *Locke. Why* (says he) *do you affirm or introduce a new and unintelligible state of the soul, whereof neither you, nor others, can have any conception?** And why is this complained of, but that men are willing to believe they know more than they do? Or how else could they think a state of *thinking, without being conscious of it*, more intelligible, than a state of not thinking at all? Or how could they conclude thinking, which is the action of the soul, necessary to the existence of the soul itself, if they did not make our knowledge the measure of things, and our not having an idea of a thing, sufficient to exclude it from being? I proceed now to the Remarker's last difficulty.

Then after all (says he) *what security can we have upon this supposition, that we shall not fall into this sleep at death, and so continue without life or thought?*† What I have said in the beginning of my discourse upon this head, might serve for an answer to this objection; but the Remarker, by repeating it, page 12, seeming to lay a great weight on it, I shall consider it more particularly.

And first (as I observed before) if our security of a future state depends upon this, *that the soul always thinks*, it has a very unsure foundation; for there is no pretence of a proof, that the soul does always think; and there are great probabilities, that it does not think in sound sleep (as Mr. *Locke* has shown.) but if the proofs of a future state do not depend upon the soul's always thinking, the contrary supposition cannot lessen our security of it; and that they do not depend upon it, I think needs not be proved, nobody, that I know of, did ever offer this proposition, *that the soul does always think*, as a proof of its immortality. And the reasons we have to expect a future state are of such a nature, that they can receive no force from it, nor lose any by the contrary supposition. The Remarker on another occasion tells Mr. *Locke*, the grounds of our expectation of *future punishments and rewards* are, that there is a presage of them from natural conscience; and that *they are*

---

*   *Second Remarks*, p. 16.
†   [*First*] *Remarks*, p. 9.

deducible from the nature of God, if we allow him moral attributes.*
Now it is evident, that neither of these two grounds can lose any of their force upon this supposition, that the soul does not think in sound sleep, and will not they secure us, that we shall not continue in this sleep after death? If not, why does the Remarker mention them as proofs of a future state? But if they do prove it, why does he say, he *could make out no certain proof of the immortality of the soul, upon this supposition, that it is sometimes without thoughts*? Since those proofs he mentions remain in their full force, notwithstanding this supposition. Thus having shown, that all the consequences the Remarker draws from Mr. *Locke*'s supposition are without grounds, I may with assurance conclude, that it is of no consequence to the immortality of the soul, nor does at all weaken any proof of it.

I cannot here forbear taking notice, how little service they do to religion, who establish the main principles of it upon such an uncertain foundation, as the nature of a thing, of which we are so very ignorant, as we certainly are, of *what the soul is*. Her operations we have clear ideas of; and therefore from our capacity of discerning and choosing good or evil; and from the power, wisdom, and goodness of God, which we may certainly know to belong to his nature; we have very good arguments, and great probabilities of a future state of punishments and rewards; such as no considering man can deny, and within every one's understanding. But when the soul's immortality is said to depend upon such suppositions as this, *that the soul always thinks*, or that it is *immaterial*; what can the consequence be, but to make men think they have very little assurance of a future life, when they find themselves so much in the dark as to those principles, upon which it is established, that the greatest proofs of them are drawn from our ignorance? As that we cannot *conceive how* matter should be capable of such and such powers as we perceive in the soul; or (as the Remarker objects) *what* the soul is, when she is without thoughts.

But could the immateriality of the soul be proved to be as certain, as it is highly probable, it can never be of good consequence, and may be dangerous, to make that the main proof of its immortality; for this is an argument of no use to the generality of mankind, who want either leisure, or capacity, for such nice speculations; and if they are convinced on other grounds, that the soul is immortal, it is no great matter, whether they think it immaterial, or no. But if they are persuaded, that it

---
* *Third Remarks*, p. 13.

cannot be immortal, if it is not immaterial, 'tis easy to see of how ill consequence that must be, if the proofs of the soul's immateriality should not happen to convince them; as it often falls out by the different cast of men's heads, that the same arguments, that are very strong and persuasive to one man, have no force at all with another, especially in abstract reflections. Those, therefore, who are zealous for truth, should endeavour to establish it upon the plainest, and clearest, principles, and such as are most adapted to common apprehensions. This is not the only instance, in which I have observed, that truth does not suffer less from those, who would maintain it upon false or uncertain grounds, than from those, who openly oppose it. I have known several, who have been carefully enough instructed in their duty, who yet for want of being taught at first, or applying themselves to consider the true grounds of it, have been easily argued out of their good notions, though some of them persons of no mean capacity; for if the foundation fail, the best superstructure will fall, though strong and immoveable, when established upon its proper grounds. And this does not only happen, when the foundation is in itself weak or uncertain, but when truths are taught upon principles, which, though true, and solid in themselves, are not the ground or reason of those truths; which some have done out of a good design of rendering the truths they teach the more sacred. But everything stands firmest on its own foundation: and I believe, if it were rightly considered, it would appear, that the reasons of all moral truths are plain and clear, and within the reach of the lowest apprehensions. These things, which I have only hinted at, are of great consequence to be thoroughly considered by all, who have the instruction of others under their care, that they may not think they sufficiently acquit themselves of their duty by inculcating good maxims, when their negligence, or *mistaken zeal* in teaching the grounds of them, may at least give too great advantage to those, who make it their business to corrupt the *principles*, as well as the *practice* of their companions, which are but too many in this libertine age.

This being a matter of so universal concern, I hope I shall be excused, if I have led the reader a little out of the way for it. We now return to the Remarker, who, after he has repeated his last difficulty, *i.e. If the soul be sometimes without thoughts, why may she not be so, thoughtless, and senseless, after death?* he adds, *it is some comfort, indeed, that we shall at length return to life at the resurrection: but I know not how you explain* that; *nor how far you allow us to be the same* men, *and the same* persons *then that we are now.*[1] This is a great comfort indeed, and I suppose the Remarker here designed to make Mr. *Locke* amends for all the faults he has imputed to his principles, by owning, that they afford us this comfort; but I cannot guess what *that* is which he knows not how Mr. *Locke* explains. Mr. *Locke* never attempted, that I know of, to explain *how* we shall return to life, which *that* seems to refer to, nor how far we shall then be the same *men*; and he needed not have told him, that he knows not how he explains a thing, which he has not explained at all. But Mr. *Locke* has very clearly explained how far he allows us to be the same *persons, consciousness* according to him, *as far as it is extended, makes the same person,* in which, he says, *is founded all the right, and justice, of reward, and punishment, happiness, and misery.** And thus, he says, *we may without any difficulty conceive at the resurrection, the same* person, *though in a body not exactly in make or parts the same he had here, the same* consciousness *going along with the soul that inhabits it:*† Which may be sufficient to satisfy the Remarker how St. *Peter at the resurrection will be the same*;‡ and how Mr. *Locke* conceives the resurrection, as far as is revealed of it, and to all its ends and purposes, which is our *happiness, or misery*. Further than this he does not pretend, nor are we concerned to know; and I think, in a matter, which can only be known by revelation, no man ought to determine, or enquire farther than the Holy Spirit has thought fit to reveal. Mr. *Locke* knows too well the vanity and presumption of such an attempt, to offer at it. "It is enough,§ (says he) that every one shall appear before the judgment seat of Christ, to receive according to what he had done in his former life; but in what sort of body he shall appear, or of what particles made up, the Scripture having said nothing, but that it shall be a spiritual body raised in incorruption, it is not for me to determine." The Remarker must be contented** *to walk in the dark* as to these things, though he says he does not love it, since there is no way

---

* *Essay*, B. ii. c. 27. [2.27.18.]
† *Ibid.* § 15. [2.27.15.]
‡ *Vid. Second Remarks*, p. 15.
§ *Reply to the Bishop of Worcester*, p. 182. ["Mr. Locke's Reply to the Bishop of Worcester's Answer to his Second Letter" in *The Works of John Locke*, 10 vols. (Germany, Scientia Verlag Aalen, 1963) 315.]
** *Second Remarks*, p. 15.

---

1 *Second Remarks*, p. 12.

to have farther light in them than the Scripture has given. And if he thinks Mr. *Locke*'s doctrine of the soul obscure, because he does not pretend to be certain by his natural faculties, of things, which they cannot certainly discover (a way to knowledge, which some are very fond of) I believe Mr. *Locke* will be content not to be understood by him, rather than write what he does not understand himself, to appear intelligible to others.

The Remarker* next proceeds to the second supposition, which he thinks weakens the proofs of the immortality of the soul, *viz. That God may give, or have given, for anything we know, to some systems of matter, a power to perceive, and think.* And here one would expect he should have shown how this supposition weakens the proofs of the soul's immortality; but all his objections are against the probability of the supposition, and to show the difficulties of conceiving how matter should have such a power; which he enlarges upon in his third remark, and has several pages to that purpose, for what reason I know not, since Mr. *Locke* allows it to be highly probable, that the soul is immaterial, but where he is speaking of demonstration, only says, that it is not *impossible, for anything we know,* that God may give, or have given, to some systems of matter, disposed as he sees fit, a power to perceive and think. But my design being only to vindicate Mr. *Locke*'s principles from the dangerous consequences imputed to them by the Remarker, I shall not enter into that dispute; and I think Mr. *Locke* has said enough, in his last additions, to silence the triumph of such sort of arguments, drawn from *the unconceiveableness of something in one hypothesis,* which cannot be a proof of the contrary opinion, in which there are things altogether as inexplicable, and as far remote from our comprehension. All the demonstration we can have from such difficulties, is of the weakness and scantiness of our knowledge, which should not make us forward in determining positively on either side, much less to establish the immortality of the soul on so uncertain a foundation; which is a consideration I have before insisted on, and I cannot but think Mr. *Locke* has done much more service to religion in that discourse, *B.* iii. *c.* 4[1] where, after he had said, that he "sees no contradiction in it, that Omnipotency should give to certain systems of matter a power to perceive and think, though it be most highly probable, that the soul is

---

* [*First*] *Remarks,* p. 13.

1 This quote is actually found in *Essay,* 4.3.6

immaterial;" he adds, that "if our faculties cannot arrive to demonstrative certainty about it, we need not think it strange: all the great ends of morality and religion are well enough secured, without philosophical proofs of the soul's immateriality; since it is evident, that he, who made us at first begin to subsist here, sensible, intelligent beings, and for several years continued us in such a state, can and will restore us to the like state in another world,* and make us capable there to receive the retribution he has designed to men, according to their doings in this life; and therefore it is not of such mighty necessity to determine one way or the other, as some overzealous for or against the immateriality of the soul have been forward to make the world believe." These are Mr. *Locke*'s words; and I appeal to all unbiased men, whether he does not better secure the belief of a future state, by establishing it on such grounds, as give an equal assurance of it, whether the soul is immaterial, or no; than those, who take pains to persuade men, that a future state is less certain, if the soul is not immaterial.

But besides the uncertainty and danger of this argument, which I have before taken notice of, the uselessness of it, to the generality of mankind, sufficiently shows, that it cannot be the foundation of the belief of a future state. That it is not so to the Eastern Pagans at this day, we have the evidence of a† judicious author, both from the information of the missionaries, who have been longest among them, and his own conversation with them, who tell us, that they believe the *immortality* of the soul, but have no notion of its *immateriality*; and that they only suppose it of a *matter* subtle enough to escape being seen or handled. And that many of the old philosophers, who expected a future state, had no thoughts of the soul's being *immaterial*, any one must observe, who has read them with attention. And I believe, if well examined, it will appear, that those among them, who had a notion of the soul's being immaterial, did not believe its immortality upon that foundation, but only sought an explication, how the soul by its own nature might be capable of that immortality; which they found great reason to hope for, on other grounds much more firm and persuasive.

---

* *Vide* the 4th edit. [Cockburn's reference here is not correct. This quote can be found in the *Essay*, 4.3.6.]

† *Loubere* du Royaume de *Siam*. [La Loubere, de. *Du Royaume de Siam* (Paris, Coignard: 1691). La Loubere was an envoy from the French King to the King of Siam in 1687 and 1688. In this work, he recounted the geography, customs, and social structure of seventeenth-century Siam.]

But what is yet more considerable, were this proof of the soul's immortality as certain and as universally received, as any self-evident proposition, it would not all serve to the chief end of our assurance of the soul's immortality, *viz*. The expectation of rewards and punishments in a future state according to our doings in this life; without which 'tis no matter, whether we think the soul immortal or no. And this we could never have by the most attentive consideration, and the clearest knowledge of what kind of substance the soul is. It must be established on far different grounds, such as the consideration of ourselves as rational and free creatures, of which we have an intuitive, infallible perception; and of an omnipotent Being, from whom we are, and on whom we depend, of which we have a demonstrative knowledge within everyone's understanding to whom it is proposed. And if the consequences drawn from them are not sufficient to assure men of a future state of rewards and punishments, as the clearest proofs of the soul's immortality can signify nothing without them, so neither can they add any force to them, and therefore are of no use to the great ends of morality and religion. For suppose to convince an intelligent heathen, who thought the soul material, and doubted of a future state of rewards and punishments, arguments were used to prove the soul in its own nature undissolvable, and that therefore it must remain after death; he might then reasonably enquire in what state it remains, how he may be sure, that it is in a state of rewards and punishments, and that it does not return to the universal soul, of which it may be an effluence; or inform the next parcel of matter it finds fitted for it as some philosophers have thought. This, it is plain, must be still in doubt to him, notwithstanding those proofs of the soul's immortality; and arguments of another nature must be used to satisfy him in this point, whatever may be most proper to work on his understanding. Suppose those I have before hinted at; That 'tis reasonable to think that the *wise and just* Author of our being, having made us capable of *happiness* and *misery*, and given us faculties of discerning and choosing good or evil, designed we should be accountable for our actions, and *happy* or *miserable*, according as they are conformable, or not, to that law, which he has established in our very natures, that his will might be certainly known to us; and since it is visibly not so, in the ordinary course of his providence, but all things happen alike to the righteous and the wicked, in this world, 'tis most consonant to reason to think this is only a state of probation, and that the dispensation of rewards and punishments is reserved for a future life;

there being no other way to reconcile the partial distribution of things here to that order which we know is agreeable to the divine will, by the conformity it has to our reason, which is a ray of his own wisdom. We will suppose the heathen convinced by these arguments, or others to the same purpose; that he owns it is highly reasonable to conclude there must be a future state of rewards and punishments; but he does not so well digest the soul's being immaterial; he has no notion of a substance without any extension. Suppose then the Remarker should tell him, as he does Mr. *Locke*, if the soul is not *immaterial*, there can be no certain proof that it is immortal. And I desire him to take this dilemma for the heathen's answer: Either the arguments, by which I have been convinced, that there will be punishments and rewards in a future state, are proofs of it, or they are not; if not, then tho' the soul should be immortal, I have no assurance that it will be a state of rewards or punishments; and if they are proofs of a future state, then a future state is equally certain, tho' the soul be not immaterial, since that does not make it less consonant to the justice and wisdom of God, nor less within his power. I believe the Remarker will find he has no way to solve this dilemma, but must either give up the certainty of rewards and punishments, or the necessity of thinking the soul is immaterial, to prove a future state; and I defy him to establish the belief of rewards and punishments in a future state on any arguments, that will not be equally conclusive, whether the soul is immaterial or not.

This then is evident, that Mr. *Locke*'s supposition, that God may have given (for anything we know) to some systems of matter a power to perceive, and think; does not at all weaken any proof of the soul's immortality, that can be of use to the great ends of religion, for which alone we are concerned to know, that the soul is immortal. And perhaps the insignificancy, as to those ends, of our knowing what kind of substance the soul is, may be the reason we are left so much in the dark about it. Our wise Maker has proportioned our faculties only to our necessities, and has made his will known to us by a light of nature clear enough to render any one inexcusable, who does not follow it; tho' the full assurance of an eternal retribution is only given us by *Jesus Christ, who has brought life, and immortality, to light, through the Gospel,* which I have already shown, that Mr. *Locke*'s principles give us a sure foundation for, both of natural and revealed religion. So that I think no more remains to clear the Remarker's difficulties; his doubts of *natural conscience,* (which is the chief subject of his third

Remark) being easily resolved from what has been already said. But the Remarker being a little unlucky at drawing inferences from Mr. *Locke*'s principles, I will give him some help in his enquiry what *natural conscience* is, according to them.

But first, I must take notice of a cavil he begins with, at Mr. *Locke*'s defining conscience to be nothing else but* *our own opinion of our own actions*, without expressing what sort of actions are the subjects of it. Now anyone, who reads that part of his *Essay*, will find that discoursing of† *innate practical principles*, he all along mentions only such actions, as are to be referred to moral rules; and that he had no reason to apprehend being misunderstood, or that it could be supposed he included any other sort of actions, no other being at all to the purpose in that question.

Before I proceed to speak of what I think the true notion of natural conscience, of what authority, and of what use it is; it will be fit to consider what the Remarker says he understands by it, which he next proceeds to tell us, but defines it more particularly in another place thus: *A natural sagacity to distinguish moral good and evil; or a different perception and sense of them, with a different affection of the mind arising from it; and this so immediate, as to prevent and anticipate all external laws, and all ratiocination.*[1] This, he says, he takes to be *the foundation of natural religion, without which he does not know how it can subsist;*[2] tho' he approves of Mr. *Locke*'s account of natural religion, so far as it goes. *You place natural religion* (says he)‡ *I think in the belief of the being of a God, and of obedience due to him. This is good, so far as it goes, and is well supported. But the question is, what laws those are that we ought to obey, or how we can know them without revelation, unless you take in natural conscience for a distinction of good and evil, or another idea of God, than what you have given us.* Having already anticipated this doubt, by showing how the moral attributes of God are deducible from Mr. *Locke*'s principles, and how we know what his will is, by the conformity or repugnancy of things to our reason, and with respect to human nature, of which he is the author, I need not give a particular answer to this question. But since the Remarker

---

* *Third Remarks*, p. 5. [This discussion begins on p. 4.]
† [*Essay*], B. i. C. 3.
‡ [*Third Remarks*], p. 5.

---

1 *Third Remarks*, p. 7.
2 *Third Remarks*, p. 5.

lays so great a stress upon his *principle of natural conscience, in that sense and notion*, which he has given of it, that he* *takes it to be the foundation of natural religion*, and thinks *the distinction of good and evil, is manifested, and supported by it*; let us farther consider it.

It would be too tedious to repeat all that the Remarker says on this subject, from the beginning of his third letter to the 16th page. I need only hint at some observations, by which it will appear, that he has not settled in his own mind a determinate idea of his *principle of natural conscience*, but argues for it sometimes in one sense, and sometimes in another; that Mr. *Locke* is not at all concerned in the greatest part of his argument; and by which the weakness of the whole will be obvious to every reader.

After his definition, he gives us a notable illustration of his principle in the soul of distinguishing *morally good and evil*, without ratiocination, by the power we have of distinguishing *sensible qualities* without reflection, or ratiocination.† He might every whit as well have told us, that since we have a power we have a power of distinguishing *moral relations*, without making use of our eyesight, we may distinguish red, and yellow, without eyes; they being no more the proper and only inlets of our ideas of colours, than reflection is of moral distinctions; which the Remarker says we may have without reflection, since we can distinguish colours, and other sensible qualities without reflection. But if this were so, Mr. *Locke* may very well say, what the Remarker believes he will not,‡ that then children would be able to distinguish moral good and evil, for they very clearly distinguish all the objects of sensation, that come in their way; and this principle could never be *improved*, or *corrupted*, as no one can be persuaded, that any sensation he has is more or less agreeable, or that a disagreeable sensation is an agreeable one; which if we could, it is evident, that our senses would not be sufficient to their end, to give us notice of what is convenient, or inconvenient to the body. And it is reasonable to think, if there were such an inward sensation designed, as the Remarker says, to direct us as to what is good or hurtful to the soul, it would operate as constantly as those others do: no man could prefer vice to virtue, any more than he can pain to pleasure; otherwise it would not answer the end it was designed for.

Another thing to be observed is, that most of the Remarker's arguments were anticipated by Mr. *Locke*, tho' he takes no notice

---

* [*Third Remarks*], p. 4 and 5.
† [*Third Remarks*], p. 8.
‡ Ibid.

of the answer to them; as to the same purpose we were now upon, Mr. *Locke* having owned, *that there are natural tendencies imprinted on the minds of men, and that from the first instances of sense, and perception, there are some things grateful, and others ungrateful to them;** the Remarker takes occasion from thence, to desire he *will grant such alike impression on the soul, with reference to moral good and evil, as a rule or direction to our actions*; though Mr. *Locke* there says,† that those impressions he speaks of, are so far from confirming the like, with relation to moral good and evil, that *this is an argument against them*; since if there were any such impressions, *we could not but perceive them constantly operate in us, and influence our knowledge, as we do those others on the will and appetite, the desire of happiness, and aversion for misery, continuing (as innate practical principles ought) to influence all our actions without ceasing, and are in all persons, and all ages, steady and universal.* But this the Remarker takes no notice of.‡ In another place he argues, that exorbitant practices against natural conscience are no proof, that there is no such principle;§ which Mr. *Locke* grants, nor does he contend against a *natural* rule. But the generally allowed breach of a rule anywhere, he says, is a proof, that it is not INNATE, which he had given instances of in several nations. This objection not being easily answered, the Remarker chooses rather to oppose an argument, which Mr. *Locke* does not use, but on the contrary owns that it is none. But anyone, who considers what** Mr. *Locke* objects, will easily see to how little purpose the Remarker takes so much pains to show, that the same arguments, which he brings against *innate principles*, may be used to prove, that the law of Christianity is not known among Christians; for besides the great difference of an *innate law*, which men must always carry about with them, from any other, that they may avoid reflecting on, or misunderstand; the case of Christians acting against a known law cannot be the same with that, which Mr. *Locke* represents, unless the Remarker can show any Christians, *who constantly, without the least remorse, or shame, offend against that law, which they believe; and that all the bystanders, even lawmakers, and governors, silently connive at it, nay affirm that it is their duty to do so*: For this is the case of those nations, which

---

* [*Third Remarks*], p. 9. [*Essay* 1.3.3.]
† *Essay*, B. i. C. 3. § 3.
‡ *Third Remarks*, p. 11.
§ *Essay*, B. i c. 3. [*Essay*, 1.3.12.]
** [*Third Remarks*], p. 14.

Mr. *Locke* mentions.* But the Remarker has a shrewd objection against this argument: they are *barbarous people*, he says, and he excepts against them for witnesses, as *personæ infames*. I find, if Mr. *Locke* would convince him, that there are no *innate principles*, he must show him some polite nation, where the people have diligently, and rightly employed their faculties, and yet are ignorant of the law of nature. This might be required, if Mr. *Locke* denied a law of nature, knowable by our natural faculties; but to prove what he affirms, that this law is not knowable to men, but by their making a right use of their faculties, it is sufficient to show, that there are men, who are absolutely ignorant of the clearest principles of that law. No, says the Remarker, they are barbarous ignorant people; and therefore are no good witnesses, that there are no innate principles. But are they not men, I pray? What is it then, that makes them more barbarous, or ignorant than others, but their not having made a right use of their natural faculties? This is Mr. *Locke*'s argument, that there are no innate principles, since some nations, for want of making a right use of their faculties, are so *barbarous*, or *ignorant*, as to have no notion of the clearest of those principles, which are esteemed innate. To which the Remarker's objection, that they are a barbarous people, not fit to be admitted for witnesses, is indeed very extraordinary. If he pleases to consider what he means by *barbarous*, and what is the cause, that these people are so, I believe he will better see the force of Mr. *Locke*'s argument, and allow them to be very good witnesses in this case; though perhaps he might with reason except against them at the bar. All he is desired to take upon their credit is, that men do not know their duty, without making a right use of their natural faculties; and that therefore there are no *innate principles*, or *none to any purpose*, since they do not operate, till men by reflection discover that law, which is to be the rule of their actions. To prove this, Mr. *Locke* mentions some vicious practices approved in several nations; which the Remarker calls† *raking up their dirt and filth, to throw in the face of human nature*. It shows men indeed, that they should not idly, or rashly, take up with the first notions they meet with, but employ their faculties in the best manner they can, which God has given them to attain the knowledge of their duty, which they can only be ignorant of by their own fault. But what *indignity* this can be thought *upon mankind*, or what *piece of ingratitude to our Maker*, I believe nobody but the Remarker can apprehend.

---

* [*Third Remarks*], p. 10.
† *Ibid.*

He next proceeds to mention some virtuous actions of heathen states, contrary to their interest, and yet done with general applause, as a proof of natural conscience.* They are indeed proofs of a *law of nature*, which Mr. *Locke* is no less an advocate for than he, tho' he denies *innate principles*; which leads me to a very material observation, which is, that, throughout this whole discourse, the Remarker uses indifferently, as terms of the same signification, *law of nature, natural conscience, innate principles, innate powers, and natural principles*,† which all signify very different things; and of which Mr. *Locke* has only denied *innate principles*; which considered, it will appear, that he is very little concerned in the greatest part of this dispute. But I shall only instance two or three places particularly, as where he argues, that *universal consent is not necessary to declare a* principle *to be* natural; *for the sense of music, of beauty, of order, and proportion, are natural to mankind, tho' some men are not at all affected with them. Even the* power *of reason,* (says he) *has several passions,* &c *appear sooner in some than others; and if you allow these* principles *to be* natural, *and born with us, I know not why you should make such ado about the word* innate. *If you allow none at all, not these last mentioned, nor so much as* willing, or nilling *this, or that, the controversy will be changed; and I desire to know what idea you can form of a soul without any* powers, *or any* action.[1] Now here it is plain, that by natural *principles* is only meant *powers* or *faculties* of the soul; which is a very different sense from that, in which Mr. *Locke* denies any *principles* to be *innate*, tho' he does not deny them to be *natural*. But in this sense of them he will make no ado about the word *innate*: if the question be, whether there are innate *powers* or *faculties* in the soul, the controversy will not be *changed*, for there will be no controversy at all. Mr. *Locke* only contends against those, who say there are principles of metaphysical or moral truths originally imprinted on the mind; by which if they only mean, that there is an *innate* power or capacity in the soul of knowing those truths, they mean nothing different from Mr. *Locke*, who denies *innate principles*; for he does not deny, that there is a power in the soul of perceiving, and assenting to those truths, or of distinguishing good and evil; tho' he is not so ready at it as the Remarker, without employing his faculties about it, or

---

* [*Third Remarks*], p. 11.
† [*Third Remarks*], *Vide* p. 5. 9. 12.

---

1 *Third Remarks*, p. 12.1

without ratiocination. So there is no occasion for him to *form an idea of the soul without any powers*, nor for that supposition, which, with a seeming charitable wish, the Remarker would so groundlessly fasten on Mr. *Locke*.*

The next place I shall mention, where *innate* principles, and *natural* principles, are used in the same sense, and both only for *powers* or *faculties* of the soul, is p. 15. where he pretends to answer a *dilemma*, which Mr. *Locke* proposes concerning *innate principles*. But any one, who takes the pains to consider what he there says, will find, that he uses those terms in a quite different sense from that, which Mr. *Locke* understands by *innate principles*; and that therefore Mr. *Locke* is not at all concerned in that argument. Neither is it any thing to the Remarker's purpose of establishing *natural conscience* in his own sense and notion of it, if we may take it from his definition, p. 7. But, indeed, his uncertain use of these, and those other terms I have mentioned, makes it very difficult to know what he means by his *principle of natural conscience*;† for those principles, which he here affirms to be *innate*, are powers of the soul, the *exercise* of which, he says, is *conditional, and depends upon the disposition of the body*, culture, *and other* circumstances: which, as they are very different from those *principles*, which Mr. *Locke* denies to be innate; so are they also from the Remarker's‡ *principle of distinguishing in moral cases without* ratiocination, *sufficient for a general direction of our lives, and the foundation of natural religion*. For how can it be sufficient for those ends, if it depend upon contingent *circumstances*? Or how can the exercise of a power of distinguishing things *without ratiocination*, depend upon any *culture*, or be hindered by *contrary principles*,§ as, he says, this power may? For by *culture* here must be meant *a right instruction, or right* reflection; and by *contrary principles*, false maxims, or opinions, (though in the same place he uses that term in a quite different sense, for *powers* of the soul) which are all acts of *ratiocination*; and therefore to say, that the *exercise* of this power depends upon them, is the same thing as to say, that the power of distinguishing things *without ratiocination* depends upon *ratiocination*. Which if the Remarker understands, I believe he will hardly make it intelligible to anybody else.

From all these observations compared, and rightly applied, it will plainly appear, that Mr. *Locke* is very little concerned in this

---

* [*Third Remarks*], p. 13.
† [*Third Remarks*], p. 16.
‡ [*Third Remarks*], p. 5, 8, 9.
§ [*Third Remarks*], p. 16.

discourse, which, the Remarker says,* is in defence of natural conscience, against whom I know not, the most part of it being arguments for things, which Mr. *Locke* no less affirms than he, though he appear to oppose him, by using Mr. *Locke*'s words in a different sense from that, which he understands them in; and those arguments, by which the Remarker really does oppose him, being anticipated, and fully answered in Mr. *Locke*'s *Essay.*

And from the inconsistency of his definition of *natural conscience*, with his illustrations of it in several places, and his loose and undetermined use of those terms, which are of greatest consequence in this discourse, I must take leave to conclude, that he has not fixed in his own mind a clear idea of that principle which he contends for; though he thinks he has given *rules, and marks*,† by which it may sufficiently appear to others what he means by it. And therefore by those *marks* I will endeavour a little to clear his own notion to him; and for his satisfaction to establish what I think natural conscience is, according to Mr. *Locke*'s principles, and in the true notion of it; though Mr. *Locke* is without reason brought into this dispute, as is evident from the Remarker's own words; *I do not remember* (says he)‡ *that in this sense you have once named natural conscience in your book.* Why then, I pray, are so many arguments used, as if he had written a whole book against it? By what rule is a man concluded to deny everything, that he has not affirmed? But the Remarker is not the first, who has thought this good logic, and fair dealing against Mr. *Locke.* Whatever he writes next, if it should be of *gravitation*, or the *motion of the planets*, I think he would do well to put the articles of his religion at the end of it, for fear he should be accused of having none, if his book should not happen to name any.

But as to *natural conscience*, I desire the Remarker to examine, whether that *principle* he speaks of, or (as I had rather express it here, as less equivocal) that *power* of distinguishing in moral things *without ratiocination*, be not a consequent of a *previous* ratiocination, or instruction; by which, having not some clear or *confused* ideas of good and evil, a different affection of the mind constantly arised from them, and this so immediate, as that it may be truly said to be *without* ratiocination; from which the mistake may come, that it prevents, or is *before any ratiocination*, though it is really an effect of it, only operating without taking notice of its

---

* Ibid.
† [*Third Remarks*], p. 8.
‡ Third Remarks, p. 5.

cause; as in other cases, the likings or aversions of the mind, to things, or persons, may be observed to do, which having been at first produced by some outward cause, some good, or evil, we have found, or heard, or apprehended of those things, or persons, the same affection constantly exerts itself at their presence, without any reflection on the cause, or perhaps the least sense, that it ever had a known cause.

And this sudden affection in moral cases is indeed of excellent use, when it is once *set on work by an enlightened judgment,* to keep up the distinction of good and evil; to incite, or to be a check upon men's actions, in the heat of a temptation, when they have neither time nor power to reason the case, or to reflect upon the instructions, that have been given them; and thus may be truly called *the support of natural religion;* or, as the apostle says, *a witness accusing or excusing those, who have no other law but that of nature;* but must not therefore be taken for the law itself, or as the Remarker calls it, the *foundation of natural religion,* but rather *natural religion for the foundation of it;* and then it may with safety be relied on. Therefore philosophers, and divines, having mostly written for such, as have had in some measure a knowledge of their duty, do with good reason give great authority to this witness, and frequently send men to consult their consciences, as if it were the original rule and an infallible director. For it is not easily perverted, or silenced, when once rightly set on work; and has a great influence on men's actions, nothing being more insupportable, than to stand condemned in our own judgments; or more delightful, than the approbation of own minds: and therefore this monitor may prevail, when our passions have misled or silenced reason; or the hopes of escaping future punishments made us for a while secure.

But powerful and faithful as this witness is, since it may by false opinions, or vicious habits, take a wrong bias, (which the greatest assertors of its authority confess) and is always set on work by the first persuasions, which happen to take possession of men's thoughts since it does not direct their opinions, but is influenced by them; this not only shows, that it is not designed for the original rule, and first director of our actions, or *the foundation of natural religion,* but that it is of dangerous consequence to lay the whole weight of morality upon conscience alone, independent of the occasions, from which it has taken the first bent. For no doubt there are too many, who by an unhappy early education, pursue with the same bent of conscience, or without the least remorse, what others (who have been better taught) abhor.

Now in this case, to bid these men appeal to their consciences, as an innate guide, that will infallibly direct them in their duty, can only serve to confirm them in their prejudices, and to make them go on securely in their vicious habits, without farther examination, when they find themselves acquitted by that inward sense, which they are taught to revere as the impression of God himself. That this may be the case of many, is not denied by the Remarker:* *We do not conceive* (says he) *natural conscience such a light as may not be dimmed or it may be* extinguished *in some people:*† and in another place, *appeal with sincerity to your conscience; if that be obscured,* perverted, *or feared, we cannot help it.*‡ *These principles of conscience are seeds, that may die, or may thrive, &c they may be weak in some, and* ineffectual *in others, by contrary principles, or other impediments.* This being granted, it is evident, that those people in whom these principles happen to be *extinguished* or *perverted*, will in vain appeal with sincerity to their consciences: there is no way to set them right but by rectifying their judgments; they are to be warned not to trust to so dangerous a security, and to be convinced of their errors, and their obligations, on rational grounds.

I appeal to the Remarker, whether this is not the only way of dealing with a man, who has been educated from his infancy in false principles, confirmed by vicious habits, and the approbation of all his companions; whether such a man may not by reflection and reason be corrected, and convinced of the natural obligations, which the Creator has laid on him, as a rational, sociable, and dependent creature? This, I doubt not, the Remarker will allow: his zeal for an *innate light* will not transport him so far, as to put out the *light of reason*, that it may shine alone, and leave men irrecoverably in the dark, in whom this light of conscience happens to be *extinguished*: Though, he says,§ *he does not see, by what ratiocination we can collect what the will of God is, unless we take in natural conscience for a distinction of good and evil.* I hope on farther consideration, and what I have before said on that subject, he will not deny the consistency of our duty to reason, and the evidence of it to all, who diligently set themselves to know it. That would indeed be *an indignity to mankind, and a great ingratitude to our Maker*. But all, who perceive the reasonableness of what is required of us, the necessity of it for the

---

*   *Third Remarks*, p. 10.
†   [*Third Remarks*], p. 15.
‡   [*Third* Remarks], p. 16.
§   *Third Remarks*, p. 5.

preservation or perfection of our nature; all, who read the will of God in his wisdom, must acknowledge, that he has not been thus wanting unto men, but that all the precepts of natural religion may be clearly known by the light of reason, to any one, who sets himself to search. This being what I believe the Remarker will not think fit to deny, I take for granted, and desire him to consider, whether a man, in whom the dictates of conscience (supposing them innate) have been early obscured, or perverted, being brought to a knowledge of his duty by reason, or reflection; whether, I say, this man has not a sure foundation for natural religion, without taking in his principle of conscience for a distinction of good and evil? This he must grant, unless he will say, that *general, obscure, and indistinct notices* (for so he describes his innate principles)* are a better foundation for natural religion, than clear and distinct knowledge; which if it be too absurd to assert, the Remarker must own, notwithstanding his zeal for *innate principles*, that those, who deny them, may have a sure foundation for natural religion, as long as the precepts of it are consistent with, or evident to, the light of reason.

And farther, I suppose the Remarker will very readily allow, that when a man is thus brought by reason to a true sense of this duty, his conscience, though before perverted, will then be set right, and thenceforward condemn or acquit him, according as he obeys or not that law, which his understanding has assented to; and this *without ratiocination*, by an immediate affection of the mind. But let him consider, whether this be the effect of an original impression on the mind, anticipating all reflection or ratiocination; or whether it does not plainly prove, that conscience is nothing else but a judgment, which we make of our actions, with reference to some law, which we are persuaded ought to be the rule of them. This, I believe, will, upon an unprejudiced examination, be found to be the true notion of natural conscience, and the best with regard to religion (as truth always is a surer support for it than the most pious mistaken notions) for this account cautions men not to trust to a peace of conscience, which may proceed from false opinions; and leaves all its authority in those, who have had occasions of being rightly informed of their duty.

Thus I have done with each particular head of the Remarker's enquiries, and I hope have said enough to convince him, that Mr. *Locke*'s principles of *Human Understanding* give a sufficient secu-

---

* [*Third Remarks*], p. 7.

rity against such a system, as he apprehends, *a Manichæan God,**
a mortal soul, an arbitrary law of good and evil,† and any dangerous
inferences from Mr. *Locke*'s notion of *cogitant matter, viz. That
God may, for any thing we know, give the power of cogitation to some
systems of matter.* For I have shown, that the proofs of a future
state of rewards and punishments are equally conclusive without
a demonstrative certainty of the soul's *immateriality*. And as to
that other difficulty, with which the first Remarks conclude, concerning the nature of God and his *immateriality*, upon this concession, that matter may be capable of perception and thought,
Mr. *Locke* has so well confuted the *Materialists* on that point,‡ so
strongly proved, that cogitation cannot be the power of matter, or
that the supreme cogitant Being cannot be material, that I cannot
imagine to what end the Remarker brings in those arguments
against the immateriality of God, if he means as well to religion
and Mr. *Locke*, as he would be thought to do.

But whatever he there meant, it seems he has repented upon
farther thoughts, or better seen the force of Mr. *Locke*'s proofs,
that God is immaterial; which he there fears will rise no higher
than probability, though he heartily wishes they may. But in his
third letter, his judgment is brought over to his hearty wish, and
he confesses,§ that *Mr. Locke very well refutes the Materialist, who
would have but one single substance in the world, namely matter.* And
to show his sincerity and good will the more, he owns this where
one would least expect it, when he is giving the worst insinuations
he can of Mr. *Locke*'s principles. But the manner of his doing it is
an extraordinary mark of the kind intentions, and respect to Mr.
Locke, which he professes, and which nobody can doubt of, who
observes how ingeniously he endeavours to fasten the *principles of
Deism* on Mr. *Locke*, by showing, that some of his notions are not
inconsistent with them; and that some of the questions, which he
discusses, may be raised upon their principles, though none of

---

* *Second Remarks*, p. 11. ["Manichæan" refers to the belief system of the Manichaean religion. This was a religion founded in the third century AD by the Persian Mani, according to whom there are two eternal principles in nature: good and evil. For this reason, Manichaeism is called a dualistic religion.]

† *Third Remarks*, p. 16.

‡ *Essay* B. iv. c. 10. [This discussion starts at *Essay*, 4.10.10. Materialists are philosophers who hold that the universe is constructed only of matter, and that all or most phenomena are explicable in material terms. This was a controversial view in Cockburn's time, held most notoriously by Thomas Hobbes in the seventeenth century.]

§ [*Third Remarks*], p. 23.

them do necessarily depend upon those principles; and a great part of his *Essay* is directly contrary to that, which the Remarker says he cannot but think is the mystery aimed at all along, but concealed from us, *viz. That the soul of man is not a distinct permanent substance*. Let the impartial judge, whether this be to *argue fairly;*★ or whether it does not look like a *desire to make use of names* to no very fair purpose. But, that I may not be suspected to have misrepresented the Remarker's way of imputing the Deists' principles to Mr. *Locke*, I will, as briefly as possible, run over the particulars, which he compares to them.

"The grand principle of Deism (says he) is this; there is one infinite, universal spirit, that actuates matter always, without the operation of particular spirits. And if the soul of man be nothing but an influx from another principle, not a distinct permanent substance, whosoever goes upon this principle, I do not wonder, if he cannot allow innate ideas, or practical principles in the soul; for there is no permanent soul to imprint them upon.¹ *Answ.* But may not one, who does think the soul a permanent substance, doubt, that it has any ideas but what it received from sensation and reflection; because he is not conscious of any but what he can trace to those originals? And the power or faculties of receiving ideas no less require a permanent substance to exist in, than ideas themselves. *Moreover* (says the Remarker) *upon that hypothesis the soul cannot be said to be immortal.*² And what is that, I pray, to Mr. *Locke*? Has he any where told us, that the soul cannot be said to be immortal? Does he not frequently profess a steadfast belief, that the soul is immortal?† Has he not zealously contested,‡ that our ignorance of what kind of substance the soul is, does not at all weaken the assurances of its immortality? Why then is this, that *the soul cannot be said to be immortal*, brought in as an opinion of Mr. *Locke*'s, but at any rate to make that position, *that the soul is not a distinct substance*, be supposed a principle of his?

"Furthermore (says the Remarker) in consequence of this principle of Deism, and the mortality of the soul, great difficul-

---

★ *Vide Second Remarks*, p. 12.
† *Essay*, B. iv. Essay, 4.3.6.
‡ *Reply to the Bishop of Worcester's Second Letter*. ["Mr. Locke's Reply to the Bishop of Worcester's Answer to his Second Letter" in *The Works of John Locke*, 10 vols. (Germany, Scientia Verlag Aalen, 1963) 476.]

---

1 *Third Remarks*, p. 23.
2 *Third Remarks*, p. 24.

ties must needs arise to them about the resurrection, how it can be the same *man*, or the same *person*, that rises again, when both the body and the soul are new. And this would bring on nice disputes about the notions of identity, and diversity, which accordingly we find discussed at large in the *Essay*, for their satisfaction, I suppose, that go upon those principles."[1] It may be so; but the Remarker must give me leave to *suppose* too, that those notions are not discussed for their satisfaction alone, who go upon those principles; and the reason, why I take the liberty to suppose so, is, because Mr. *Locke* determines the ideas of *identity* and *diversity*, upon several very different principles; and because those, who do think the soul a distinct permanent substance, may have some *difficulties about the resurrection, and about the notions of identity and diversity*; for *identity of substance* will not determine it in all cases, as *personal identity*, and *human identity*, to those, who take the *body* into their idea of *man*; and for their satisfaction, who place *human identity* in the same *immaterial spirit*, united to such and such particles of matter, in such a shape and form, Mr. *Locke* shows, how we *may easily conceive the same person at the resurrection, though in a body not exactly in make or parts the same he had here*. But supposing, with the Remarker, that discourse was designed for the satisfaction of those, *who go upon the principles of Deism*; that does not sure entitle Mr. *Locke* to their principles; and indeed these are a sort of Deists very well worth satisfying, whatever they think of the soul, since they allow the resurrection. I suppose they are of that party, which the Remarker* tells us will own both natural and revealed religion. And to satisfy such men, how consistently with their own notions, they may conceive the same persons at the resurrection accountable for their actions in this life, is worthy of a good man's pains, though he differs from them in their opinions of the soul; and much more serviceable to religion, than those can be (whatever zeal they pretend for it) who will not allow, that the resurrection, or a future state, can be established upon any hypothesis but their own. For no doubt, if men are convinced of a future state, it is of no consequence upon what grounds they are so: their mistakes about the substance of the soul, will not endanger their morals, or their salvation. And if Mr. *Locke*'s discourse of *identity* and *diversity* was designed to resolve the difficulties, that may arise about the resurrection, that

---

* *Postscript.* [*Third Remarks*, pp. 26–27.]

1 *Third Remarks*, p. 24.

can only show his concern to secure that essential point upon every man's principles, since he determines the ideas of identity and diversity upon several contrary suppositions; and therefore there can be no reason to conclude any one of them to be his opinion, more than another, unless he has declared in favour of one, which he has done two or three times in that chapter for this, *That the soul is one individual, immaterial substance,** the direct contrary to that, which the Remarker would have thought to be his opinion.

We come now to the next and last dispute, which the Remarker mentions, as arising from that principle, "That the soul is not a substance distinct from God and matter. From this position (he says) a question springs up concerning the powers of matter, or whether matter be not capable of cogitation?"† I should rather think this question preceded that position; it seems more rational, and natural, in the ignorance men are of *what the soul is*, first to enquire, whether that power of cogitation, which they perceive in themselves, may not be communicated to matter; and if they find no contradiction in it, (and upon that think fit to determine of the nature of a thing, which they cannot certainly know) thence to conclude, that the soul is not a substance distinct from matter. But howsoever that be, it cannot be concluded, that those, who make this question, go upon a supposition, *that the soul is not a distinct permanent substance*, which is the principle the Remarker would have supposed to be Mr. *Locke*'s. The question, as Mr. *Locke* makes it, is not, *whether our cogitations are the operations of God, or of matter;* but whether God has given the power of cogitation to a *material*, or an *immaterial substance*: and which way soever this question is resolved, the soul must equally be supposed *a distinct permanent substance;* for a *material substance* is not less a *substance* than an *immaterial.*

But the fallacy, by which that supposition, *that the soul is not a distinct permanent substance*, is imputed to Mr. *Locke,* upon his doubting whether the soul may not be material, lies in this, that supposing the soul not to be a substance distinct from *matter* is taken for the same thing, as supposing it not to be distinct from *the body,* which are very different suppositions; and upon this fallacy it is concluded, that those, who think the soul may be *material,* cannot suppose it to exist after the dissolution of the body. But that one, who thinks God may have given *perception* and *thought* to some systems of matter disposed as he sees fit, may

---

* Vide [*Essay*, 2. 27] § 13. § 25.
† *Third Remarks*, p. 24.

suppose this system *distinct from the body*; and to continue in the same state of *cogitation*, when the *body* is dissolved, we have for an instance (not to mention many others) a no less eminent philosopher than *Cicero*, who in all his enquiries about the substance of the soul, went not beyond that matter, of which the heavens are made, *Aristotle's Quinta Essentia*;[1] though he finds reasons to think it may be *immortal* and survive *the body*; and plainly distinguishes it from *body*, taken for the sensible, organical parts of a man, though there is nothing of immateriality in all his considerations about the substance of the soul.

This then is evident, that none of these discourses in the *Essay*, which the Remarker mentions, as *agreeing with the notion of one universal mind operating according to different systems of matter, without any particular thinking beings distinct from the universal*;[2] none of them, I say, do necessarily depend upon, or terminate in that supposition; and some of them do necessarily suppose the contrary: for if the soul is not supposed a particular substance, distinct from the universal spirit, to what purpose are any questions made or resolved about the resurrection? There is no ground for such an expectation. Who can take account, or be accountable for actions done here, if they are all the operations of one universal spirit? And who but the Remarker could find any consistency in that supposition, with a discourse to satisfy men how they may conceive the same persons at the resurrection, and justly subject to rewards and punishments, whatever substance the soul is, or of whatever particles the body is made up? No sort of Deists, or sect of men, that I know of, did ever reconcile these two opinions.

Those sects, which the Remarker says* were noted for holding only one universal mind, consistently with themselves denied the resurrection; and to such men Mr. *Locke*'s discourse about *identity* and *diversity* could give no satisfaction in that point, nor could it be made upon their principles. But I leave the reader to judge what ground there is, from any of the particulars mentioned, for the Remarker to impute that opinion to Mr. *Locke*, and to† *think*

---

*   [*Third Remarks*], p. 13, 22.
†   *Ibid.*

---

1   *Quinta Essentia* means "fifth element." According to Aristotle there are four basic natural elements that compose the sublunary universe: earth, air, fire and water. There is also a fifth element, *aether*, which is a superior element composing the superlunary world of the stars. Unlike the other elements, aether is incapable of any change.
2   *Third Remarks*, p. 23.

that the mystery aimed at all along in an *Essay*, where upon every occasion he speaks of the soul as a real distinct substance, in too may places to be instanced; and of man as a free agent, subject to an eternal retribution, according to his doings in this life; and that so frequently, and so expressly, that it is impossible to declare his sentiments upon that grand point (for the Remarker's ease as he desires) more plainly than he has done; which, indeed, is so effectual a way of *concealing a mystery* so opposite to those notions, that I believe nobody will suspect it to be Mr. *Locke*'s *aim*, but the Remarker: And he, I hope, upon further reflection, will find *an easier key to decypher this philosophy*, and be as forward to own his mistakes of Mr. *Locke*'s principles, and wrong inferences from them, as he was to publish Remarks so injurious to him, upon *uncertain conclusions, and groundless suppositions.*

Remarks upon some Writers in the Controversy concerning the Foundation of Moral Virtue and Moral Obligation; particularly the Translator[1] *of Archbishop King's* Origin of Evil,[2] *and the author of the* Divine Legation of Moses.[3] *To which are prefixed, Some Cursory Thoughts on the Controversies concerning necessary Existence, The Reality and Infinity of Space, The Extension and Place of Spirits, and on Dr. Watts's* Notion of Substance.[4]

First printed in the Year 1743.

1   Cockburn is here referring to Edmund Law (1703–87), Bishop of Carlisle. His first work was the translation of King's *An Essay on the Origin of Evil* from its original Latin (*De Origine Mali*). Law not only translated this work but added voluminous footnotes, in which he defends a voluntaristic and hedonistic morality. According to Law, moral laws are the product of God's will and have no independent ontological status. The obligation to obey these rules arises strictly from consideration of the rewards and punishments God attaches to them. Law was a devotee of Locke's philosophy, and in 1777 he published a four volume edition of Locke's works.
2   William King (1650–1729), Archbishop of Dublin, was a well-known controversialist—a writer of sermons, letters, and religious works. He originally published his magnum opus, *An Essay on the Origin of Evil*, in Latin in 1702 (entitled *De Origine Mali*, it was only available in English with the publication of Law's translation in 1731). In this work, King addresses the problem of evil. Central to his discussion is King's view that morality is founded on God's will and that obligation arises from a system of rewards and punishments. His work came under critical attack from both Bayle and Leibniz (both of whom are discussed in Law's notes).
3   William Warburton (1698–1779), Bishop of Gloucester, was a well-known theologian of the period whose *Divine Legation of Moses Demonstrated* (4 vols: 1738–65) is a refutation of Deism. Cockburn's *Remarks upon some Writers* presents a critical evaluation of Warburton's ideas. He was so impressed with Cockburn's critiques that he published and prefaced her subsequent work *Remarks upon Dr. Rutherforth's Essay*.
4   Dr. Isaac Watts (1674–1748), was a well-known hymn-writer, who also wrote on philosophy, divinity, and education. Cockburn here addresses Watts's work, *Philosophical Essays on Various Subjects with some Remarks on Mr. Locke's Essay on the Human Understanding* (1742). John Yolton, editor of the modern edition of the *Philosophical Essays*, writes in the introduction (not paginated) that this work is largely derivative of Locke's views, although at times critical. (Watts, *Philosophical Essays on Various Subjects with some Remarks on Mr. Locke's Essay on the Human Understanding*, ed. John Yolton [Bristol: Thoemmes Antiquarian Books, 1990]). Cockburn's references have all been checked against the Yolton edition, and I have indicated any discrepancies. This work will be referred to hereafter as the *Essays*.

Preface

I have so great an esteem of the judgment and penetration of the translator, and author of the notes on Archbishop King's *Origin of Evil*; and have received so much light from him on several subjects, that I am sorry to be obliged to differ from him on any. But I am much more concerned to find, that one, who generally seems inclined to do justice to all the authors he has occasion to mention, should show a *partiality* against one of the greatest lights this age has produced; a divine, whose writings are universally allowed (except on one point of great depth and difficulty) to convey the clearest and strongest convictions of the most important truths of religion, that solid reasoning, and the most judicious explications of Scripture can give to all sober and rational enquirers. To what then can be imputed that remarkable bias against this great man in so candid a writer? I would not suppose a too partial regard for the *eminent head* of the opposition against him, whose figure in the learned world has drawn many rash adventurers to engage on his side, though few, I am persuaded, of the weight and discernment of the author of the notes. All personal regards ought undoubtedly to be laid aside, in questions of such importance, as the ultimate foundation of *Moral Virtue*, and of *Moral Obligation*; and as the following remarks on that debate were at first drawn up only for my own use, though now thought fit to be made public, I hope they may be excused, however different from the notions of some, for whose superior abilities I have not the less deference.

I have not meddled with the comparison of *moral* and *positive* duties, which first occasioned this controversy; because I think, if it be well proved, that the obligation to *moral virtue* is ultimately founded on the *eternal and immutable nature of things*, that will go a great way in deciding where the preference should be laid: and more especially, because I think our Saviour himself has determined that point with such exactness, as might well have superceded all arguments upon it.

On the more abstruse controversies concerning *necessary existence*, and the reality of *space*, the *extension* and *place* of spirits, and the nature of *substance*, I am only an enquirer; in order to which, a few cursory thoughts are prefixed to the principle subject of these papers. If they are thought late in appearing, after the books, to which they relate, have some years been published, let it be considered, that the most noted authors may be long unknown to those, who live in remote parts of the country, who, whenever they meet with them, will at all times think they have a right to examine subjects of universal concernment, and which can never be out of date.

Remarks on some passages in the translator's Notes upon Archbishop King's Origin of Evil.

Of necessary existence.

This seems a subject of too abstruse a nature for human understandings to determine upon decisively; but I venture to make a few remarks upon the dispute, as it has been managed in the late opposition to Dr. *Clarke*; and must premise, that it looks a little unfavourable to their cause, that it obliges them to contend against all proofs from reason of the *unity* of God, as well as against the *eternal immutable nature* of things; both which have been esteemed essential foundations of natural religion.

I shall next observe, that it is somewhat unfair in the author of the notes to affirm,* that the reason, for which necessity of existence was first introduced, was to exclude a *difference of persons* in the divine nature; since he could not be ignorant, that Dr. *Clarke*,† in that very place, where he first introduced the notion of necessity of existence, from whence he deduces the *unity of God*, does expressly assert, that a *diversity of persons* in that one and the same nature is not inconsistent with it; and that there is no argument, by which it can be proved impossible, or unreasonable to be supposed.

This writer farther urges,‡ that "necessity of existence as being, as Dr. *Clarke* contends, simple and uniform, should exclude all difference or variety of any sort; and may exclude all diversity of perfections in the divine nature, for the *very same reason*, that it does exclude a *difference of persons?*" But who has given *any reason*, why it must exclude a difference of persons? The Doctor affirms, that no reason can be given for it, and has professedly proved a diversity of attributes, or perfections, to be essentially in God, as this author himself owns. The unity Dr. *Clarke* contends for, and which he thinks necessity of existence proves,§ is a unity of *nature* or essence: the variety he excludes, is a difference of natures, such a variety, as appears to be in all things of the world, which are distinguished one from another by a diversity, not only of *modes*, but also of *essential attributes*.

---

* P.S. p. 31. [Cockburn's notes all correspond to the second edition (1732) of King's *An Essay on the Origin of Evil*, hereafter referred to as the *Essay*.]

† *Demonstration Of the Being and Attributes of God.* [Hereafter Cockburn refers to this work by the designation *Demonstr.*]

‡ [*Essay*], P.S. [p. 30] and Note 10.

§ *Demonstr.*, Prop. vii.

The author of the notes likewise asserts,* that "necessity of existence must exclude that perfect liberty, or absolute freedom of choice, which is a property of God, as well as of man." But I can see no manner of repugnance between these two, any more than there is between man's being determined to existence by the will of God, and yet having a perfect liberty, or freedom of choice. Why must the same principle, that is the ground of the existence of any being, be the ground of all that being's actions or determinations? Necessitated to *exist*, and necessitated to *act*, are very different ideas, and seem no way consequent one of the other. But "if we cannot admit it in one case, says he, why should we in the other?"[1] Answer: *Because it would be an imperfection in the last case, but is not so in the former.*

As to the question itself, whether the divine being exists by an *absolute necessity*, or without any cause, ground, or reason of his existence, it is a point of too great difficulty for me to determine on either side; but I shall venture to set down such reflections, as occur to me on both.

That the most perfect being, the cause of all other beings, should itself exist without any ground or reason at all of existence, is a supposition, that leaves in a considering mind such a void, as it cannot easily be satisfied with. Could the first cause possibly exist by mere chance? Then it might possibly never have existed. If it existed without any reason, it might *without reason* have existed but a day before the present phenomena; and may, without reason, cease to exist in any time to come. And how, upon this supposition, can those be confuted, who affirm, that the material world, and every existing substance, was eternal, *absolutely without any ground or reason of existence*? If some one thing can exist absolutely without any reason, why not every thing?† The author of the notes argues upon this subject, "that there was a time, when all beings, except one, were indifferent to existence, or non-existence, were nothing; and that for them to be determined to existence, is a *change*, which cannot be effected without a cause; whereas in eternal existence there is no change, no effect, and therefore, no cause wanted." But this, instead of being an answer to the followers of *Spinoza*, would be a plain begging the question, since they maintain, that the universe has

---

* [*Essay*], Note 10.
† [*Essay*], Remarks, e.

---

1 Essay, Note 10.

existed eternally, *absolutely without any cause or reason of existence*; and I see not how they can be confuted by those, who affirm the same of God. If the most perfect of all beings, can be conceived to exist absolutely without any ground or reason at all, how can we determine what may or may not be without reason? In short, may we not more justly say of *this*, what our author says of *necessity*? "It is in truth such a vague equivocal principle, that it will be hard to affirm positively what it may, or may not do."[1]

On the other hand, *necessary existence* seems to give the mind something more satisfactory to rest on: if the first cause is necessarily existent, it must have always existed, and cannot possibly cease to exist: And not only *eternity*, but several other attributes, are deducible from this principle, as *immensity*, *unity*, &c. whereas from existence without any cause or reason, nothing seems to be certainly deducible. The author of the notes affirms indeed, that there may be *two or more* necessarily existing independent beings; but I think he has not proved it, nor answered what Dr. *Clarke* alleges to show, that such a supposition implies a plain contradiction.

However, it must be confessed, that *there is a great difficulty attends* the notion of *necessity*, considered as a ground or reason of the existence of the first cause, since the existence must be coetaneous[2] with the supposed reason of it. Nothing can be really antecedent in the order of nature, (whatever it may be in the order of our ideas) to an eternal being. The author of *An impartial enquiry of the being and attributes of God*,* who allows the first cause to be necessarily existent, yet requires some ground of that necessity, which ground is, as he asserts, *the perfection of the divine nature*. Some perhaps will be apt to require another ground for that; but whichever part we take, the difficulty seems no way removed. Whether we suppose *perfection* the ground of necessary existence, or found the existence on an *absolute necessity*, still the perfection, the necessity, and the existence must be *coetaneous*, how then can we conceive either of them antecedent to the other, so as to be the reason of the necessity, or of the existence?

But we may not perceive, that the first cause must exist by some *internal necessity* of its own nature, so that it was not possi-

---

* Clarke, *A Demonstration of the Being and Attributes of God* (1705).

---

1 P.S., p. 31.
2 *Coetaneous* means coming into existence at the same time; originating simultaneously.

ble for it not to have existed, tho' the *manner* how this is, be above human comprehension? Do we not allow *necessity of existence* in the divine being, when we suppose, that it cannot be destroyed, even by his own omnipotent will, that can annihilate all other things? Why then may he not have existed by the same *necessity* from all eternity, whatever it is, or whencesoever it arises? But if we can perceive such a necessity of the divine existence, *the perfection of his nature* seems most reasonably to be supposed the ground of it, or rather to be itself the same with that *absolute necessity.*

The author of the notes argues,* that necessity is a term merely relative, and that no ideas can possibly be fixed to these terms, *necessity absolute in itself.* The same he says of *truth,* that truth is relative, and all such phrases as *true in itself, absolutely such &c.* are very absurd ones. I should be glad to know, what this gentleman thinks of self-evident truths, such as are no way deduced from any other truths, neither require, nor will admit of any proof. Can they be said to be *relative?* Or would it be any absurdity, to say of them, that they are *true in themselves?* For instance, may not this proposition *I exist,* be said to be, by everyone that affirms it, true in itself, or absolutely true? Most of our knowledge indeed is acquired by a deduction of one truth from another; and therefore, most of the truths we are acquainted with, may be called relative, with respect to our manner of discovering them, tho' many of them may be in themselves *absolutely true.* Thus we deduce the existence of an independent being from the existence of dependent beings; but when we have demonstrated this truth to ourselves, by a deduction from other known truths, we may then perceive, and without absurdity affirm, that it was always true in itself, absolutely true, that this independent being existed from all eternity, when there was no other being but himself.

And may not something like this be the case of relative and *absolute necessity?* We perceive, that the first cause must necessarily have always existed, from the absurdities, that would follow the contrary supposition. This is indeed a *consequential* necessity, which infers nothing of the *modus* of the divine existence: but may not this lead us to see, that there must be some *absolute* necessity in the divine nature itself, which made it impossible, that he should ever not have existed, or that he should ever cease to exist, tho' the manner or ground of this necessity surpasses our comprehension? Perhaps it would be no less difficult for an unpreju-

---

* [*Essay*], Note 4.

diced mind to conceive, that we should be forced to allow the *necessity* of an eternal existence, (tho' only a consequential one) and yet that there may be no cause, reason, ground, or absolute necessity at all of that existence. O! eternal being, who can speak without error of thy incomprehensible nature, unless enlightened by thee!

Remarks on the Notes by Archbishop King's *Translator concerning* Space, *&c. With a digression on Dr.* Watts's *Notion of Substance.*

Those, who maintain the real existence of space, seem to me to have given great advantage to their adversaries, by calling it *extension*; which being a term, that stands for an abstract idea, they have taken occasion from thence, to treat of space as such, as having no existence but in the mind. Mr. *Locke*, in asserting the reality of space, might, I think, have denied it to be the same with extension, for the same reason, that he denies *matter* to be so; for that cannot be the same with either, which may be predicated of both; and it may be said of space as well as of matter, that it is extended, which would be nonsense to say of extension itself. Space I take to be one of the particulars, from whence that general idea is abstracted.

The learned writer* quoted by the translator, owns, that the idea of space is not the idea of extension, but of *something extended*; yet he will have it to be nothing more, than an *ideal substratum* of extension. "When the mind," he says, "has been considering the idea of extension, abstracted from extended bodies; it is a very easy step to *frame* an *imaginary substratum* to support an imaginary extension." But this seems to me a very *imaginary* account of our getting the idea of this extended something. I rather think we have the idea before we have any of extension in general, or are capable of abstracting: Nor does the mind *frame* it to itself; it is an idea early obtruded upon it by the senses, and unavoidably perceived by it, as something without itself. This is all the proof we have, that matter is anything really existing without the mind; and if the translator will not admit of this evidence in behalf of space, but† require some other proof, that it is more than *mental*, he may be in a fair disposition entirely to embrace Bishop *Berkeley*'s

---

* [*Essay*], Note 3. [This is actually found in Note 9.]
† See P.S. p. 12.

scheme,[1] to deny, that there is any such thing as *matter* or motion but in idea. We cannot well conceive motion to be possible without space; so that if bodies are allowed really to exist and move, space will not easily be discarded. We should methinks admit or reject them all together; and to say the truth, the arguments against the reality of each of them seem much of the same kind; they serve rather to puzzle than to convince.

The only ground I can apprehend for denying the real existence of space, is, that we know not in what class of beings to place it. And indeed Dr. *Watts*, who has with great ingenuity discussed all the several opinions about it, seems at last to determine space to be *nothing*, chiefly because he cannot find out what kind of being it is. But sure our ignorance of its nature is no sufficient reason to exclude from existence a thing, which so forces itself upon the mind, that we cannot annihilate it even in imagination. It is enquired, whether space is a substance or a mode? If a substance, whether spirit or body? But how are we assured, that this is an adequate division of being? "Who has told us (as Mr. *Locke* asks)* that there was, or could be nothing but solid beings, which could not think, and thinking beings, that were not extended? which is all that is commonly meant by body and spirit." To this question I have met with no answer, but (if that may serve instead of it) a great exclamation against *Gassendus*, quoted from *Bayle*,[2] by the author of the notes,† where it is said, that to avoid asserting, that a vacuum is nothing, he chose rather to plunge himself "into the *hideous abyss* of conjecturing, that all beings are not either substances or accidents; and that all substances are not either spirits or bodies; and of placing space among the beings, which are neither corporeal or spiritual," *&c*. Whether all beings

---

* [Watts's] *Philosoph. Essays*. [This discussion is found in Essay II.]
† [*Essay*], Note 6.

---

1 George Berkeley (1685–1753). Berkeley was a well-known philosopher of the period, who was famous for his *idealism*—the view that nothing exists in the universe but ideas. In Berkeley's account, there are no "material" objects, only ideas placed in our minds by God.
2 Pierre Gassendi (1592–1655) was an empiricist, famous for reintroducing Epicurean atomism into early modern science. Pierre Bayle (1647–1706) was a sceptic, who was strongly critical of rationalistic philosophical theories. His most famous work was the *Dictionnaire historique et critique* (Historical and Critical Dictionary) (1697).

must be divided into substances or accidents, I shall not here enquire; but as to the other part of the conjecture, I see no absurdity in supposing, that there may be other substances, than either spirits or bodies. Why is this thought such a *hideous abyss*, but that the learned are afraid to suppose there may be anything in nature that they are ignorant of? For my part I am inclined to take the hint from *Gassendus*, and venture to propose a consideration, which may perhaps serve to confirm his conjecture.

It has been observed by the curious, and beautifully described by Mr. *Addison*[1] and Mr. *Locke*, that in the scale of beings, there is such a gradual progress in nature, that the most perfect of an inferior species comes very near to the most imperfect of that, which is immediately above it: that the whole chasm in nature, from a plant to a man, is filled up by such a gentle and easy ascent, that the little transitions from one species to another are almost insensible: That if the scale of beings rises by such a regular progress so high as man, we may, by a parity of reason, suppose, that it still proceeds gradually through those beings, that are of a superior nature to him; that there is no manner of chasm left, no link deficient in this great chain of beings.

Now according to this observation, which is apparent through all the known works of God, and by a parity of reason presumed of those above our knowledge, there should be in nature some being to fill up the vast chasm betwixt body and spirit; otherwise the gradation would fail, the chain would seem to be broken. What a gap between *senseless material*, and *intelligent immaterial* substance, unless there is some being, which, by partaking of the nature of both, may serve as a link to unite them, and make the transition less violent? And why may not space be such a being? Might we not venture to define it, *an immaterial unintelligent substance, the place of bodies, and of spirits, having some of the properties of both.*

I should think, that space might be more fitly called the *place of spirits*, than, as Dr. *Clarke* has termed it, the *place of all ideas*, which, the author of the notes believes, few besides the doctor can apprehend. But whatever may or may not be apprehended of the place of *ideas*, to suppose, that *spirits are in no place*, seems to me utterly inconceivable, by whatever subtle or plausible argu-

---

1 Joseph Addison (1672–1719). English essayist, poet, dramatist and statesman. Addison was greatly influential in his time, particularly with respect to his aesthetic theories; in his view (broadly speaking), the refinement of personal taste contributes to moral and political stability.

ments it may be maintained. Dr. *Watts** has supported this notion with all his force, whose candour in representing the side he opposes, and modesty in defending his own opinion, are very insinuating. But all his reasonings on this point amount, I think, to nothing but *difficulties*, that seem to follow from allowing spirits to be in a place; as that they must be *extended*, and if so, they must have some *shape or figure*, and consequently be *divisible*. These consequences follow indeed from supposing spirits to be extended in the same manner that bodies are; but may not beings, of whose nature we have but a partial knowledge, have some other kind of extension, consistent with that indivisibility, which we suppose essential to thinking substances? Is not space an instance of extension, or expansion, without figure or divisibility, to those, who allow it any being? However, we are not to reject what is *clear*, for the sake of *difficulties*, that may be raised against it. The learned know, that there are insuperable objections against demonstrable truths; and perhaps there are few truths more clear and evident than this, that whatever has a real existence must exist *somewhere*; nor does any difficulty or inconsistency appear greater to me, than the supposition of any being really existing, yet existing *nowhere*. This author† argues, that tho' a body cannot be without being somewhere, yet a spirit, which is a conscious and active power, may have a real existence, and yet have *no proper place*. i.e. as he explains it, have *no proximity of situation to bodies, or fill up no supposed dimensions of space*. This qualifying expression, *no proper place*, which the doctor often uses, seems to me to imply, that he supposes spirits to be in a place after *some manner or other*; and I would ask him, whether he can really conceive, or have any idea of a *conscious active power*, exerting its consciousness and activity, or even barely existing, without being somewhere, any more than he can conceive a body to be, without being somewhere? Should we allow him, that spirits have no proximity of situation to bodies, (a subject, which he has curiously enlarged upon, but is too far out of my way to engage in) yet I would farther enquire, whether he can possibly conceive, that they have no proximity of situation, or distance, with respect to one another? Can he suppose, that a human soul, as soon as it is free from the prison of the body, and finds itself in the world of spirits, is in that moment equally present to all the myriads of spirits, that may exist in the universe? That it can communicate its thoughts to them all in that instant, and receive communica-

---

* [Watts's] *Essay[s]* VI. [Section II.]
† *Ibid.* Sect. iv.

tions from the whole creation of spirits at once? This surely would be to make them infinite, which, he justly says, *we know they are not*. If then finite spirits cannot be present to all of their kind at once; if they can communicate their thoughts only to some limited number at a time, what ground can we conceive of such a limitation, but that they are nearer to and farther from some spirits than from others? And that, I think, implies being in a *place*. The manner, how spirits *possess place*, we are undoubtedly ignorant of, and may content ourselves so to be, till we enter into the world of disembodied minds. But when we venture to affirm, that they are *nowhere*, I fear we go beyond our clear and distinct perceptions; as this ingenious author* owns we are in danger of doing, when we endeavour to turn from sensible ideas. I should be apt to think, with Mr. *Locke*,† that spirits must possess a place, so as to exclude any of the same kind from it, otherwise all distinction between them must be lost. To this Dr. *Watts*‡ answers, that every spirit is sufficiently distinguished from all others, by its particular cogitations and consciousness. But I cannot see how the particular consciousness of any being can distinguish it from others, to any but itself. But to return to the author of the notes.

This learned writer asserts, that "space and spirit, and the distinct properties of each, appear to him as distant and incompatible, as the most remote and inconsistent things in nature; and an *extended soul* seems just another phrase, as a green sound," *&c.* Yet a few lines after he owns, "that it is perhaps impossible for us to imagine any such thing as an *unextended substance*;"[1] which is, I think, not very consistent with the former assertion. If it is as impossible for us to imagine an *unextended* soul or substance, as it is impossible to imagine the colour of a sound; then it should rather follow, that an *unextended soul* must seem just such a phrase as a *green sound*, since they both express things, of which we can have *no idea*. This judicious writer frequently blames others, for going beyond their ideas for knowledge: why does he go beyond his ideas, or why would he have us do so, in this case? I confess I see no reason for it, extension not seeming to me inconsistent with indivisibility, the allowed property of thinking beings. A simple uncompounded, therefore indivisible, yet extended sub-

---

* [Watts's] *Essay[s]* VI. Conclus.
† In his chap. of ident. divers. Sect. 2. [Locke's *Essay* 2.27.]
‡ [Watts's] *Essay[s]*, XII, s. vii.

---

1 *Essay*, Note 7.

stance, carries with it no contradiction, that I can perceive; and if ascribed even to the deity himself, as some have done, I should apprehend no inconvenience in it, provided the properties belonging to compound finite substances, be excluded from the idea.

If the author of the notes should admit of my conjecture, that there must be some being to fill up the vast chasm betwixt body and spirit, for the sake of that beautiful gradation, which he makes so good use of, to confirm an argument of Bishop *King*'s; I fear he would scarce allow, that *space*, which he treats of as a mere nothing, may possibly be such a being; much less would he admit it for the *place of spirits*; since he, as well as Dr. *Watts*, contends, that spirits are in *no place*: Nor would either of them, I suppose, allow, of an immaterial being, without the *power of thinking*; for, according to the author of the notes, "the substance of spirit consists in the powers of thinking and acting; the aggregate of the properties of any being is the being itself."[1] But if thinking is the *action* of spirits, as it is acknowledged to be, even by those, who contend, that it is their very substance; how is it possible to conceive, that the actions of a being are the being itself? Dr. *Watts* likewise maintains, that *a power of thinking is the substance of spirit*; that this is sufficient to support all the properties of spirit, and that therefore there is no need of supposing any other *unknown* subject of them. On this point he is very large; and tho' it does not directly relate to that which I am upon, he has several passages, that incline me to go a little out of my way, to take some notice of them.

This author argues,* that if a *power of thinking* be only a mere mode or property, then it may be destroyed, and yet the substance will remain: but destroy *thinking power*, and nothing at all remains; *we have no idea left.* We have *no idea* left indeed of what remains, unless the obscure one of something, to which that power did belong. But does it follow, that therefore nothing can remain? If there is ground, from reason and the nature of things, to conclude, that a power of thinking cannot subsist of itself, but must be the property of some being; our ignorance, or having *no idea* of what the substance of that being is, will not hinder it from remaining, if God should think fit to take from it the power of thinking. *Logical* ways of speaking, to which this ingenious author

---

* [Watts's] *Essay[s]* II. Chap. 3.

1 *Essay*, Note 7.

imputes our prejudices against allowing a power of thinking to subsist without a subject, seem, in this case, forms of speaking founded on reason and truth; for what idea can we frame of a *power*, without supposing some being, to which it belongs? What is a *power of thinking in perpetual act*, but an ability or capacity perpetually exerted? And how can this be conceived, but as the property and action of some being, that exerts its ability, and therefore must be distinct from it. I do not find myself so prejudiced by logical or grammatical ways of speaking, but that I could easily agree with this author, that *solid extension* may possibly be the very substance, or only *substratum* of all the properties of *matter*; I see nothing repugnant to reason in this supposition: But I cannot so well reconcile my reason to the notion, that a *power of thinking* may be the substance of spirit: actions and abilities (and I have no other idea of powers) seem unavoidably to imply some subject of them, some being, that exerts its powers in different ways of acting.

I confess myself ignorant indeed of what the substance of that being is, but cannot think *that* a sufficient reason to exclude it from existence, as this new philosophy would do, tacking properties and actions together, without any subject of either; somewhat unphilosophically, as it seems to me. Nor have I found any arguments from the maintainers of this new notion, that oblige me to alter the sentiments I had, when I formerly* endeavoured to show, from what we know of the human soul, that thinking cannot be the substance or essence of it; and that it may continue to *be*, though it should sometimes cease to *act*. It has long been my opinion, that, from our ignorance of the nature of things, or of their manner of acting, how they cease to act, or how they resume their actions, no other reasonable conclusion can be drawn, but of the narrowness of our understandings. This is a lesson I learnt from Mr. *Locke*'s *Essay*; and if others would make the same use of a work so adapted to teach us, where to set bounds to our pretences to knowledge, there would be no fear of the dangerous consequences Dr. *Watts* apprehends from admitting, with that great man, an *unknown substratum* of the properties of matter and of spirit. Is it suitable to our limited understandings to conclude, that because we know not what the substance of either is, therefore they may be the same? Is there not at least the same ground for the very contrary conclusion? But if we must argue about the *nature* of things, which we know not, let us form our reasonings from what we do know of them;

---

* *Defence of Mr. Locke's Essay*, printed in 1702.

let us rather conclude, that properties so essentially different as those of matter and spirit are, must certainly belong to substances as essentially different in themselves.

'Tis but too common, I confess, to frame an hypothesis, and even to establish the most important truths, upon the nature of things we are unacquainted with. And this is what Mr. *Locke* seems to me designing to *ridicule*; not the notion of *substance in general*, as Dr. *Watts* supposes, but forming arguments, and drawing conclusions from the *nature* of substance, which we are as ignorant of, as the *Indian* was of his unknown something, that supported the tortoise, *&c.*[1] A design, which agrees very well with the* title of the section, where he introduces that comparison! It is certain, Mr. *Locke* always allows, that there is a real ground in nature for our general notion of substance; as that, which supports all the properties, that we observe in different beings, and which we cannot conceive to subsist of themselves; and therefore I think he could never intend to ridicule that notion. Yet I do not see how his insisting on this *unknown something* should lead his readers (as this author apprehends) into a belief, that there is such a real being as *substance in general*, the common support of all the properties of particular different beings, unless his readers mistake what he says of *our idea* of substance to be meant of the *real nature* of substance; which, perhaps, is often the case, tho' there are very different things. The Bishop of *Worcester* seems to have fallen into that mistake; and I fear this author has done the same; for what he quotes from Mr. *Locke*'s first letter to the bishop for his notion of a *general substance*, plainly relates to our *general idea* of substance, which is indeed *the same everywhere*; an abstract idea, in which all substances must agree, though in other respects they may be essen-

---

* Substance and accident of little use in philosophy. [The discussion referred to here can be found in Locke's *Essay* 2.23.]

---

1 This refers to an example found in Locke's *Essay*, 2.23.2. Locke is here examining the concept of substance, or substratum—that aspect of an object in which all of the object's qualities are supposed to inhere, but which is not itself perceivable. According to Locke, substance would seem to be a term for which we can have no clear experiential ideas. He recounts the story of an Indian philosopher who asserts that the world is supported by an elephant, which is in turn supported by a tortoise. When asked what supports the tortoise, he is said to reply "something I know not what." This phrase is used by Locke to describe our notion of substance.

tially different. *A real universal* cannot sure be deduced from his principles, who has sufficiently exploded that notion, and expressly maintains, that every real existence is particular: And individuals of all kinds he often speaks of, as particular *distinct substances*. He* treats it as no small absurdity to suppose, that substance, when applied to God, to created spirits, and to material beings, signifies the same thing, that is, the same in its *own nature*; though we are so far from having three distinct meanings of it, that we have but one common, and that a *confused obscure idea*, not of what it *is*, but of what it *does*. Yet, as unknown as he supposes the nature of substance to be, I cannot but think he has sufficiently obviated all the objections to that notion, and secured it from any *unhappy consequences*, by his clear demonstration, that the eternal mind cannot possibly be material; that no system of matter can of its own nature be capable of thinking; and that our certainty of the immortality of the soul does not depend upon our knowledge of what the substance of it is. And I am sorry to find, that the weight of these arguments did not give satisfaction to so candid and judicious a writer. But to return from this digression.

Among many eminent philosophers, Mr. *Locke*, in particular, as I just observed, has demonstrated, that the first cause of all things must be immaterial. He too maintains it to be in the highest degree probable, that the soul of man is also immaterial, grounding the possibility he supposes, that some systems of matter may have a power of perception and thought, tho' we cannot conceive how matter can be capable of it, solely on that omnipotent will, which, in uniting the human soul and body, has given them powers of acting on each other, which we can no more conceive how they can be capable of. Other learned men have professed to demonstrate, that *all thinking beings* must necessarily be immaterial; and we should in reason allow of their demonstrations, as agreeing with our best conception of things, so far as may be without limiting the divine omnipotence. But from the strongest proofs, that *all thinking beings* must be immaterial, it does not follow, that every immaterial being must think; thinking not being a necessary consequence of immateriality, for aught that can appear to us, till the new philosophy is better established than it yet seems to be, which would make a power of thinking and immaterial substance to be the same thing. The author of *Enquiry into the nature of the*

---

* [Locke's] *Essay*, Book II. Chap. xiii. Sect. 18.

human soul,[1] in diffusing immaterial beings through the whole sensible creation, (though he has much laboured to prove, that every being capable of perception must always actually perceive) has brought them down to so low a degree of sensation or perception, according to the bodies they inform, so very near to none, that it seems but an easy step farther to imagine with me, some *immaterial* beings placed in such circumstances, as to have no perception at all; thus linking the *intelligent* and *material* world together by an easy gradation; into which class I would willingly introduce *space*, the subject from whence I have insensibly wandered.

Of infinite space.

Most of those, who have maintained the real existence of space, (perhaps all of them) have likewise asserted it to be *infinite*; and it may be thought a bold singularity to dispute it. But, as the translator of the *Origin of Evil* judiciously observes, the equivocal use of that word, by jumbling mathematics and metaphysics together, has occasioned a great deal of confusion in subjects of this kind; and, in regard to our ignorance of the extent of space, I think it is more fitly styled *indefinite*.

Some have ascribed a *positive* infinity to space; others only a *negative* one, which are very opposite things. If by the former Dr. *Clarke* meant a metaphysical infinity, *viz.* absolute perfection, to which nothing can be added, I see not how positive infinity, in that sense, can be applied to anything but the deity and his attributes. The Doctor seems indeed to make infinite space something near a divine attribute, when he calls it,* an *abstract idea of immensity*, which I confess I do not understand.

As to that other kind of infinity, which Mr. *Locke* has explained at large, and ascribes to space, that perpetual addibility or increasableness without end, it seems utterly inconsistent with being positively or absolutely infinite; and, according to my notions, that kind of negative infinity cannot, without a contra-

---

* *Demonstr.* Prop. iv.

---

1 Andrew Baxter (1686?–1750). *An Enquiry Into the Nature of the Human Soul; Wherein the Immateriality of the Soul Is Evinced From the Principles of Reason and Philosophy* (1st edition, 1730[?]; 3rd edition, 1745). Baxter was a Scottish metaphysician who argued that all matter is inert, moved by immaterial force which he identified as God.

diction be applied to anything, that has a real actual complete existence; and therefore I think it should not be ascribed to space, by those, who allow space to be a real particular being, and not a mere *idea*. *Negative infinity* can only be applied to *general abstract ideas*, as number, duration, extension, *&c.* which have no existence but in the mind. To those *ideas* we can always add indeed, without ever being able to come to an end; and *there is no great mystery in that*, as the author quoted by the translator observes.*

But it is not the power the mind has of enlarging its idea of extension *in infinitum*, that is the ground of ascribing infinity to space, as that author seems to suppose;† for we have the same power of adding to number, and yet are not apt to think there is any such thing as a number actually infinite. The true reason, that has inclined so many great men to think, that space must be boundless, seems to be, that they cannot conceive what should set bounds to it; as Dr. *Clarke* and others have argued. 'Tis impossible, say they, since that would be to suppose space bounded by something, which itself occupies space, or else nothing, both which are contradictions; and Mr. *Locke* has reasonings, that tend to the same purpose. But these kind of arguments seem to me to prove nothing but the narrowness of our understandings. As I cannot conclude space to be *nothing*, because we know not *what* it is, neither can I conclude it to be *infinite*, because we are ignorant *what can set bounds to it*. May there not be many ways of setting bounds to space, that we know nothing of? It may be bounded by its own nature, or by the will of God, or by some kind of beings, that we are not acquainted with. In short, whatever *contradiction* may be supposed in setting bounds to space, nothing can seem a more palpable one to me, than to imagine an actual complete being, which implies existing in all its parts together, and yet to be increasable without end, or absolutely boundless, an idea, as I think, utterly inconsistent with real existence.

O thou sole infinite being, *whom the heaven of heavens cannot contain*! how art thou hid in impenetrable darkness! or how shortsighted are we! and with what diffidence should we reason upon things, which you have placed out of our reach, when *that*, which some have thought to be the divine *immensity*, nay thy very *essence*, and to which most have ascribed *infinity*, is by others pronounced to be a mere *nothing*!

---

* [*Essay*], Note 3.
† *Ibid.*

Remarks upon some writers in the controversy concerning the foundation of Moral Virtue, and Moral Obligation, particularly the translation of archbishop King's Origin of Evil, *in his notes on that work.*

The translator of archbishop *King*, when he opposes in his notes those, who maintain the reason, nature, and fitness of things to be the foundation of virtue, and of moral obligation, seems to have forgot that due candour* himself recommends, of not always taking the words of writers on morality in the common acceptation, but in the sense we find they are used by the author we are reading. A little of this candour might have spared his cavilling at the word *fit*; for however it may be commonly applied, it is very evident, that the authors he opposes mean by it, *a suitableness of actions to the relations of things*, and by *fit* or *unfit in themselves*, that this fitness or unfitness depends not on the will of any being, or on any reward or punishment annexed to them. When this is sufficiently explained to be the meaning of those expressions, it seems not very candid to cavil at them as solecisms, or an absurdity of language: and after all, whatever dispute there may be about the truth of their notion, can any words be found more proper to express what they contend for? That there is a moral fitness and unfitness in actions, resulting from the nature of things, antecedent to all positive appointment, and to any consideration of reward and punishment.

The defender of Dr. *Clarke*, as quoted by this author, in the[†] postscript to his notes, gives for instance on this subject, "that it is absolutely right and fit in itself, antecedent to any command, that a creature should reverence his creator. Where (says he) can be any absurdity in this proposition? Is not reverence from a creature to his creator suitable to the nature of each of them?" To this the author of the notes answers, "It is suitable to the nature of the *first*, as productive of its happiness, and to that of the *second*, as agreeable to his will, who originally designed the happiness of his creatures, and therefore bound this and the like duties on them."[1] Thus he resolves all moral fitness into *will* on the one hand, and interest on the other. But surely this is reversing the order of things. Should we not rather conclude, that reverence from a creature to his creator is therefore productive of happiness to the

---

* [*Essay*], *Preliminary Dissertation*.
† P.S. p. 21.

---

1 *Ibid.*

one, and agreeable to the will of the other, because suitable to their respective natures? If this were not so, if there was no fitness or suitableness in the thing itself, antecedent to the will of God, or the happiness it produces; then God might *originally* have annexed the happiness of his creatures to their *irreverence* towards him, and *bound that as a duty upon them*. If this appears an absurd or impossible supposition, to those, who deny any antecedent fitness or unfitness in things, (as Dr. *Waterland*, and some other writers on his side, affirm such suppositions to be),[1] 'tis a plain giving up their cause; for what absurdity can there be in that supposition, if the suitableness of reverence from a creature to the creator depends solely on the creator's will, and the happiness he has made consequent upon it? Since, in that case, his willing the direct contrary would make *irreverence* as suitable to the nature of both.

The opposers of Dr. *Clarke*, who have of late introduced the doctrine of founding moral good and evil on the sole will of God, in order to establish *positive duties* on the same ground with *moral*, seem labouring to overthrow the most solid and immutable foundation of moral virtue, and even to take away our only certain criterion of the will of God, the *eternal immutable nature, and necessary relation of things.*

"We cannot (says the author of the notes,)* imagine these relations to be *strictly eternal*, or independent of the will of God, because they must necessarily presuppose a determination of that will, and are in truth only consequences of the existence of things proceeding from that determination."

To this I answer, the necessary relations of all possible things are *strictly eternal*, as they are eternally perceived by the divine understanding to be unalterably what they are. This depends not on a determination of the will of God, tho' the bringing any possible nature, with its necessary relations, into *actual* existence, proceeds solely from that determination. This distinction the writers on the other side are very apt either *weakly* or *willfully* to overlook, though a very obvious and a very important one in this controversy. Whether God will bring into actual existence a particular system of beings, of any determinate nature, depends

---

* [*Essay*] Remarks i.

---

1 Daniel Waterland (1683–1740), a theologian. In his work *A Vindication of Christ's Divinity* he attacked what he perceived to be heretical tendencies in Clarke's views.

undeniably on his sole will and pleasure; but whether that system of beings shall have such and such relations, from whence certain fitnesses and unfitnesses must result, depends not on his will, but on the nature of the beings he is determined to create. To suppose, that he may will them to have other relations, *&c.* is to suppose, that he may will them to be another kind of beings than he determined to create; for if they are the same, the relations and fitnesses resulting from their nature, are necessary and immutable.

This writer further adds, "much less can we apprehend how these relations, *&c.** are to be chosen for their own sakes and intrinsic worth, or have a full obligatory power antecedent to any reward or punishment, annexed either by natural consequence, or positive appointment, to the observance or neglect of them*; since the natural good or happiness consequent upon, and connected with, the observance of them, is to us their sole criterion, the argument and indication of their worth, the ground of all their obligation."[1] And what then? There is nothing in this at all inconsistent with what Dr. *Clarke* maintains in those words quoted from him: he does not say, that those things are to be chosen, *&c.* antecedent to any *natural* good or happiness consequent upon them, but antecedent to any *reward or punishment* annexed to the observance or neglect of them, either by natural consequence, or positive appointment; and it sufficiently appears in many places of the Doctor's works, that *natural good* is to him the criterion of *moral good*, as it respects ourselves, or our fellow creatures; though *reward and punishment* is not. A distinction, which it is strange so penetrating a judgment should have been at a loss to *apprehend*.

But let it here be observed, that though the fitness of moral actions conflicts in their general tendency to produce natural good to the objects of them, yet there are particular cases, where the fitness remains, though no natural good should be consequent upon it. Respect to parents, gratitude to benefactors, are always fit in themselves, that is, have a rectitude in them, that makes them fit to be chosen, whether any benefit can accrue from them to either side or not. And in whatever regards our duties to the supreme being, *natural good* seems not at all the criterion of them: the object of them we are sure can receive no advantage by

---

* These are Dr. *Clarke*'s words.

---

1 *Essay*, Remarks i.1.

them; and I would ask those gentlemen, who assert,* that *nothing can be our duty, that is not our interest into the bargain*, whether reverence and gratitude to the creator would not always be the duty of a creature, though we should suppose him unalterably placed in a state of the utmost happiness he was capable of? Whether there is not a rectitude in such behaviour, a fitness necessarily resulting from the relation he stands in to his maker and benefactor, which a rational mind must be *conscious* is his duty, though (as in the supposed case) there could be *no interest into the bargain*.

The author of the notes allows this conscious approbation and disapprobation, to be of itself both *rule and obligation*; but to make this consistent with his scheme of resolving all obligation into interest or private happiness, he† founds the obligation of moral sense upon the *uneasiness* we feel, when we neglect what it approves, or practice what it disapproves, as it makes our conformity to it necessary to our happiness. But the obligation seems plainly founded on the *approbation* itself: the uneasiness we feel upon the practice of anything contrary to what moral sense approves, is a *consequence* of the obligation, not the *foundation* of it, and only shows, that we are conscious of being obliged to certain actions, which we cannot neglect without standing self-condemned; self-condemnation manifestly presupposing some *obligation*, that we judge ourselves to have transgressed.

But though Dr. *Clarke* and his followers maintain, that the *fitness of things*, and conscience or the *moral sense* (by which they never understand, nor would I be understood to mean, a blind instinct, but a consciousness consequent upon the perceptions of the rational mind) have *in themselves* an obligatory power, yet it must be allowed, and they as earnestly maintain, that the *will of God*, with the sanctions of his laws, can only enforce this obligation, so as to extend to all times and all cases. These therefore, as Mr. *Warburton*‡ judiciously observes, make a threefold cord, that ought never to be untwisted. The consideration of the *will of God*

---

*   *Turner*, quoted by Author of the Notes in Remarks i. [In the *Remarks*, Law refers to Turner's *On the Laws of Nature, and their Obligation*. This is possibly Daniel Turner (1710–98), a friend of Isaac Watts, a hymn-writer and poet, who also wrote works on morality and divinity. It is not certain this is the same Turner to whom Law refers, however, given his association with Watts, whom Cockburn refers to above, there is a likelihood that this is the same person.]

†   *Ibid.*, Remarks, i.

‡   *Divine Legation.* [Volume 1, Book 1, Section 4.]

must necessarily be taken into all schemes of morality, as the author of the notes justly says; but an endeavour to establish it upon that alone, exclusive of the other principles, seems to me no less a defect in *some*, than the want of that has been in *many* of our modern systems.

Remarks on Note 53, in the second part of the Origin of Evil, *concerning the Foundation of Virtue, and of Moral Obligation.*

This large note has suggested some farther reflections on the foregoing subjects. 'Tis strongly urged, both by archbishop *King*, and in the notes by his translator, that it depended solely on the will of God whether he should create any world, and, among many possible worlds, which he should choose, there being no *best* among created things, that could absolutely determine him. All which, I think, is very justly argued, and solidly refutes Mr. *Leibnitz*'s notion, of there being nothing equal or indifferent in nature. But I do not see how this at all affects the arguments of those, who maintain a fitness in things antecedent to the divine will; though the artful mingling this contest with the other, which has no dependence on it, casts a mist upon the subject that a little perplexes it. The defenders of this antecedent fitness, have no need of supposing, that the present system is *absolutely best*. There may be many possible, indeed actually created, worlds as good or perhaps better than this: each of these may have different systems producing different relations, and fitnesses resulting from them, which will be as eternal and immutable as those of our system are asserted to be; for the relations of all *possible* systems must be eternally in the divine *mind*, as the translator owns; they cannot therefore be dependent on *will*.

God is indeed perfectly free to choose, which of them he will bring into actual existence; but when he has fixed on any particular system, the relations and fitnesses resulting from it are necessary; and to act suitably to them, must be an immutable rule to that system of beings. To this reason, nature, and fitness of things, the divine will always conforms itself. God cannot, for instance, will, that pain shall be suitable, and pleasure unsuitable, to a sensible being; or that it shall be morally good to give causeless pain to such a being. Nor can he will the existence of innocent creatures on purpose to make them miserable; not because *this would be contrary to what he has willed already*, (as this writer* argues) *or inconsistent with* what he supposes to be *the sole end of God's acting,*

---

* [*Essay*], Note 53.

viz. *a communication of happiness*; but because there is an *unfitness* in the thing itself, inconsistent with *rectitude*, and therefore morally evil. If there was no unfitness in this, if making creatures to be happy or miserable was indifferent in the nature of things, antecedent to the will of God, no reason can be given, why he may not change his will concerning them, or make *misery* instead of *happiness* the *end of his acting*. But let us suppose God to have had some other end in the creation, as the *exercise and manifestation of his power*; this end might be answered by making innocent creatures on purpose to be miserable: but can anyone think this would be equally fit, right, and good, as to design them for happiness? And yet this must be the case, if the fitness or goodness of things depends merely on God's willing them, as Dr. *Clarke's* opposers maintain. But further; if this was so, if there was no essential difference in the nature of good and evil, we could never be certain, either that God would deal with us according to truth, justice, and the reason of things, (if upon that supposition there would be any meaning in those words) or that we ourselves were under any obligation of dealing equitably with our fellow creatures. He might decree us to eternal misery, merely to show his sovereignty; or have a secret will contrary to his revealed one, as some upon this very principle have taught: So that we could neither know what we might expect from God, or what he required of us, by any kind of declaration, that he could make of his will; since, according to this notion, it would be no more *unfit from the nature of things*, that he should will to break his promise, and to deal deceitfully with us, than that he should will to act with faithfulness, with equity, and veracity.

When the author of the notes finds himself pressed with the danger of this principle, of founding good and evil, and placing the obligation to virtue, on the mere will of God, he owns, that* *mere will* would of itself be no ground of obligation at all, and that *the will of God must not be separated from his other attributes*; which is, I think, giving up all that is contended for. The moral attributes of God, his goodness, justice, truth, and rectitude, are chiefly understood by us with relation to his dealings with his creatures, suitably to the nature he has given them, and to their demeanour in it. To say then, that the will of God *must not be separated* from these attributes, *i.e.* must be considered as determining itself agreeably to, or in conformity with them, is the same thing, in other words, with conforming itself to the reason, nature, and fitness of things.

---

* *Ibid.*

What ill consequences this author* apprehends, from founding moral obligation on the fitness of things, antecedent to any consideration of reward and punishment, (for which he has taken so much pains to oppose it) he has not been pleased to tell us: but the ill consequences of the contrary notions, of making good and evil depend upon *mere will*, and all obligation to virtue upon *private happiness*, are obvious enough, though he so earnestly contends for them. Upon his scheme, the Heathens, who considered not the law of nature as the will of the supreme being, and knew nothing of a future recompense, could have no obligation to virtue at all; and consequently could not be justly punishable for the neglect of it. The blessed in heaven, as we suppose them confirmed in unalterable bliss, can have no duties to perform; there can be nothing fit or right for them to do, since they can have no advantage by it. But we have good reason to believe, that they are worthily employed in acts of gratitude to their creator, and of benevolence to his creatures, who in a lower or more imperfect state may need their assistance; and therefore we are taught to pray, that the will of God may *be done on earth as it is in heaven*. But what is worst of all, upon this scheme (as I had occasion before to observe) if there is nothing right or fit in itself, but only as it tends to the happiness of the agent, we could never depend upon being equitably dealt with by the deity, since he could receive no addition of happiness from it.

The author of the notes indeed supposes, that "God was always determined to pursue the best end, and by the best means: but why he is so determined, and in what sense this was *better* and *fitter for him*, who could receive no addition of happiness from it, I confess, says he, I do not understand."[1] In truth, upon his principles, this is not only unaccountable, but must be very doubtful. There could indeed be no such thing as *best end*, or *best means*, nor any motive or action, to a perfectly happy being; which he sufficiently shows, that the principle itself must be false. Whereas those, who maintain the *essential difference* of good and evil, right and wrong, and the immutable relations of things, as they were eternally in the divine mind, will easily understand, why a perfectly happy being, of infinite knowledge and power, who unerringly sees, what is in its own nature good, right, and fit, and can be under no influence to bias the rectitude of his will, should

---

* *Ibid.*

---

1 This is a paraphrase of a comment made in Note 53.

always determine himself to do what he perceives to have a goodness in it. Nor will they be at a loss to know, in what sense it is *better and fitter*, that such a being should pursue the best ends, should promote order, rectitude, and happiness; these things being necessarily approved, and consequently objects of choice, to every rational mind, that is under no wrong influence.

And as the most perfectly *happy being* has thought it fit, right, and good to communicate happiness to his creatures, tho' himself could have no advantage by it; may it not seem to be a part of that image of God, in which he is said to have created mankind, that he has made us capable of taking delight in doing good to others, without any regard to our own interest? If it be said, that this *delight* is our reward for doing good, and that therefore our own happiness is the real end of our acting; let it be observed, that the delight of doing good is never the end in view. A benevolent agent has no other prospect, but the interest or happiness of another. The delight he finds in having obtained that end, is either the *consequence* of his benevolence, or of the approbation of his own mind, for having done what was right and fit; but in no case the motive of his acting.

Tho' the author of the notes will not allow, that there is any such thing as *disinterested benevolence* in nature, yet he owns,* that it is matter of fact, that there are great variety of instances of men's practicing virtue, without knowing, that it tends to their own private happiness, indeed even when it appears destructive of it. And he argues very justly against Mr. *Hutcheson*, that this is no proof, that the *moral sense and public affections* (in his language) are mere *instincts* implanted in us, since they are all resolvable into *reason*, and are undeniably cultivated and improved, by making a right use of our faculties. But when he goes on to say, that "they are resolvable into reason *pointing out private happiness*; and that whenever this end is not perceived, they are to be accounted for from the *association of ideas*, and may properly enough be called habits,"[1] I question whether this is reconcilable either to reason or matter of fact. There are many instances of benevolent affections; and a disinterested approbation of virtue, that cannot be accounted for by any supposed *association of ideas*; nor does reason direct a social creature to think, that there is nothing fit for him to aim at, but his own private happiness. On

---

* [*Essay*], *Preliminary Dissertation*.

---

1 *Essay, Preliminary Dissertation*.

the contrary, right reason will inform him, that it is suitable to the nature of such a being, and worthy of approbation, to do all the good he can do for others, whether his own advantage is included in it or not.

Mankind is a system of creatures, that continually need one another's assistance, without which they could not long subsist. It is therefore necessary, that everyone, according to his capacity and station, should contribute his part towards the good and preservation of the whole, and avoid whatever may be detrimental to it. For this end they are made capable of acquiring social or benevolent affections, (probably have the seeds of them implanted in their nature) with a moral sense or conscience, that approves of virtuous actions, and disapproves the contrary. This plainly shows them, that virtue is the law of their nature, and that it must be their duty to observe it, from whence arises *moral obligation*, tho' the sanctions of that law are unknown; for the consideration of what the event of an action may be to the agent, alters not at all the rule of his duty, which is fixed in the nature of things. Thus, as St. *Paul* tells us, *those who had not the law* (the revealed law) *were a law unto themselves*: the obligation of living suitably to a rational and social nature was plain: the consequence was to be trusted to the author of that nature.

Thus undeniably stood the cause of moral obligation, where revelation was not known. But our beneficent creator, foreseeing, that many would be drawn by irregular passions, to deviate from the rule of their duty, by which those, who steadily adhered to it, would be liable to great disadvantages, determined, agreeably to his goodness and rectitude, to make suitable retributions in a future state, that no one should be finally a loser by obeying the law of his nature, or a gainer by transgressing it. This determination, it is plain, introduces no *new moral obligation*, in the usual sense of that word; and I see not why we should give up to this writer his *arbitrary definition* of it: on the contrary, the very notion of reward and punishment implies an *antecedent* duty or obligation, the conforming or not conforming to which, is the only ground of reward and punishment. These cannot, therefore, be the foundation of the obligation; tho' the translator supposes all obligation to arise solely from a prospect of them.

When God was pleased to declare to the world this his determination, in making known to mankind more explicitly, that the law of their nature was likewise *the will* of their creator, he brought them indeed under an *additional* obligation to observe it, obedience to his will being one of the principal fitnesses resulting from the nature and relations of things. But in declaring, that he would eternally *reward or punish* those, who obeyed or disobeyed, he gave them only a new *motive* to the performance of their duty, but no new *foundation* of it: the rule, and reason, and obligation of virtue remained as before, in the immutable nature and necessary relations of things.

At the end of this long note, the author asks, "What will become of the obligation, in cases where virtue fails to produce happiness, which must often happen in the present state?" for in such cases, according to his explication of the word, there can be no obligation. "To deduce one," continues he, "from the prospect of a future reward, is having recourse to the *will of God* to supply *defects*: It is owning, that the obligation supposed to arise from the relations of things, is not in itself adequate and indispensable, and seems to be quite giving up that full obligatory power of theirs, antecedent to any reward or punishment."[1] But by what has been said above, the inconclusiveness of this reasoning may appear. Having recourse to the *will of God*, and the prospect of a *future reward*, is not to supply the *defects of the obligation*, but the defects of our strength and resolution to comply with it. The *right* of obliging may be full, the obligation indispensable, and yet there may be great need of assistance to our frailty, for the discharge of it in cases of severe trial. The prospect of future rewards and punishments is allowed to be the only motive suited to all capacities and conditions: And therefore, no divines have more strongly pressed the consideration of the will of God, and of future retributions, than those, who maintain a full obligatory power in the relations and fitness of things. Dr. *Clarke*, in particular, constantly insists on them, throughout all his admirable practical discourses; and very judiciously refutes the notion of those, who would depreciate the principle of practicing virtue, with a view to future rewards, as mercenary or selfish.

The assurance of equitable retributions in another life is of too great importance to be neglected in any schemes of morality, where revelation is known: but to place all obligation to virtue solely on that, seems to be confounding the *sanctions* of a law with the *reasons and grounds* of it. To make *private happiness* the only foundation of moral obligation, as the author of the notes does, is, I fear, setting it on a principle, that, in case a future state is not known, or not attended to, would leave men free to every kind of

---

[1] Note 53.

profitable wickedness, that they could commit with impunity. Whilst, on the other hand, I see not how there can be any danger in asserting, that there is an indispensable obligation to virtue, founded on the nature, relations, and fitness of things; since that leads us to conclude, that it must be likewise the will of our creator, who gave us a nature, from whence such relations arise; and that himself will act suitably to those necessary relations, in every dispensation to his creatures through all eternity.

Remarks upon an Essay *on* Moral Obligation.[1]

The author of this *Essay*, who writes on Dr. *Waterland*'s side, against a reply to his supplement,* pretends, that *moral obligation*, as built upon the supposed fitnesses of things, must resolve at last into conscience, or the *moral sense*; and that the scheme of Dr. *Clarke* and his followers (which this author opposes) is no otherwise intelligible, but upon that supposition. On this account he has taken† a great deal of pains to confute the notion of an *innate moral sense*: a labour, that might well have been spared in opposing Dr. *Clarke*, since there cannot easily be imagined two schemes more different, than that of founding virtue and *moral obligation* on *a moral sense*, considered as an *innate instinct*, and that of founding them on the nature, reason, and relations of things. These are the objects of the understanding, and can only be apprehended by reasoning and reflection, not by sense, or a *blind instinct*. On what grounds then can this author be persuaded, that "if Dr. *Clarke* and his followers had gone *deeper* in their enquiries, they must have got to this *natural instinct or moral sense*."[2] This would indeed have been going much *lower*, if he means that by *deeper*. But "some of them," says

---

* [Johnson], p. 43.
† [Johnson], p. 30.

---

1 Thomas Johnson (d. 1737). *An essay on moral obligation, with a view towards settling the controversy concerning moral and positive duties in answer to two late pamphlets: The one entitled, The true foundation of natural and revealed religion asserted: being a reply to the supplement to the Treatise on the Christian sacraments: the other, some reflections upon the comparative excellency and usefulness of moral and positive duties, by Mr. Chubb* (1731). (I have checked Cockburn's references against this edition and have indicated any discrepancies.)
2 Johnson, p. 30.

he, "I know do readily grant it."¹ What do they grant, that the nature of virtue, or the obligation to practice it, is founded on a *moral sense*? If they grant this, they are no followers of Dr. *Clarke*, having entirely departed from his principles. But perhaps they may grant, that there is such a principle or faculty in man; for a *moral sense* or *conscience* (if these mean the same thing) is not inconsistent with their foundation of virtue, and *moral obligation*; nay, they may even maintain, that it has an obliging power; for Dr. *Clarke* has gone so *deep* in his enquiries as to tell us,* that natural conscience is founded on the perception, that every rational mind necessarily has, of the natural and essential difference between good and evil. But 'tis sufficiently plain through all his works, that by conscience he does not mean *a blind sense or instinct*, but some principle or faculty, the operations of which depend on the judgment of the understanding.

That there is such a principle in man, whatever it be called, or whether innate or acquired, something that distinguishes between right and wrong, and condemns or approves of actions accordingly, is undeniable. Whether this is a faculty of the understanding, or anything distinct, I presume not to determine; but am inclined to think the faculty *innate*, since it operates in some measure on all mankind, whether they will or not: Though I allow it to be very evident, that the exercise of it, the manner of exerting itself, depends upon custom, education, or whatever means and opportunities it has had of being informed; and agree with this writer, that "its determinations therefore can be no certain rule to act by, no solid foundation for morality."² To which I add, nor can it possibly be admitted for such, but those, who with Dr. *Clarke* found morality on *the immutable nature of things*. But as this faculty is of great use, when duly informed, and rightly set on work, they may allow its proper place in their scheme. Their principle is not of the *excluding* kind; they readily admit whatever can be of *additional* obligation, or assist to the practice of virtue. The will of God, the sanctions of his laws, benevolent affections, and the *moral sense*, have each their weight and importance with them. They leave to their opposers to exclude from having anything to do with virtue, every principle, but their favourites, self-love and self-interest.

---

* Vol. vii. Serm. XV. [Samuel Clarke, *One Hundred and Seventy Three Sermons on Several Subjects and Occasions in Two Volumes* (1734).]

---

1 *Ibid.*
2 Johnson, p. 43.

This author begins chap. iv. (in which he is to show, that his adversary's scheme must resolve into an innate moral sense) with this preliminary remark: "'Tis very observable," says he, "that the maintainers of this natural, necessary, or independent fitness of things and actions, have constantly declined letting us know, what they mean by *moral obligation*, except a synonymous term can be called a definition."[1] But this seems to me a very groundless observation. Dr. *Clarke* and his followers use that term in the plain well known common acceptation of it: if they have not defined it, 'tis perhaps because they could find no words more clear and intelligible than itself. Nor have I met with any definition of it, that has not rather obscured it. A plain man, of an ordinary capacity, readily understands what is meant, when he is told, that he is *obliged* to do to everyone as he would be done by: he apprehends that he *ought*, that it is his *duty* to do so. If there are *synonymous* terms, who can help it, when no other can be found to explain it better?

If it be said, that though a man may know *what* is meant by his being obliged to do a thing, that will not make him understand *why* he is so, or on what grounds he is under such an obligation; this is very true; but then this is not the defect imputed by the author of the *Essay* to the writers he opposes. He cannot pretend, that they have declined to let us know, what they understand by the *foundation* of moral obligation; for it is their plain declarations of that, which he so strenuously contends against. What is it then, that they have declined to do? Truly nothing, that I know of, unless it be an omission not to have put their *grounds* of moral obligation into a definition of the term, as their opposers do, and they might with as good reason have done. They might have told us, that by moral obligation they mean a necessity of action arising from the nature and relations of things; which would have been as just an explication of the term, as that, which Archbishop *King*'s translator, and after him this author gives us, when they say, that by moral obligation they mean a necessity of action, arising from a prospect of obtaining happiness or avoiding misery. But in a controversy, about what is the true original ground of moral obligation, this would have been in them, as I take it to be in these authors, a plain *begging the question in debate*: An error, which did not fall in my way to take notice of, in my remarks on the translator's notes.

---

1 Johnson, p. 25.

However, our present author gives us the reason, from whence he concludes, that he has hit on the true meaning of moral obligation. "Before it can be determined" says he, "what can bring such a necessity upon an agent, as is consistent with perfect liberty, which *moral obligation* is supposed to do, it must first be known, what it is he would choose or refuse as an intelligent free agent: and as it is self-evident, that to every *sensible* being happiness is preferable to misery, and consequently that happiness must be his choice, and misery his aversion, it is plain, that *moral obligation* can be founded upon this principle *only*."[1]

This may be a true conclusion, if there are any intelligent free agents, that are to be considered as *sensible* beings *only*; but that seems to be a very partial consideration of *man*. He is a *rational* and *social* as well as a *sensible* being, and may, nay must be under some obligations as such. Let man be allowed as a sensible being, to choose natural or sensible good, and even to be under a *moral obligation* of so doing; but let him likewise be allowed in his other capacities to have other views, and to be under other obligations. A rational being ought to act suitably to the reason and nature of things: a social being ought to promote the good of others: an approbation of these ends is unavoidable, a regard to them implied in the very nature of such beings, which must therefore bring on them the strongest *moral obligations*. To ask, why a rational being should choose to act according to reason, or why a social being should desire the good of others, is full as absurd, as to ask why a sensible being should choose pleasure rather than pain. If such a question is to be answered, the answer will be the same in either case, these ends are to be chosen, because suitable to the nature of beings with such and such capacities. To act contrary to the reason, relations, and fitness of things, may not improperly be called the *pain* of rational beings. Vice would naturally be the *misery*, and virtue the *happiness* of such beings, if there was no reward or punishment appointed for them.

But this kind of refined happiness these writers seem to have no notion of. This, I presume, is not the happiness the author of the *Essay* has in view, when he tells us,* "that in the case of moral ideas, to say it signifies nothing whether I am to be gainer or loser, seems to me to be *banishing morality* out of the world; as all the relation in moral ideas, that I can possibly discern, is the rela-

---

* [Johnson], p. 59.

---

1 Johnson, p. 3.

tion of certain actions to the agent's happiness." If this gentleman cannot *possibly discern* the relation of fitness of gratitude to a benefactor, of fidelity to trust, of relief to a miserable object, unless the agent is to be a gainer by these virtues, I believe nobody else can possibly discern, how requiring the practice of such moral virtues, without a regard to self-interest, can seem to be *banishing morality* out of the world. If he had said it seemed to be *banishing happiness* out of the world, there might have been some more appearance of ground for it; though I dare venture to engage, that neither of them will be in danger by it.

I readily grant, however, in answer to this author's question,* that the relation of things to our own happiness, as the *sensible* beings, is a very material relation, worth examining into; but it does not follow, that there is no other worth considering; which seems to be the judgment of all this class of writers; and very particularly of the author of the *Essay*, as appears by many passages in it, of which the following is not the least worth noting.

"If," says he, "we must talk in the language of these advocates for fitnesses, we should call the fitnesses, which they speak of, partial fitnesses, or rather *unfitnesses*, as wanting the most essential part of the fitness of an action, *viz*. Beneficialness to the agent himself. God's command supplies that part of fitness before wanting, and makes it now wise and fitting to choose what before could not have been *wisely* chosen; for what is not fit upon the whole, is *really unfit*."[1] This writer seems to have had a mind to outdo all, who had gone before him on his side of the controversy; they have contented themselves with maintaining, that man would have been under *no obligation* to practice virtue, if God had not promised a reward for it. None of them, that I have met with, have ventured to affirm, that without such a prospect the practice of virtue would have been *foolish* and *unfit*. This seems to be a peculiarity of the author of the *Essay*. It was indeed sufficiently contrary to our natural notions of the *essential* difference of good and evil to affirm, that moral virtues are in their own nature *indifferent* till God commanded them, and that he might, if he pleased, have made the direct contrary to have been our duty, as some of the writers, who found virtue solely on the *will of God*, have maintained. But if it was not only *indifferent*, but *unwise* and *really unfit* for a moral agent to be just, to be grateful,

---

*   [Johnson], p. 58.

---

1   Johnson, p. 56.

faithful to a trust, or any way beneficent to his fellow creatures, before God commanded it, as this adventurous writer asserts; on what grounds can God be supposed to have commanded it at all? Or how can this be made to agree with what himself had before affirmed?* *viz.* that God could not have given to man any other rule of action but the law of virtue. "If," says he, "God determined to create man, that is, a rational and social being, 'tis impossible, or rather absurd, that he should give him any other rule of action, than what he has given him: 'tis impossible he should have made it his duty to act unjustly, ungratefully, &c. or to live viciously, intemperately, &c. because this would have destroyed the very end and design of his being, and frustrated that very scheme, which God himself had purposed." One would think the author was arguing here for the other side of the question, that the fitness of moral virtue, of justice, gratitude, temperance, &c. and the necessity of these to the well-being of mankind, did not depend upon the will or command of God but upon the nature of the things themselves; (which, by the way, is all the necessity and independence contended for, by Dr. *Clarke* and his followers.) But if it is granted, that the practice of moral virtue was so *necessary*, as is here said, that without it the very end and design of God's creating man, yea his whole scheme, had been *frustrated*, how could it have been *unfit* for man to practice it *antecedently* to God's command? It could never be unfit or unwise for man to act with the same views his maker had, to pursue what was *necessary* to the well-being of the creation. This sure must have been right and good, though there had been no command about it. Nor can a wise and good being make a thing, that is *really unfit* in itself, the subject of his command. Virtue therefore does not acquire its fitness from *command*: But God commanded it, because he saw, that it was absolutely right and fit, the indispensable duty of a rational and social being.

Though our author allows this, agreeably to the sentiments of Archbishop *King*'s translator, (whom he closely copies in everything but his prudence) though I say they both allow, that moral virtue is the necessary consequence of the nature of man, they notwithstanding maintain, not only that *moral obligation* but that *moral virtue* too, is founded on the will of God. But with such inconsistencies their principles seem to me to abound. The great argument, by which they support their notion, is thus expressed in the *Essay*:† "Everything, every relation, every fitness, is owing

---

* [Johnson] *Essay*, p. 28. [This reference is actually found on p. 21.]
† [Johnson], p. 22

to God's will in its first instance: he sees, at one view, through all the causes, effects, and consequences of things; and therefore in that very act of volition, whereby he determines the existence of certain things, he determines their modes, relations, and everything else belonging to them: and therefore if morality be supposed to flow *immediately* from those relations, yet still it must be *ultimately* resolved into the *will of God*, the author of nature, as its first and true foundation." To this I answer, that if God saw with one view, (as he undeniably did from all eternity) the *necessary* relation of moral virtue to a rational and social being, saw, that he *could not possibly* give any other rule of action to such a being (as this writer asserts) if according to that view he determined to create man; then morality may indeed be *ultimately* resolved into the divine *understanding*, (that is the nature of things, as they exist in it) but cannot be resolved into the *will* of God, in any other sense, that that it depended solely on his will, whether any beings should exist, whose nature required the practice of morality, which I believe nobody denies.

But the *will* of God must be supposed at any rate to be the foundation of *moral virtue*, by those, who will allow no other ground of *moral obligation* but rewards and punishments; by those, who, with this author, can see no fitness in any action, that brings no advantage to the agent. All concern for the good of others is, with him, unreasonable and unaccountable; every generous benevolent action, would be *madness and folly*, setting aside the consideration of a future reward.* "Without that," he says, "no single reason can be given why one ought to suffer the *least* degree of pain to remove from another the *greatest*;" and page 64 he puts this question: "What can induce a man to communicate happiness to another rather than not? What is the exciting reason? You must either assign one, or tell me 'tis preferable in itself as an ultimate end, and then the *pleasure of doing it* will be the true reason: now this," says he, "is recurring to a moral sense." Not at all. Though pleasure may be generally consequent upon doing a right or morally good action, that is not the true reason of doing it, is not the end the agent has in view; the rectitude or goodness of the action makes it preferable in itself, and is the *exciting reason*. To ask, why a man should choose to do good rather than not, or rather than do evil, is to ask, why good is better than evil, and why a man perceives it to be so. That a man should choose to do what his understanding perceives to be good, worthy of approbation, and consequently of choice, carries its own reason

---

* [Johnson], p. 61, 66.

with it. *If no single reason can be given* for such conduct, it must be upon the same grounds, that no proof can be given, that it is daylight, when the sun shines, if anyone should take it in his head to deny it; not on account of the uncertainty or obscurity of the thing, but because no evidence can be stronger than the glare of its own light.

'Tis surprising to observe, that judicious, and (as I am willing to believe) well-meaning men, can argue against the common sentiments of humanity, contradict the most natural perceptions of their own minds, and admit the greatest inconsistencies into their schemes, to support a favourite hypothesis.

The author of the *Essay*, according to the general scheme or the writers on that side, (who are for taking away every motive to virtue but self-interest) denies,* that there are any benevolent or disinterested affections natural to man: but as he cannot deny, that there are some *appearances* of such affections, and that men are apt to think they find in themselves; he accounts for this, after Archbishop *King*'s translator, from an early *association of ideas*. "The great Mr. *Locke*," he says, "was the first, who gave any hint towards a solution of this phenomenon in human nature; and his scheme has lately been improved upon, in a preliminary dissertation to an *English* version of Archbishop *King*'s *Origin of Evil*."[1] Which *improvement* is adopted by our author.

I dare say, when that great man wrote his very useful chapter *Of the association of ideas*, in which he so rationally accounts for the groundless fears, *unnatural aversions*, whimsical affections, and obstinate adherence to error, observable among men, by an *accidental association of ideas*, not at all united in nature, he little imagined any *hint* could be taken from thence, to account in the same way for the most reasonable affections, the most *suited to our nature*; so general, and even so necessary, that if they were wanting, it might justly be esteemed a defect in the forming of a social being.

But our author can supply this *defect* with his *association of ideas*. 'Tis but to suppose, that† "at first a man perceives, or is taught from his infancy, that as he lives in a social state, so his happiness is necessarily connected with that of other men; that the esteem of others is useful to him; this esteem only to be pro-

---

* [Johnson], p. 35.
† [Johnson], p. 40.

---

1 Johnson, p. 37.

cured by beneficent actions, and an inward concern manifested by his outward actions for the good of others. Hence he desires the happiness of others, and joins pleasure to that idea: thus the association is formed, thus benevolence is rooted in our minds; and, forgetting how it came there, we are apt to think it *natural*, and act upon it as a principle entirely distinct from self-love."

This detail of an *unnatural* progress of the mind, in acquiring benevolent affections, will scarce satisfy anyone, who consults *nature*, or what in fact passes in the world, or in his own mind; however plausible it may seem to a speculative recluse, shut up in his study, only to *imagine* by what means such affections might possibly arise. Our author thinks, they so wholly depend on this *imaginary association*, that he tells us,* that "they, who are not sensible how nearly private and public happiness are united, (as a great part of mankind, 'tis to be feared, are not) have no benevolent *affections*, but are indifferent to the happiness or misery, the virtue or vice, of everyone else."

I am persuaded this remark was made in the *study*, with the above *detail*, without looking into what really passes in the world; for though it may be pretty true, that the bulk of mankind have no distinct notions of the connections of public and private happiness, that is, they form no general propositions about it, and perhaps such kind of maxims enter into the education of very few, even of the better sort; yet, 'tis far from being true, that for want of this they have no *benevolent affections*. If these depended on such notions or instructions, as this author has imagined, 'tis to be feared they would be much rarer than we find them. When we examine the real fact, those, whose understandings are least improved, and who reason least, will perhaps be often found to have the strongest affections. Men need not be *taught*, they *feel*, that their happiness is not independent of that of others; they find themselves unavoidably involved, or affected with the miseries of others, and can form no idea of happiness, into which some kind of communication with others does not enter. The very supposition of being happy alone, without regard to any person in the world, or whilst all about him were miserable, must appear a contradiction to a social nature: But this dependence of his happiness on that of others is the *effect* of his benevolent affections, not the *cause or ground* of them.

Can anyone think, that the fondness of a mother, and her tender concern for the happiness of her child, is owing to her "having perceived, or been taught from her infancy, that her hap-

---

* [Johnson], p. 36.

piness is necessarily connected with that of others; that their esteem is useful to her, this esteem only to be procured by beneficent actions, &c."¹ How far unequal to such an effect are reflections of this nature! The connection of her happiness with that of her child must be owing solely to her kind affections, an association of *nature's* forming, quite different from that, which Mr. *Locke* has observed of ideas *accidentally* united, that have *no connection in nature*. Is it possible, from the hypothesis of these writers, to account for parents sacrificing a great part of their ease and happiness in this world, to provide for the welfare of their children; and sometimes by methods, that allow them no title to a reward for it in the next? What desire of esteem, what secret aim at their own happiness, can lurk at the bottom of this?

But it seems we have not the whole of their scheme at once; the parts of it are not consistent enough to be shown together: benevolence, in their view, wherein it has hitherto appeared, is nothing but a secret aim at *our own* happiness; but we are now to have a prospect of it as entirely disinterested. "We maintain* (says the author of the *Essay*) that in this social state benevolence or disinterested affection is a proper *principle of action*; and how it comes to be so, we have shown before; nay, we farther maintain, that a disinterested benevolence is *rational, commendable*, and indeed the very thing, that gives the name or character to virtuous actions among mankind." This, he pretends, is not in the least inconsistent with what he has said before, of *private happiness* being the *ultimate end* and *true principle of action*; "for doing good to others, says he, is a necessary means to *that end*; these means are valuable, therefore desired, approved, hence by habit loved; but the object of love is a real end, or desired for its own sake, without an *immediate* view to anything else. This is what *we mean* by disinterested benevolence; 'tis not necessary, that the agent should have no *remote* view towards *his own happiness in the main*."² All I can gather of these gentlemen's meaning, in whose name this author speaks, from his account of it here, compared with what has been before quoted from him, is, that men first deceive the world, and then *themselves*, with an *appearance* of disinterested benevolence, to gain esteem, and the character of virtuous, though there is really no such thing in nature. But if this

---

* [Johnson], p. 66, 67.

---

1 Johnson, p. 40.
2 Johnson, p. 68.

scheme were true, how could it come to pass, that all mankind should expect from one another what none of them has? How did they agree in making the *name and character* of virtuous actions to consist in what they all must know had not a being? Why should they not rather esteem one another, for doing beneficent actions upon an avowed principle of self-interest, if that were really the only *natural and reasonable motive of action*, as these gentlemen professedly maintain?

But it is at last pretended, that upon their principles a disinterested benevolence is *rational and commendable*, which was before said to be "madness, folly, and unfit, as wanting the most essential part of fitness, beneficialness to the agent." Doing good to others is now become, "an object of love, a real end, or desired for its own sake;"[1] though but two pages before it was asked, "What can induce a man to communicate happiness to another rather than not?"[2] And his adversaries affirming it to be *preferable in itself as an ultimate end*, is exploded, as *recurring to the moral sense*. These passages seem to me *absolute inconsistencies*; but if our author can find a way to reconcile them in his scheme, it may help to reconcile him, at the same time, to those who, more consistently with their own principles, maintain virtue, rectitude, or the fitness of things, to be *an object of love*, and as such, *a real end, desirable for its own sake*. And he may come to a better understanding of this *enthusiastic, unintelligible* language, which he finds fault with in them, since himself begins to talk at the same rate, though at the hazard of overthrowing the doctrine he is labouring to support.

Several of the writers in this controversy argue against the followers of Dr. *Clarke*'s doctrine, from the *ill use* they pretend has been made of it; tho' nothing can be more fallacious, than to condemn a principle for the *abuse* of it, or for the consequences *falsely* drawn from it, which the most sacred and uncontested truths cannot be secure against.

The author of the *Essay*, in particular, reasons thus:* "'Tis easy to see what *pernicious tendency* the scheme of independent fitness is of, from what use has been made of it by a late advocate for Deism. His whole book is built upon this principle, that duty and obligation arises from the nature and relation of things,

---

* [Johnson], p. 71. [This reference is actually found on p. 70.]

1 Johnson, p. 68.
2 Johnson, p. 64.

which are so independent, that no command can alter them, or make that fit, which is in itself unfit; and consequently man must always have the same religion." This is a very false consequence, from a very true principle. Our author is so charitable as to believe, that neither of the persons he writes against, were aware of this consequence; but he "can't see how they will get off it, if the premises are granted; because what is once fit in itself, must be always *fit in itself*, not having relation to any *end*, and not being alterable by any change of *circumstances* whatever."[1]

But who has maintained such *independent* fitness, as these writers have imagined? It is affirmed indeed, that there is a fitness in things independent of any *positive institution*, and of all *consideration of reward and punishment*; and on that account they are said to be fit in themselves, or fit without being commanded. But how does it follow, that they are independent of everything else, or that they have no relation to any end? This is as false a consequence as that of the late advocate for Deism; and yet the premises, from which both *pretend* to be drawn, are undeniably true, even from these authors' own concessions. For though they maintain, that virtue is founded ultimately on the will of God, they yet own (as has been before observed, how consistently need not here be said) that "when God determined to create a rational and social being, it was *impossible* he should give him any other *rule of action* than what he has given him." The moral law then is equally allowed to be *necessary and unalterable* upon either scheme; and if it be a true consequence, that therefore *man must always have the same religion*, it follows as much from the concessions of these authors, as from the principles of those they oppose; and therefore cannot reasonably be urged by them, as an argument of the *pernicious tendency* of their adversaries' doctrine, since it would equally involve their own. But in truth it is no just consequence of either.

It is undeniably true, that what was at first a law to man necessarily resulting from his nature, *is still*, and always must continue to be. But the error of the author of *Christianity as old as the Creation*[2] lay, in not seeing, or being willing to see, that notwith-

---

1 Johnson, p. 71.
2 Matthew Tindal (1657–1733), *Christianity as Old as the Creation* (1730). Tindal's work espouses Deism, a view according to which God's laws are imprinted on the human soul, accessible by human reason. For Tindal, all truths of religion must be identified as truths of reason. William Law's work was strongly critical of Tindal.

standing this, some change might happen in the circumstances of man, as a free agent, from whence new duties, new wants, might arise, or new assistances be requisite. And the mistake of the author of the *Essay* lies, in supposing, that independent fitnesses (as he affects to call them, though improperly) have no relation to any end, and are not alterable by any change of circumstances. Whereas the fitness of moral actions has always a respect to some end, and is entirely *dependent* on the nature and relation of things, considered in their various *circumstances*. The same action may be fit and right in some circumstances of things, which would be unfit in others; for an action is then only morally fit, when it is suitable to the agent, and the object, according to their respective relations and circumstances.

If then any change has happened in man, that introduced new wants, and required new assistances, *revelation* might be necessary to supply them, notwithstanding the false reasoning of that author; and new duties, *new fitnesses*, might arise, notwithstanding the mistakes of this. *Repentance*, for instance, is a fitness introduced among mankind by sin, the sinner standing in a different relation to God from that, which he had as an innocent person: But this does not hinder the moral law from retaining its *immutable nature*, or the fitness of moral actions from being *independent of positive appointment*, or of rewards and punishments; their fitness resulting *necessarily* from the nature, relations, and circumstances of things. Nor would there be any absurdity in saying, that repentance for sin was *eternally fit in itself*.

The opposers of Dr. *Clarke* in general are, I find, greatly prejudiced against the word *fitness*. Let us consider it therefore a little more particularly. Absolute fitness, or *fit in itself*, is an absurdity with them. The term is relative, they say, and must be unintelligible, when used without relation to an *end*; (for it is a mistake, common to all the writers on that side, to suppose, that the words *fit in itself*, are meant to exclude all manner of *end*, or relation to anything;) and some of them, particularly the author of the *Essay*, complain of "a mist and confusion in the language of the advocates for fitnesses."[1] Perhaps there may be some ambiguity in applying the term indifferently to the foundation of virtue in the *abstract*, and to the practice of it by moral agents, which may have given ground for such a complaint: But as these authors, in whatever respect they speak of the *fitness of things*, have expressed their meaning with great clearness, it seems a needless trifling to cavil

---

1 This would seem to be a paraphrase of Johnson, pp. 44–45.

so much about words. Those, who speak of the abstract idea of virtue in general, as a conformity to the reason of things, and the proper ultimate end of moral agents, use the word *fit*, when so applied, in an *absolute* sense; for, as a* fine writer upon these subjects says, why must this term be confined to a *relative* signification, any more than the *aequum* and *rectum*[1] of the ancients? But when they speak of the practice of particular virtues, tho' every right action may be said to be absolutely fit in itself, yet this cannot be so understood, as to exclude such actions from having any relation to an end: for instance, if it should be said, that to relieve a distressed person is *fit in itself*, could this be reasonably understood to mean, that it is fit, without a relation to any end? Or where would be the difficulty to apprehend, that the goodness of the end made the action right and fit in itself, *i.e.* fit without being commanded, fit without a prospect of advantage to the agent? What is there *unintelligible* in this? The absolute fitness of virtue in general consists in its tendency to promote the order, harmony, and happiness of the world; and every particular virtue, (such at least as respects our fellow-creatures) tends to some

---

* Mr. *Balguy*, author of several tracts on these subjects. [John Balguy (1686–1748), philosopher and theologian who defended *Clarke's* ethical doctrines. His works include *The Foundation of Moral Goodness* (1728) and *Divine Rectitude* (1730).]

---

1 The latin terms *aequum* and *rectum* have a variety of meanings, but in the context of Balguy's discussion, to which Cockburn here refers, they mean *equality* and *proportion*. Balguy talks at length about fitness and necessity throughout his works, especially with respect to the idea of virtue. In his work *The Second Part of the Foundation of Moral Goodness* (a follow-up volume to his original *Foundation*), Balguy offers a discussion that uses the mathematical terms *equality* and *proportion* to make his case. He offers the example of gratitude as the most fit and proper disposition that ought to arise in a person in bountiful circumstances. In an effort to show that fitness is not a strictly relative term, he argues that the ideas of bounty and gratitude, for example, arise from the necessities of nature. He explains as follows: "[The agreement between these terms] springs from the same *Necessity of Nature* that makes the Three Angles of a Triangle equal to Two Right ones.... Can then such an *Equality* or *Proportion* be ascribed to those Moral Ideas, as belongs to these Mathematical ones? Those Terms are used and applied to both Kinds, but not precisely in the same Sense. They belong originally to Ideas of Quantity; and when they are used to denote *Moral Fitness*, their Signification is somewhat figurative" (*The Second Part of The foundation of Moral Goodness* [London: Printed for John Pemberton, 1729] 6).

good or other, towards the object of it; but the immediate, the proper end of a moral agent, is the rectitude or moral fitness of the action, whatever other ends that action may respect. In this it is the mind finds a complacence: And therefore, the followers of Dr. *Clarke*, often speak of virtue itself as a real end, amiable and desirable for its own sake; and that sometimes with a rapture, that may seem to favour more of the enthusiasm of poetry, than of the sedateness of philosophy, tho' there is a real and solid foundation for it.

This their opposers call *the error of the Stoics*,[1] and accuse them of falling into the same folly, of mistaking *means for ends*. But these authors mistake the error of the *Stoics*; it did not consist in taking means for ends, but in a *partial* consideration of human nature: an error, which themselves have fallen into, though in another instance. They consider man only as he is a sensible being, and conclude, that he can have no other views but to his own happiness as such. The *Stoics*, on the other hand, considered man as a rational and social being *only*; and as such, they rightly judged, that virtue must be his *end* and his happiness; but then they neglected to consider, that he was likewise a *sensible* being, liable to many external accidents, to pains and sufferings, under which virtue alone, with all its excellence, could not be sufficient for his happiness. This consideration might have led them to the knowledge of a future state, where virtue would meet with no impediments; but whilst they were ignorant or uncertain of *that*, and yet plainly saw, that virtue had an intrinsic goodness, independent of any external advantages or disadvantages, that might attend it, they were forced into the absurdities of maintaining, that *pain was no evil*, that a wise man was master of his own happiness, and that virtue was itself a sufficient compensation for all the sufferings in the world. This was the real, and, if the expression may be allowed, the *noble* error of the *Stoics*.

But in this Dr. *Clarke*, and those who adhere to his principles, having the advantage of a better light, have been far from following them: they have, with great strength of reason and variety of argument, insisted on the necessity of having recourse to the

---

1 Stoicism describes a school of thought founded by the ancient Greek philosopher Zeno of Citium (335-263 BCE). According to the Stoics (its adherents), the world is governed by divine providence, and everything that happens in this world is part of a preordained system of events. The Stoics proposed living in accordance with nature, as discovered by reason, as a means of achieving happiness.

expectation of rewards and punishments in another life, for the support of virtue under the temptations and calamities of *this*. They tell us indeed, that virtue will be a great part of the happiness of that future state; and if their opposers would a little refine or exalt their notions of happiness, (which surely does not wholly consist in *sensible pleasure*) they might perhaps come to see, that there can be no absurdity, in making *that* to be the *end* of rational agents *here*, the perfection of which may probably be in a great measure their *happiness hereafter*.

Some observations on a pamphlet, entitled, The eternal obligation of natural Religion, *&c. being an Answer to Dr.* Wright's *Remarks upon Mr.* Mole's *Sermon.*[1]

This author, who styles himself *Phil-orthos*, is an instance, that happening to be on the side of truth, does not secure warm heads from running into extravagancies in the defence of it. His chief design is to maintain, that morality is founded on the eternal truth and the immutable nature of things. But in order to do this, instead of considering those eternal truths, and immutable natures, in the view, that some eminent* authors have done, as *proofs* of the existence of an *eternal mind*, there being no other intelligible support of eternal *abstract ideas*; he has fallen into the unintelligible whimsies of those, who assert, that *universal natures*, *abstract ideas*, and the moral *differences* of things, are real entities

---

* Dr. *Cudworth* and Mr. *Norris*. [Ralph Cudworth (1617–88) was a philosopher who held that the human mind can know universal and necessary truths since these truths are impressed upon the mind by God. According to Cudworth, these truths exist independently of our minds, in the mind of God. It is this divine origin that guarantees their truthfulness; John Norris (1657–1711), another philosopher who held a similar view regarding the nature of eternal truths. He argued that these truths are knowable by the human mind and are inextricably connected to our knowledge of God's divine nature.]

---

1 George Johnston (1732–33). *The eternal obligation of natural religion; or, The foundation of morality to God and man. Being an answer to Dr. Wright's Remarks upon Mr. Mole's sermon. By Phil-orthos [pseud.].* This work was written in response to Samuel S. Wright (1683–1746), *Remarks on a sermon preached by the Reverend Mr. Thomas Mole, occasioned by his insisting on a foundation of righteousness among men, independent on, and previous to, the will of God. With a defence of the author against whom the preface to the said sermon is written* (1732).

subsisting of themselves, independent of any mind. But as these visionary gentlemen have not been pleased to tell us the place of their residence, I fear those, who go to look for them, will be at a great loss where to find them.

However, according to this author, their existence is rather more necessary and certain, than the existence of God himself; for he says:* "Whether there were a divinity or not, any creator, creature, or not, such moral entities would always subsist, and be just the same that they are now." But if these moral entities, the moral natures and differences of things, refer, as this author says they do,† to *possible existences*, he should have considered, that by supposing there were no divinity, no creator, he supposes away the only ground of *possible existence*; if there was no divinity, there could be no possible existences, and consequently no truths concerning them.

In maintaining these self-existent moral entities, this author has three main arguments;‡ first, "That to speak of abstract ideas arising from any mind, is a flat contradiction in terms,—because *we understand* by them such moral entities, as are self-existent, or that do not depend upon any being for their existence, but may be considered abstractly or separately, without the consideration of any subject: and therefore to say, that they must arise from the mind of God, is to destroy *our notion* of them; or to say, that they are both abstract, and not abstract, at the same time; which is absurd."

Answer. Who can help it, if asserting truth destroys people's *false notions* of things? Where can ideas exist but in some mind? And whatever this writer *understands* by *abstract ideas*, what *should* be understood by them, but the general natures of things, *considered by some mind*, separately form particular existences? For the nature of things is never in *fact* separate, or abstracted from particular existences: that is only done by an act of the mind: The *consideration* of them, separate from any subject, is that, which makes them *abstract ideas*, and their being *in the mind*, that abstracts them from their subject, cannot make them at the same time *not* abstract. To speak of them therefore, as existing *out* of mind, may with much more reason be said to be *a flat contradiction in terms*.

His second argument is, "That whatever ideas did arise in the mind of God, before the creation of the world, must be supposed

---

* [Johnston], p. 15.
† [Johnston], p. 31.
‡ [Johnston], p. 27.

to have had some moral nature or entity for their object: otherwise they could not be ideas or images of anything but mere *reveries*, floating at random, and corresponding to nothing at all."[1]

Answer. If God perceives by *ideas*, there is no need of looking out of the *divine understanding* to find objects for them. Abstract ideas are not images of anything without the mind, as ideas of *sensible* things are supposed to be, but are formed by the mind itself: *possible* existences are real objects to it; and tho' there is nothing in being to represent them, they are no *reveries*, if they correspond to some power adequate to the production of them. Before all creation, God undoubtedly had ideas of all *possible natures*, not by looking out of himself for objects of them, but by contemplating his own infinite power and wisdom; for he must necessarily see all the objects, and the whole extent of his own power. But to imagine, that whilst things were only in *possibility*, their general natures and essential differences had an actual existence, I know not where, *out* of the divine mind; that they were self-existent objects of the divine ideas, tho' themselves are allowed to be only ideas; seems indeed to be a mere *reverie, corresponding to nothing at all*; and which I doubt if our author can form any *image* of. If he can, I should be glad to be informed, what sort of entities the *differences* of things are. The *essential difference* between a circle and a square, an angel and a man, or between a moral good and evil, I allow to be eternal, immutable, and independent of any will; but cannot comprehend this to mean anything else, than that it was eternally true, that none of these things are the same with those, from which they essentially differ; or can be made so by any will. But that their differences should be something subsisting distinctly from the things themselves, real self-existent entities, or, in plain English, *real beings*, is, I think, utterly inconceivable.

Nor is there any occasion for such an unintelligible supposition, to support the truth, which this author chiefly designs to maintain. The eternal and immutable nature of things, their necessary relations, and essential differences, unalterable by any will, are sufficiently secured by being in the divine understanding, eternally and unchangeably what they are. If God sees the possible existence of a triangle, he sees, that it must *necessarily* be different from a circle, and that he cannot will it to be the same; for to will a thing to be the same with that, from which it is essentially different, is a contradiction, and therefore no object of power.

---

[1] Johnston, p. 27.

His third argument is, "That,* if the moral natures and differences of things did primarily *arise* from the *mind* of God, or if his *mind* were the foundation or support of them; he must as naturally will evil as good, and approve of vice and virtue alike. There is no avoiding this consequence, says he, unless it can be proved, that there may be a difference, without different ideas or objects." In the same paragraph he expresses his argument thus: "If the nature of moral good, or of truth, did wholly *arise* from the divine *will*, then the nature of moral evil and of falsehood, by parity of reason, must arise from it, and be equally conformable to it."

Here he quite changes the state of the supposition, and whatever consequences he may draw† of *rank Epicurism*[1] or *downright Manicheism*, from supposing the moral nature and truth of things, to arise from the divine *will*, they no way concern those, who assert these things to have been eternally in the divine *mind*. If this author takes these two suppositions to be the same, he very much mistakes them. But indeed I cannot guess what he understands by the moral nature of things, *arising from or in* the divine mind, when he draws so absurd a consequence from it. The expression itself I think very exceptionable, as it seems to imply things coming to the mind of God, which were not always there: but if he means by it what sober writers mean, who maintain, that the abstract natures or ideas of all things were eternally in the divine mind, or that God eternally perceived in his own comprehensive understanding, the moral natures of things to be what they are, I see not how it will follow from thence, that *God must as naturally will evil as good, and approve of vice and virtue alike.* There is no avoiding this, he says, *unless there may be a difference without different ideas or object.*[2] But what ground is there to imagine, that because good and evil are equally perceived by the divine *mind*, therefore he has not *different ideas* of them, or that they must be equally *conformable to his will*? How wild a conse-

---

* [Johnston], p. 28.
† [Johnston], p. 29.

---

[1] A system of thought founded by the ancient Greek philosopher Epicurus (341–270 BCE). The central goal of life, according to Epicurus, ought to be happiness, defined as minimization of pain and freedom from disturbance. One means to this end was the realization that death is nothing to fear. Epircureans lived in simple, private communities ruled by the primacy of friendship and kindness and the moderation of desires.

[2] Johnston, p. 28.

quence is this! Our author sure knows of no distinction, between the divine *understanding* and the divine *will*. Let him consider, that if God saw before the creation the possible existence of an intelligent *free agent*, he must see, that the idea of such a being necessarily implies a power of choosing either to act suitably to the nature of things, and agreeably to his will, which is moral good; or to act unsuitably to both, which is moral evil. These ideas must be essentially different in his mind, and their being equally perceived by him can by no rule of logic or metaphysics infer, that they are equally conformable to his *will*, or equally approved by him. How far this reasoning may affect those, who maintain, that truth and falsehood, good and evil, depend on the *mere will* of God, I need not enquire: But it is a sufficient defence against that erroneous notion, to show, that these things must necessarily be, from all eternity, in the divine *understanding* immutably the same. We need not have recourse to unintelligible self-existent entities, *abstract ideas*, that yet are *objects* of ideas independent of any *mind*; and which I am persuaded no rational mind can comprehend.

The same author, if I remember right, (for I have not his performance by me at present) has run into another extravagance, tho' in maintaining a solid truth; affecting to talk of God, as under a moral *obligation* of making nature, and the essential difference of things, the *rule* of his actions;[1] with many daring and unusual expressions, which must give great offence to those, who have accustomed themselves to join with the term *obligation*, the idea of a *superior will*, and of reward and punishment: Since it will not only appear to them an absurdity, but the highest irreverence, when applied to the supreme being; and therefore ought in prudence to be avoided.

The truth which this author should, and which perhaps he did mean, has been asserted by the best writers on these subjects; but then they did it with decency and dignity. They did not subject the supreme being to rule his actions, by imaginary self-existences, that have no dependence on him: acting in conformity to moral truth is, with them, acting in conformity to *himself*, in whom all essential truth exists. And I think, it can no way derogate from him to assert, that the perfection of the divine nature *obliges* him to acting conformably to the essential difference of things, because acting contrary to them would be an imperfection: it is the same as acting contrary to goodness, justice, truth,

---

1 Johnston, p. 24.

or, in one word, the rectitude, which everyone, who allows the immutable nature of these things, readily owns to be inconsistent with absolute perfection.

And if the supreme being may be thus *obliged* by his own essential perfections, to act conformably to the immutable nature of things, on the same grounds it is maintained, that every rational being must be *obliged* to act suitably to his perceptions of those things; because, in doing otherwise, he must fall short of that degree of *perfection*, and consequently of happiness, which belongs to his nature: For the happiness of every being is dependent on, and in proportion to the perfection, which belongs to it.

This consideration leads me to reflect, that the writers on the other side, who maintain, that nothing can induce *moral obligation*, but rewards and punishments annexed to the law of a superior, can only mean, that if there was no such expectation, should men disregard the perfection of their nature, fall from their moral character, and forfeit the happiness of rational beings, by choosing to act contrary to the reason and truth of things, they may do it with impunity. And that indeed is very true. But does it follow, that there is nothing *wrong* in such a choice? Is it not unsuitable to, and unworthy of such a being, and inconsistent with the true happiness of a reasonable nature? And is virtue nothing but mere aiming at reward, or a care to avoid punishment? I do not know what notions the partisans of that doctrine can have of virtue and moral goodness, whilst they talk of it as nothing but a regard of *interest*. Could they think anyone a virtuous and truly good man, who would willingly counteract his sense of right and wrong, and all the dictates of his reason, from the nature and fitness of things, if he might do it with impunity? I am persuaded they could not; the *natural* sentiments of their hearts, I doubt not, get the better of their *artificial* schemes; and whilst they contend, that nothing can *oblige* them to do just or kind actions, but the prospect of a reward, they feel the charms of rectitude and benevolence determine them to act independent of other views, with all the force of *moral obligation*.

Eternal truth! Instruct us so to learn thy *perfect will*, in the essential difference of good and evil, that aspiring to perfect our nature *here*, by a conformity thereto, we may be qualified for that blessed state *hereafter*, which thou hast promised as the *reward*, and which is itself *the perfection of virtue*.

Remarks on some passages of the first book of the Divine Legation *of* Moses.

Since I drew up the foregoing remarks, I have met with the second edition of the *Divine Legation,* in which I find a great deal upon the *foundation of morality and of obligation,* which either was not in the first edition, from whence I have quoted a just observation relating to those subjects, or I did not then advert to it. Otherwise the sentiments of so great a writer would not have been the last in my consideration: but I cannot allow myself now to omit taking notice of them, and it may be no improper conclusion of these papers.

This penetrating author with great judgment observes all the extremes, into which the contenders about the true foundation of moral virtue have run, whilst each would advance his own favourite principle upon the ruins of others. But tho' he judiciously avoids all their extravagancies, some of which have been taken notice of in these remarks, I am sorry to find, that, in establishing morality and obligation of the *will of a superior,* he too acts upon the *exterminating model,* will not allow, that a *moral difference* of things, or *obligation* to practice, can be deduced from either of the other two principles, the *moral sense,* or the *eternal relations and essential difference of things.*

If the important point he is proving, required his argument to be carried thus far, I should very unwillingly oppose it: But there is no need of it: he has strongly proved, throughout the course of this learned work, the absolute necessity of religion to society; and particularly, in opposition* to Mr. *Bayle,* the insufficiency of the *moral sense,* and the knowledge of the *essential difference of things,* to influence society to the practice of virtue. Against this I am far from contending. My only purpose is to plead, that these principles have so far a *right* of obliging, that whosoever is not so influenced by them, deserves blame and punishment, tho' he knows nothing of a superior will with power to inflict it. The contrary notion seems to give the Atheists a greater advantage, than I am persuaded was ever intended them by an adversary, who had attacked them in their strongest holds, and turned their own artillery against them, with abilities equal to his arduous undertaking. I beg leave therefore, to examine the grounds, upon which

---

* [*Divine Legation*] From p. 53 to 58. [This and all subsequent references to Warburton's *Divine Legation* are found in Volume 1, Book 1.]

this great author maintains, "That an Atheist is not under any obligation to act agreeable to right reason,"[1] *i.e.* to practise virtue.

And first he urges, that an Atheist cannot arrive at the knowledge of morality properly so-called: that tho' he may have a knowledge of the *natural* essential difference of things, this does not induce the knowledge of the moral difference:* That this distinction has been much unobserved, the contenders for this principle, as well as their adversaries, being under the same prepossession, that *one* inferred the *other*. But that is a mistake, for nothing but *will*, or the law of a superior, can constitute the morality of actions. This in short is the sum of what is insisted on in several pages.† To which, with submission I reply, that which properly constitutes the morality of an action, is the free choice of the agent, judging it to be right or wrong, praise or blame worthy. The law of a superior does not make an action morally good or evil; it only declares what is so, or restrains and incites by the sanctions of punishment and reward, (I speak not of *positive duties*, the morality of which depends solely on the law of a superior). Neither do I find, that the contenders for the *natural essen-*

---

* In order to judge of this point, let us suppose of a society of Atheists, one fallen into a pit, where he must inevitably perish if unassisted; and another of them happening to travel that way, who could with great ease relieve him. Will these two persons perceive nothing, but the *natural* essential difference between leaving a man to perish in a pit, and helping him out of it? Would not the distressed consider one of these as inhumanity to be detested, and the other as a good action deserving grateful return? Might not the traveler be too conscious, that one of these actions would be better than the other, have a goodness in it more to be approved? Yet we will suppose some business or pleasure he is intent upon, stifles this consciousness and prevails with him, to leave the distressed to his miserable fate; and that he afterwards relates to the rest of the society, how he had hurried from the melancholy object, in pursuit of his inclinations. Can it be imagined, that they would coldly consider this action, only as not agreeable to reason? Or would they not rather judge it to be wrong, inhuman, and worthy of detestation. It cannot, I think, be doubted, that such a society might be capable of these sentiments. And what is this but to perceive the *moral difference* of things, tho' they have not discovered *a superior will* to enforce the observance of them? Or tho' they may think the guilty secure from that punishment, which they must be conscious so great an immorality deserves.

† [*Divine Legation*], See p. 42, 46, 52.

---

1 *Divine Legation*, p. 45.

tial *difference of things* have* mistaken it for the *moral difference*; they plainly saw, that these were distinct things, but they saw too, that one was so dependent on the other, that when they had clearly demonstrated the former, they needed not give themselves much trouble to prove the latter: For perhaps this great author is the first, who, acknowledging *the natural essential difference*, has denied, that the *moral difference* was deducible from it.

"The natural essential difference of things, he says,† if we mean anything by the terms, hath this apparent property, that it creates a *fitness* in the agent to act agreeably thereto: As the moral difference of things creates, besides this fitness, an obligation likewise." But what is this fitness and unfitness, that results from the natural essential difference? Not indeed the same with that, which creates it, but surely the very same with the *moral difference*; or else I know not what we mean by either. An action fit or unfit, made the object of choice, is morally good or morally evil. And therefore it is maintained that *fitness* creates an *obligation*, because it implies, or is the same with moral difference, from which our judicious author allows, that *obligation* is inseparable.

He further argues, "that the essential differences of things are the adequate objects of the understanding; and for this reason, the understanding is necessitated in its perceptions, but the will is not necessitated in its determinations: For instance, that three are less than five, the understanding is necessitated to judge; but the will is not necessitated to choose five before three: Therefore the essential differences of things are not the adequate objects of the will; the law of a superior must be taken in, to constitute obligation in choice, or morality in actions."‡ But if this reasoning holds good, it will prove too, that *the law of a superior* is not the adequate object of the will; for neither does such a law *necessitate* the determinations of the will: if it did, there would be no longer any *choice*, and consequently no morality in actions; *obligation* would then differ nothing from *compulsion*. But all the *necessity* that a *free-agent* can be laid under, either from the law of a superior, or from the essential differences of things, is that of standing self-condemned, if he chooses to do what he cannot avoid judging, and in the case of another, would pronounce to be unfit, wrong, and deserving punishment. This judgment of his therefore brings him equally under the strongest of *obligations*, upon whatsoever principle it

---

* [*Divine Legation*], p. 52.
† [*Divine Legation*], p. 44.
‡ [*Divine Legation*], p. 46.

is founded, or how inconsistent soever it may be with the absurd notions of an *atheistic fatalist*.

It is urged in the preceding page, that *obligation* in general necessarily implies an *obliger*. And elsewhere,* that, "upon the discovery of a superior will, and not till then, human actions became the subject of *obligation*." To this I answer, that, in the common acceptation of the word, obligation implies only a perception of some ground or reason, upon which it is founded, but not necessarily a superior will. When we say a man is under an obligation to be grateful to a benefactor, we mean, that the relation interceding between them requires it of him; and so that he is obliged to do to others, as he would have them do to him, implies an *equity* in the thing, that brings him under such an obligation. Again it is urged, "That the *obliger* must be different from, and not the same with the *obliged*. To found *obligation* upon *reason* is an absurdity, because reason is only an attribute of the person obliged: To make this then the obliger, is to make a man oblige himself."[1] Very true, but it is just the same, whatever principle we suppose obligation to be originally founded on; a free-agent must be always the *immediate* obliger of himself: Whether he judges, that the will of a superior is to be the only rule of his actions; or that he ought to act conformably to the necessary relations, and essential differences of things, or to his consciousness of right and wrong; or that a prospect of rewards and punishments should solely influence his actions; in either case it is equally the perception and judgment of his own mind, or his *reason*, that obliges him to act accordingly; and this is so far from being an absurdity, that it is essential to *moral choice* and *free agency*.

But it does not follow, because that a man's own reason has a right in this sense to oblige him, that therefore *he may relinquish that right*. That maxim, which Mr. *Warburton*† says, "is an unexceptionable rule of right reason, that whoever acquires a right to anything from the obligation of another towards him, may relinquish that right," takes place I suppose in those rights alone, that are acquired by voluntary compact, not in those, which are deduced from the nature of things. But it is the nature of things, the essential differences, which is maintained to be the original ground of obligation; over which reason has no power, tho' by its

---

* [*Divine Legation*], p. 37.
† [*Divine Legation*], p. 45.

---

1 *Divine Legation*, p. 45.

perception of them it becomes the *immediate obliger* to act suitable thereto.

This great writer farther argues,* that "from the *nature* of any action morality cannot arise, nor from its *effects*: Not from the *first*, because, being only reasonable, or unreasonable, nothing follows but a fitness in doing one, and an absurdity in doing the other: Not from the *second*, because did the productive good or evil make the action moral, brutes, from whose actions proceed both one and the other, would have morality." To this last I reply, that from the *effects* of an action, where there is no *choice*, or *free-agency*, (of both which brutes are supposed incapable) no morality can arise: But where these are, morality does arise from the *effects* of an action made the objects of choice. To the *first* I reply, that if from the *nature* of an action follows a *fitness*, from *fitness* follows *obligation*, and consequently morality, in actions.

This methinks our judicious author should readily assent to, as agreeable to his own principles; for tho' he founds obligation on the *will of God*, he disclaims the error of those, who place it solely on a view of rewards and punishments. "The true principle of morality,† he owns, should have the worthiest motive to enforce it; and the legitimate motive to virtue on that principle is compliance with the will of God. It is a mistake,‡ he says, that will could not oblige without happiness; will could not indeed oblige to unhappiness, but it would oblige to what should produce neither one nor the other, tho' all considerations of the consequences of obeying or disobeying were away." Now if this be so, (and one would scarce imagine it could be denied) this obligation to obey, *independent of all consequences*, which our author justly contends for, can be founded on nothing but a *fitness* resulting from the relation of a creature to his creator and benefactor. To argue from hence, that therefore *it is fitness, which obliges, and not will*, is indeed a *metaphysical quibble*, and, as§ this author has represented it, not a little absurd, fit only, as he designed it, to *divert* the reader. But I think it may with great solidity be concluded, that if the will of God obliges from a fitness, that arises on account of the relation of a creature to his creator, whatever fitnesses arise from other relations, and the essential difference of things, will likewise oblige in their proportion.

---

* [*Divine Legation*], p. 47.
† [*Divine Legation*], p. 38.
‡ [*Divine Legation*], p. 49.
§ [*Divine Legation*], p. 50.

This great writer* urges, indeed, "that the fitness, that a creature, who depends entirely on his creator, should obey him, is infinitely different from any other fitness, that arises to a supposed independent being, from the comparing and perceiving the relations between his ideas." But if these relations, or our perceptions of the essential difference of things, are, as he farther argues,† the rule, that God hath given his creatures to bring them to knowledge of his will, then it must be a rule to all his creatures, whether they consider it as his will or not; and therefore, as reasonable beings, the fitness of obeying the creator's will must be so far from being *infinitely different* from the fitness of complying with a man's perceptions of the necessary relations and difference of things, that, supposing all consideration of the consequences were away, there must be an equal obligation to either, according to the opportunities of discovering them: Besides that without a regard to the right, and reason, and equity of the case, whatever men's actions may be, there is no virtue or real goodness in the person, that does them: the nature and reason of things therefore should seem to be the genuine principle of true morality.

That the knowledge of the *essential difference of things* would not alone be generally effectual to influence a society of Atheists to the practice of virtue, I readily grant. But that is no more an objection against the truth of the principle, and its *right* to oblige, than it is against the right, which the *will* of God has to oblige, *independent of its consequences*, that the knowledge of it would not be effectual to keep the bulk of mankind to the practice of virtue, without enforcing it by the sanctions of reward and punishment. 'Tis nevertheless true, that there is an indispensable obligation to obey the will of God, *though all consideration of the consequence of obeying and disobeying were away*, as this author justly maintains: And the same obligation there is without consideration of the consequence, to act suitably to that fitness, which results from the essential difference, and relations of things; and to the unavoidable judgment of our own minds, that actions are accordingly right or wrong, worthy of reward or punishment.

Now an Atheist is undeniably capable of these affections of the mind, by which this great author‡ accounts for men's being disposed to place morality in the essential difference of things, *viz.* "that sense of *right* and *wrong* so strongly impressed, as to be

---

* [*Divine Legation*], p. 51.
† [*Divine Legation*], p. 53.
‡ [*Divine Legation*], p. 51.

attended with a consciousness, that the one deserves reward, and the other punishment, *even though there were no God*." This consciousness therefore, which the Atheist is allowed to be capable of, though he is so blind as not to see, that that very sensation is the plainest indication of *will*; though, from the eternal truths which he perceives, he is so absurd, as not to discern an *eternal mind*, from which they result; yet this consciousness of his brings him under obligation to act suitably to what he *does see*, to do, or to forbear what he unavoidably judges to be right or wrong; for no stronger obligation can be laid upon a *free-agent*, than that of standing self-approved, or self-condemned.

If this not be so, I should be glad to be informed, whether we are to suppose, that an Atheist is not accountable in a future state for any enormities he may commit here? Or if this be too great a privilege to allow him, upon what principle he can be justly punishable for doing or not doing, what it is maintained he is under *no obligation* to do or to forbear? If the author of the *Divine Legation* is pleased to take occasion of giving an answer to this question, when he publishes the impatiently expected remainder of his valuable work, it will be acknowledged a great instance of goodness and condescension, to overlook the obscurity and low abilities of the enquirer, in regard to the importance of the *difficulty*.

Appendix

There are two arguments relating to the subjects of the foregoing *Remarks*, that seem to be of great weight with the opposers of Dr. *Clarke*, being frequently insisted on, and repeated by the best writers among them; though one of them is a mere *fallacy*, (which perhaps themselves are not aware of) and the other at least a very precarious supposition. It may therefore be of some service in this controversy to set them both in a true light, which I shall here endeavour to do, having but lately had occasion to observe the importance they are thought to be of.

It is maintained by Dr. *Clarke* and his followers, that there are eternal and immutable relations, essential differences of things, and fitnesses resulting from them, independently of the will of God, which are obligatory to all reasonable beings, *antecedent to any positive appointment* or *declaration* of the will of God concerning them. In opposition to this, several of their adversaries, in order to establish virtue and moral obligation *solely* on the will of God, have argued in different forms of expression to this purpose: That those relations and fitnesses *&c* cannot be eternal, or independent on the will of God, since they are *consequences of the existence of things*, proceeding from the determination of his will. And, for the same reason, they urge, that moral obligation cannot be *antecedent* to the will of God, because it could not commence, till *after the will of God* had exhibited certain relations and fitnesses in the creation, from whence morality arises. Now here is the plain *fallacy* of substituting a quite different consideration of things in the room of that, which they pretend to oppose, viz. *particular existences*, instead of *general abstract ideas*; and the will of God, *as expressed or implied in the creation*, for the will of God *explicitly declared* by the command of moral virtues. And who is concerned in this argument I know not, for surely Dr. *Clarke* or his followers never pretended, that particular existences were eternal, and independent of the will of God; or that the eternal reason and truth of things were obligatory to reasonable creatures, before the will of God had brought any such into existence. The relations and fitnesses, they speak of, are *truths eternally in the divine understanding*, which proceed not from any determination of his will, but are the rules, by which his will is itself determined. The *antecedency* they speak of respects only the explicit declaration of the will of God, by the command of moral virtues. And what can be a greater fallacy than to object to this, that *the will of God is expressed in the creation*, exhibiting those relations and fitnesses, from whence morality arises? For the will of God, as expressed, or rather implied in the creation, is the very same with that reason and truth of things, which are said to be obligatory *as such*; that is, antecedently to any explicit declaration of the will of God concerning them. If these writers will allow the will of God in that sense, viz. *as expressed in the creation*, to be obligatory to morality without any positive appointment, or explicit command, the controversy would be at an end. But if they deny this, why do they amuse their readers or themselves, by seeming to oppose their adversaries with an antecedency of the will of God, when they really mean nothing more, than that the *existence* of creatures capable of moral obligation is a consequence of the determination of the will of God? which is indeed very true, but nothing to the purpose in this debate.

The other argument, which I design here to consider, is urged by those, who acknowledge no moral obligation, but what is founded on self-interest, or a prospect of *future rewards and punishments*. First they lay it down as a *postulatum*, that *the sole end of God in the creation was to communicate happiness*, and that he appointed the practice of virtue to be the necessary means of obtaining that end. In consequence of this they argue, that man ought to make *that his end*, which God has made so, that a consideration of the end must be the motive to choosing the means, and therefore virtue should only be chosen with *respect to the recompense of reward*, without which view it would neither be beautiful nor orderly, nor reasonable, nor fit.*

That happiness was the *sole end* the creator had in view, is too precarious a supposition to be taken for granted. Had that been so, probably the utmost possibilities of it would have been produced; which does not seem to be the case. However, *rewards and punishments* have not the least pretence to be the sole end of God in the creation, tho' necessary for the *after* government of degenerate creatures. The very notion of reward and punishment implies merit or demerit arising from a compliance with or neglect of some end, which moral agents were *previously* obliged to have pursued; so that obligation must be founded on some principle *prior* to all consideration of reward and punishment, otherwise there could be no ground for them. And why should God have so over-rated virtue, as to propose inestimable rewards for the practice of it, if it had no self-excellence, or if it had not been one great end of his creating moral agents? If an earthly king should promise some great honours or privileges to such of his subjects as amidst a rebellious people had continued faithful to him, or would timely return to their duty; would anyone doubt, that the king's *chief end* was to preserve, or to recover his subjects to their obedience; and that the proposed rewards were intended as *means* the better to secure that end? And if some of his subjects should profess, that they would have persisted in their fidelity, or returned to it, from a sense of the reasonableness of their duty, though his majesty had made them no such gracious promises; would the king think them the worse men, or the worse subject for this, or that they were the less worthy of the honours he intended them? I dare say nobody will imagine it. Why then should not the rewards proposed by the king of heaven for the practice of virtue, be esteemed as *means* to promote universal rectitude? And that contributing each his

---

* This point is largely insisted on, in *The Cure of Deism*, Chap. xvi. [Rev. Elisha Smith (1683?–1740), author of *The cure of deism: or, the mediatorial scheme by Jesus Christ the only true religion. In answer to the objections started, and to the very imperfect account of the religion of nature, and of Christianity, given by the two oracles of deism, the author of Christianity as old as the creation, and the author of the Characteristicks* (1740).]

part towards that great end ought to be the *chief view* of all his reasonable creatures?

That *one* design of God in the creation was to communicate *happiness*, so far as was consistent with *order and rectitude*, or as it is a consequence of them, I believe will not be questioned. But since the infinitely *happy* Creator is likewise infinitely *perfect*, I think there is as little reason to question, that *one great end* he had in view was to communicate some degree of all his communicable *perfections*, to produce beings capable of imitating his moral attributes, of conforming to that sacred rule of truth and rectitude, by which his own unerring will is always directed; that they might be perfect *even as he is perfect*. And if this was one design of God in creating mankind, which can scarce be doubted; then certainly they ought to have the same end in view; and if, in order to it, God could give them no other law but that of moral virtue, as these writers allow, then the obligation to practice it must arise, with virtue itself, from the very nature of such a system, not solely from a prospect of rewards and punishments.

I am far from intending to depreciate a proper regard to future retributions, as they are gracious assistances to the frailty of man; but let them not change place with that, which they were appointed to promote; be made *sole ends*, whilst virtue is degraded into *bare means*; tho' if doing right actions purely *because they are right*, is not the proper idea of virtue, it will be hard to say what is; but aiming *solely* at a reward certainly is not. Where the will of God is known, there is an additional obligation, that strongly enforces the practice of virtue, from a desire of being acceptable to the supreme being, who wills the perfection of his creatures, in which their chief good consists; and therefore the consideration of the will of God ought never to be omitted in any Christian schemes of morality. But neither ought moral virtue to be established solely on such principles, as would leave men loose from every obligation, who are either not so *wise*, as to discover the will of God in the *nature of things*, or not so *happy*, as to be acquainted with his *revealed will*, and the *sanctions of his laws*.

These Remarks are, with the utmost Deference, inscribed to Alexander Pope, Esq. *by an admirer of his* Moral Character.[1]

---

1 Alexander Pope (1688–1744), English essayist, critic, and poet; best known for his works *The Rape of the Lock* (1712–14) and *An Essay on Man* (1734).

Remarks upon the Principles and Reasonings of Dr. Rutherforth's Essay on the Nature and Obligations of Virtue:[1] *In vindication of the contrary principles and reasonings, enforced in the writings of the late Dr. Samuel Clarke.*

Published by Mr. Warburton, with a Preface.

First printed in the year 1747.

Preface[2]

The author of the *Divine Legation* had observed, that God, in order to secure the practice of moral virtue, had been graciously pleased to bestow on man an instinctive approbation of right, and abhorrence of wrong; to which some philosophers have given the name of the *moral sense*: That God had further established a real, essential difference in the qualities of human actions, whereby some are seen to be fit and right, and others wrong and unfit. But, as this author thought, that *obligation* without an obliger, and an *obliger* without agency, were mere jargon, he therefore had recourse to a superior *will*, as the proper and real ground of *moral obligation*. For tho' *instinct felt* a difference in actions; and *reason discovered* that difference to be founded in the nature of things; yet it was *will* only, that could make *compliance* with such difference to be our *duty*; whereby that, which was, before, a *fitness*, now became *virtue*. On these *three principles*, therefore, he supposed the whole edifice of practical morality to be erected. He observed further, that this admirable provision for the support of virtue had been, in great

---

1   Thomas Rutherforth (1712–71), *An Essay on the Nature and Obligations of Virtue* (1744). Rutherforth was a professor of divinity at Cambridge. His *Essay*, which was critical of Clarke's rationalistic natural fitness theory, presents a brand of hedonism, wherein moral principles are said to reflect considerations of pleasure and pain/happiness and unhappiness. Cockburn's references have all been checked against the 1744 edition. Any discrepancies have been noted. *All* notes referring to Rutherforth are references to his *Essay*—although I have retained Cockburn's occasional inclusion of the title in her notes.
2   William Warburton published and prefaced this work. Warburton (1698–1779) was a well-known theologian of the period whose *Divine Legation* was a refutation of Deism. Cockburn discusses his work in her *Remarks upon some Writers* (included in this volume).

measure, defeated by its pretended advocates; who, in their eternal squabbles about the true foundation of morality, and the obligations to its practice, had sacrilegiously untwisted this threefold chord, and each (whether he placed it *falsely*, in the moral sense or essential differences; or *truly*, in the will of God) running away with the part he esteemed the strongest, had affixed *that* to the throne of Heaven, as the golden chain, which is to draw all unto it.

Since the making of these observations, the writer here confuted hath afforded one of the most notable examples of the folly there condemned. He seemed indeed to aim at placing, the foundation of morality rightly, in the *will of God*: but then he would not so much as allow the other principles to be even a *rule*, to direct us in the knowledge, and, consequently, in the observance of that will. And see, the mischiefs of separating what the divine wisdom had united; for, to support the extravagance of his scheme, he was forced to entrench himself in a vile and abject selfishness; by which he hath not only degraded human nature, and defiled moral virtue, but hath even slipped beside his professed foundation, the *will of God*; by which miscarriage he hath fallen, before he was aware, into the most impious, as well as most absurd system, that ever entered into the head of professed religionist; as may be seen by a perusal of the following sheets.

But his answerer, the author of them, proceeds with much greater discretion; as intent only on the advancement of truth and piety. This writer, though placing the foundation of moral virtue (I think, wrongly) in the *eternal relations* of things; yet allows the other principles all their efficacy; and so sagely secures the interests of practical morality. And by this means, seconded by a fine genius and infinite superiority in reasoning, hath given so thorough a confutation of this exclusive, exterminating system, as is rarely to be met with in controversies on these subjects. Indeed, there was little or nothing in the work confuted, but sophistical wrangling, and disingenuous tergiversation; embarrassed by an understanding more than ordinarily condensed with the frigid subtlety of school-moonshine. To make amends for this, you have, in the confutation, all the clearness of expression, the strength of reason, the precision of logic, and attachment to truth, which make books of this nature really useful to the common cause of virtue and religion.

But after all, on this subject it would not be amiss, for disputants to attend to the advice of M. *Bayle*: "Disputez tant qu'il vous plaira sur des questions de logique; mais dans la morale contentez-vous du *bon sens*, et de la lumière, que la lecture de l'*Évangile* repand dans l'esprit."[1]

Remarks upon the Principles and most Considerable Passages of Dr. Rutherforth's Essay., &c.

One, who has been accustomed to an awful sense of religious duties, as founded on the eternal reason and nature of things; and to consider mankind as a system of social beings, designed to promote each other's welfare, no part being made for itself alone; cannot, I am persuaded, without a good deal of uneasiness, take a view of the unamiable and degrading picture of both, given us by some late moralists, who profess to do honour to religion by establishing it on the *lowest* motives, upon pretence, that they are the *strongest*; and to consult the happiness of mankind, by maintaining, that every individual is concerned solely for his own; that there is no such thing in nature, as a disinterested desire of the good of others; and that no man does, or ought to do, the least beneficent action, or has any sense of gratitude for those done to him, without a prospect of farther advantage to himself. These doctrines are so contrary to the appearances, that are in the world, as well as to the natural feelings of our own minds, that the assertors of them are obliged to account for all the disinterested actions, that seem to be done and the sentiments we imagine we have of them, by an unnatural *association of ideas*, or a far fetched string of reflections, that never entered into a benevolent heart; and which (however those writers have found out these distant secret springs) they will never find one virtuous man in the least conscious of.

In this no one has laboured with more advantages of learning, of plausible argument, and all the arts his cause requires, than the author of a late *Essay on Virtue*. The great design of his book, he tells us, is to lead his readers to see, that revelation is necessary,

---

[1] Pierre Bayle (see footnote 20, *Remarks upon Some Writers*). This quote is found in Bayle's renowned work, *Dictionnaire historique et critique* (Historical and Critical Dictionary), originally published in 1697. The following translation was found in one of the numerous English editions of Bayle's *Dictionnaire*: "Dispute as long as you please upon logical questions; but in morality be content with good sense, and with that light, which the reading of the Gospels sheds on your mind." (*The Dictionary Historical and Critical of Mr. Peter Bayle, Vol 3*, 2nd ed. [London: Printed for J.J. and P. Knapton, 1734–38] 894.)

both to teach us how to make ourselves happy, and to oblige us to be virtuous: in which I would heartily concur with him, but see not the necessity of depreciating religious duties, or human nature, in order to that end. Let the God of truth, who has *written his laws in our hearts*, be honoured by the dictates of our nature, as well as by the assistances of revelation.

This author is not unaware, that the most* eminent of the advocates for the obligations to virtue, arising from the relations and fitnesses of things, do, as strongly as he, assert the necessity of revelation; for he has taken advantage of their concessions on that point to argue against the sufficiency of their principle. But supposing their principle insufficient, if it is not *inconsistent* with an acknowledgment, that revelation is necessary, why must it be entirely discarded? Supposing mankind incapable of steadily performing their duty in *all* cases, without a prospect of future retributions, how does it follow, that therefore there is no duty in any case, but what arises from such a prospect?

Or even granting the author of the *Essay* his main principle, "That every man's own happiness is the ultimate end, which nature and reason teach him to pursue,"[1] why may not nature and reason teach him too, to have some desire to see others happy as well as himself, or give him some delight in doing what seems fit and right, if these things do not interfere with his own happiness? Why indeed may they not make a part of it? At least, if he finds them suitable to a social nature, and commanding his approbation, why may he not amuse himself by the way with such gratifications (as most of us do with very trifling ones) without considering, whether they lead directly to his ultimate end? Why may he not, with the pursuit of that end, join some other pursuits not inconsistent with it, instead of transforming every benevolent affection, every moral view, into self-interest? This surely neither does honour to religion, nor justice to human nature. But let us examine, as concisely as the subject will allow, on what grounds the learned author of the *Essay on Virtue* establishes a scheme, which appears so injurious to both.

He begins chap. i. with a very just observation, "That virtue, which we expect all mankind should practice, must be some-

---

* Dr. *Clarke*, and Mr. *Balguy*. [John Balguy (1686–1748), a defender of Clarke's ethical doctrines. His works include *The Foundation of Moral Goodness* (1728) and *Divine Rectitude* (1730).]

---

1 Rutherforth, p. 153.

thing, which all mankind either are, or easily may be, acquainted with." And that with regard to the vulgar and illiterate, "common sense, joined to most ordinary helps of instruction, must afford a more obvious notion of virtue, than any, that is to be met with in the writings of the moralists."[1] And thus far I go along with him. It is not indeed to be expected that the vulgar or the illiterate should be acquainted with general definitions, or abstract reasonings. Their guides to virtue must be something plain and familiar to them; and these I take to be common sense, their natural notions of right and wrong, and the approved customs of the society they live in, by which they commonly know well enough what ought to be their practice, as particular occasions offer, tho' they have little or no notion at all of what virtue in general is. And perhaps if this writer's* way of life allowed him to be more acquainted with the world, he would find, that the definition, which he has given us of virtue (tho' traced, as he imagines, from the common opinions and sense of mankind) is far less the ground, on which *men of low and unimproved parts* act themselves, or judge of the actions of others, than those *relations and fitnesses of things* are, which he thinks beyond their understanding, nay so unintelligible, that he scarce ventures to mention them without† making an apology to his readers. But let him not be afraid: however abstruse or obscure the discourses of learned men may have been about them, the things themselves are obvious, and level to most capacities; and much surer guides to the bulk of mankind, than his own‡ definition, that *virtue is that quality in our actions, by which they are fitted to do good to others, or to prevent their harm*. For (besides that this is far from taking in the entire system of virtues) there may be cases, in which actions *fitted to do good, &c.* may not be virtuous; but in no case an action suitable to the relations and fitnesses of things can be otherwise.

However, in support of the definition, the author has taken a great deal of pains in chap. ii. of this work, to show, that the name of *Virtue* is given by common consent to that sort of behaviour *only*, that is fitted to do good, or to prevent harm; expatiating on the good and evil consequent upon several instances of behaviour approved or condemned as virtuous or vicious. And truly here is

---

* [Rutherforth], *Vide* Page 3.
† [Rutherforth], p. 3, 12.
‡ [Rutherforth], p. 6.

---

1 Rutherforth, p. 1.

field enough to enlarge upon; virtue is, without doubt, sufficiently fruitful of good, and vice of bad effects, to afford ample matter for declamation. But this is no proof, that the whole of virtue consists, or that it is *commonly supposed* to consist, in a fitness to do good to others. Those, who maintain, that virtue consists in acting suitably to the nature and relations of things, can show too, that in every instance of virtue there is a suitableness to certain relations, *&c.* and, on the contrary, an unsuitableness in every vice, without exception; and that actions are accordingly judged to be right or wrong, virtuous or vicious, by the natural notions of mankind; which will more strongly prove on their side.

Ask an honest labourer, why he wears himself out with toils and cares to provide for his family, to feed and clothe a parcel of troublesome children. Would he answer, that this action was fitted to do good, and to prevent harm? No, certainly, for he would easily see, that as much good might be done by taking care of some other family: but he would readily answer, that truly he thought it behoved him to take care of his own; that his wife and children were very dear to him; and who should take care of them, if he did not? Tell him again of a jolly neighbour, who enjoys himself at the ale-house, drinking and playing away all he can get, whilst his family is left to go naked and starve; would he not instantly cry out, What an unnatural wretch is that! The very beasts take care of their young! These are the most natural sentiments of a well disposed, though uncultivated mind; and they arise directly from the relations and fitness of things, and a disinterested benevolence, which guide him to virtuous practice, tho' he never heard of any of those terms. And that most perfect rule of life, *To do unto all men, as we would they should do unto me*, which is the sum of all the social virtues, is plainly deduced from the natural relation of equality we bear to each other, and a fitness resulting from thence: yet nothing is more easy and intelligible to common capacities. The same might be shown of all the particular virtues, and the contrary of the vices instanced in by this author, if my designed brevity would allow me to pursue the observation so minutely.

But I am obliged to take notice of the fallacious manner, in which he pretends to* prove, that the *sensualist* is called vicious on account of the harm he may do to others; not for his acting unsuitably to the nature and relation of things, which I the rather observe here, because the same fallacy is made use of in several

---

* [Rutherforth], *Essay*, p. 16.

other parts of this *Essay* for the like purpose; changing the terms, and thereby entirely altering the state of the question. "Do we (says he) disapprove the behaviour of the sensualist, because it is contrary to the character of a man? Who then shall determine what the true character of a man is?" Really that may be pretty hard to determine. But, pray, what moralist ever made acting up to the *character* of a man, or acting contrary to it, the standard of virtue and vice? Character is too equivocal a word to be used in such an enquiry; and our author very well knows, that it is not a term used by any of the writers he opposes; whose arguments he fairly sets down in their own language, but artfully changes it, when he pretends to answer them. In the same manner he goes on a little lower; "Perhaps it would be found, that fact and experience do not put *an aversion to the pleasures of sense* into the notion of a man." And who ever put *aversion to the pleasures of sense* into the notion of virtue? "I do not remember, (adds he) to have seen it, in any of the laboured, and abstract definitions of our species." Nor anybody else, I believe, ever saw it: to what purpose then is it brought in? *Aversion to the pleasures of sense* is certainly no part of the nature of man. But did this gentleman never see or hear,* that keeping the sensual appetites in subjection to *reason, the superior faculty*, is acting up to the true nature of man? Does he not know, that this was what the ancients meant by living according to nature? And if the contrary to this, if allowing the *lower* appetites and passions, to *rule* in opposition to the governing principle, unsuitably to the relation they bear to one another, and to the nature of a reasonable being, is what we *disapprove* in the behaviour of the intemperate, or the sensualist, of which he has said nothing; then what does all he has here said, (with his characters and aversions, in which no adversary is concerned) amount to, but mere *fallacies* to amuse or perplex the reader?

He afterwards† allows, that the temperance of a man, who is thrown upon a desolate island for life, may be a virtue, notwithstanding no good comes of it to any one but himself: "Because," says he, "the nature of the behaviour is the very same, that it

---

* See Dr. *Butler*'s *Sermon on human nature*. [Joseph Butler (1692–1752) was a well-known moralist who held that moral decisions regarding right and wrong must arise from a proper hierarchical ordering of sentiment, self-interest, benevolence and conscience. The sermon to which Cockburn here refers can be found in his work *Fifteen sermons preached at the Rolls Chapel* (1726).]

† [Rutherforth], *Essay*, p. 25.

would have been, if he had lived in society; it is fit to do good, and to prevent harm." An extraordinary reason indeed! This instance might rather have shown him, that his definition is not agreeable to the true, or to the general notion of virtue; for how absurd is it to make the virtue of a man, who is always to live *alone*, consist in a fitness of his behaving to do good *to others*, and to prevent their harm? How ridiculous would it be, to suppose him forbearing acts of intemperance, upon considering of what ill consequence, such actions might be, if he lived in society? What is that to him, when he can neither do good nor harm to any one? If temperance would be a virtue in a man, tho' living alone, as no doubt it would; it must be because it is agreeable to the nature of a reasonable being, and to the fitness of things: And it will always be a virtue wherever he lives, for the very same reason.

The last instance of behaviour, this author brings in favour of his notion of virtue, is that of the griping usurer,* compared with the industrious merchant, and the cruel tyrant with the true patriot.

"Here," he says, "the very same objects are pursued, both by those, who are not vicious, and by those, who are: The merchant desires to get money, and perhaps gets more than the usurer: the patriot endeavours to acquire power, as well as the tyrant; yet these deserve our esteem, whilst the other characters are detestable." This he concludes can be for no other reason, than that, in which he supposes the general notion of virtue to consist, "That the merchant *does good* with his riches, and the patriot with his power; whereas the usurer *does no good*, and the tyrant a great deal of *harm*." But surely it is no less manifest, that the virtuous characters in these instances *act conformably to the nature, relations, and fitness of things*, than it is, that they *do good*; and that, on the contrary, there is a manifest *disagreement* in the actions of the vicious characters to *the reason and nature of things*; and in this *conformity*, or *disagreement*, consists the *virtue* and the *vice* of all *the good*, or all *the harm* they do: For where there is not this *disagreement*, there may be actions, that *do harm*, which yet are *not vicious* (as in the punishment, suppose, of a rebellious nation, where many innocents must suffer) and, on the other hand, where there is not this *conformity*, there may be actions, that *do good*, which yet are *not virtuous*. So that I must beg leave to assert, contrary to our author,† that in the dispute, whether some particular actions have any claim to be placed in the catalogue of

---

* [Rutherforth], p. 31.
† [Rutherforth], *Essay*, p. 34.

virtues, the first and most usual enquiry is not, *whether they do good, or prevent harm*; but whether they are conformable to the nature, relations, and circumstances of the agent and the objects.

To illustrate this in a particular instance: Suppose a rich miser, who had many years denied himself the conveniences, and almost the necessaries of life; hoarding up all he could get or save, and refusing the least assistance to his nearest relations, under great straights and difficulties, and this with a view of leaving all his treasure, without any regard to the ties of nature, to found an hospital after his death, for the maintenance and education of a large number of poor children. I choose to instance in this case, because I have known it to be fact. Here then is an action *fitted to do good, and to prevent harm*. But I presume the generality of mankind would, *upon the whole*, perceive such a disagreement in it to nature, and reason, and fitness, as would not allow them to esteem it a virtuous action.

The author of the *Essay** approves of the common division of duties, into those, which we owe to God, to our neighbour, and to ourselves; but I think not very consistently with himself. For† he admits those, that are called *self duties*, into the catalogue of *virtues*, solely on account of their being fitted *to do good to others*; and he‡ allows them to be *duties* on this single consideration, *that God has commanded them*; neither of which can be any ground for accounting them duties, that *we owe to ourselves*; for (according to his distinction) as *virtues*, they must be ranked among those, which we owe to our neighbour; as *duties*, among those, which we owe to God; so that if his notion was right, no such thing could ever have been thought on, as *a duty we owe to ourselves*: and therefore, this *allowed* division might have shown him, that the generality of mankind place the virtue of those, that are called the *self-duties*, in a fitness to promote *self-good*, not the good of *others*; and consequently, that this is *not*, as he supposes, the only notion of virtue, that common use has established.

Our author seems likewise to§ approve of distinguishing between *piety* and *virtue*; and in this he is consistent enough; for since he has restrained the name of *virtue* to those actions, that are *fitted to do good to others, or to prevent their harm*, this must, in his account, effectually bar all our regards to God, from having any pretension to the title of virtues. But I confess myself greatly

---

* [Rutherforth], p. 21.
† [Rutherforth], p. 22.
‡ [Rutherforth], p. 20.
§ [Rutherforth], p. 20.

prejudiced against the distinction, which, I fear, has had very bad consequences. Some have been accustomed so entirely to distinguish between piety and virtue, that they have imagined they could be *religious without virtue*; and others have supposed they might be *virtuous without religion*: and therefore, I cannot but be much better pleased with that notion of moral virtue, which places it in a conformity of our actions to the nature of them, and from the fitnesses resulting from them, and from all the relations we stand in to different beings; for this, without much* *metaphysical refining*, unites religion and virtue, directing us to all the duties we owe our Creator, as well as to our fellow-creatures.

The author takes notice, in this chapter, and in other† parts of his work, "That the effect, which any action has, or may have, upon the happiness or misery of the agent himself, is not what gives the name of a virtue, or a vice to it: that the moral goodness of voluntary actions does indeed consist in their producing good or happiness, but then it is the good or happiness of others, not of him does them." A truth, which one would not have expected to find inculcated in a book, the chief tendency of which is to persuade us, that there is no such thing in nature, as doing good to others, without a regard to our own happiness. Indeed it seems matter of wonder, with what view the second chapter was writ; for if the doctrine of the *Essay* be true, I know not what use can be made of it, unless it be to conclude, that virtue is nothing but an empty speculation; that there is no such thing in reality as virtuous practice; and that the best *Christian* in the world neither is, nor ought to be, a *virtuous man*. Whatever might be the intention of the writer, this seems to be a plain consequence from his own notion of virtue, compared with the whole tenor of his book, as will appear to any one, who attentively goes through it.

At the beginning of the third chapter (which being in opposition to the *Fable of the Bees*,[1] I shall have little to do with, but in relation to that we are upon;) he says: "As I undertook, in the

---

* *Vide* [Rutherforth's], *Essay*, p. 34.
† [Rutherforth], Chap. iv. p. 67.

---

1 Bernard Mandeville (1670–1733), *The Fable of the Bees* (1723). Mandeville's work was considered scandalous at this time, for, among other things, its strongly stated egoistic morality. According to Mandeville, human beings are driven essentially by their desires for power and sensual pleasure. The disreputable nature of this work would explain Cockburn's dismissive attitude towards any discussion of it.

foregoing chapter, to determine, wherein the *nature* of virtue consists, some may object, that I ought to have enquired, not what has been *called*, but what really and truly *is virtue*; if they, who make this objection, confound the notions of *virtue* and *duty*, I will endeavour to satisfy them, when I come to explain the cause of moral obligation. But if we keep these two notions *distinct*, then I confess, that I know but little difference between what is really and truly virtue, and that sort of behaviour, which by common consent is called so."[1] And truly if we are to keep these notions *distinct*, if *virtue* is to be distinguished from *duty*, then I confess, that I know of no occasion we have to enquire either after its *name*, or its *nature*. If virtue is not that sort of behaviour, which men, as *men*, are obliged to, which God requires from us as reasonable beings, how are we concerned at all about it? In one sense, as this writer somewhere says, "Virtue can never be indifferent, for it will always be fitted to do good." But it must certainly be indifferent in a *moral sense*, if nobody is obliged from the nature of things to practise it. He talks indeed of proving hereafter, that virtue is our duty; and how does he perform this? Why, by telling us, that it becomes such, when God has promised to make us happy for it. But what consistency is there in saying, that *a prospect of our own happiness* makes it our duty to do good to others, *without any regard to our own happiness*, which is his own notion of virtue? This gentleman seems indeed to delight in paradoxes, by placing the self-duties in a fitness to do good to *others*; and the duty of doing good to others, in regard to *self-good*.

Remarks on Chap. v.

The arguments in this chapter are peculiarly levelled against Mr. *Hutcheson*'s scheme,[2] which I have no intention to defend; for tho' I have a great esteem for that ingenious author's writings, in which are many useful truths; yet I cannot agree with him, that a *blind instinct* (if that is what he means by a *moral sense*) or that the public affections (as he calls them) are the proper *foundations of virtue*. But since the design of the author of the *Essay on Virtue* is

---

1 Rutherforth, p. 35.
2 Francis Hutcheson (see Introduction of this edition, pp. 21-22) held that human beings are naturally disposed towards acts of benevolence, or virtue. Human response to virtue, according to Hutcheson, is regulated by the "moral sense," a perceptual faculty which produces feelings of approbation upon the perception of benevolent acts.

to maintain, that there is no such thing as a disinterested affection for, or approbation of virtue, I shall consider what he has offered to that purpose, distinct from the relation it bears to the particular writer he opposes.

Before we proceed, it may not be amiss to look back upon the fourth chapter, which I had passed over, it being chiefly employed in explaining terms. But there is a passage in it, occasioned by a definition (the author gives us from Mr. *Hutcheson*) of moral goodness, which having some relation to the subject we are going upon, it may not be improper to observe here the fallacy of his reasoning, independently from any regard to the justness of the definition it is intended to confute, about which I have no concern.

"If," says he, "moral good was a quality, which made us desire the happiness of every one, who shows it in his conduct; then, as this quality appears in our own conduct, our love towards ourselves must increase; the more we practice moral good, the more we must desire our own happiness; we must grow selfish in proportion as we are virtuous, and be the more interested, the more benevolent we are. Either, therefore, our sense of moral good, and our affection for it, do not reach to our own behaviour; or else the practice of virtue must be fatal to itself, by strengthening that self-love, which is represented by these very moralists, as the only thing, that can stop the operation of the public affections, and keep the balance always inclined towards the side of private interest."[1]

The self-love, which those moralists represent as dangerous to the public affections, is that degree, or rather that *wrong application* of it, which *solely* regards private interest, exclusively of all public affections; or, in more intelligible language, which regards *self* alone, without the least concern for the good of any other. This is so vicious a misapplication, that on the account of it, instead of distinguishing the use from the abuse of an innocent principle, all *self-love* has been absurdly and unnaturally exclaimed against, as a vice, that ought to be entirely eradicated. Those enthusiastic writers, who (perhaps misled by the schoolmen) have fallen into this error, considered not self-love as a part of our nature, and consequently the work of God; and saw not, "That true self-love and social are the same."

But this is now so well understood, that the former sort is come to be commonly distinguished from it, by the name of *self-*

---

[1] Rutherforth, p. 64.

ishness; a distinction, of which I presume the author of the *Essay* is not unaware, tho' he argues here, without taking notice of the difference, that if we approve and love ourselves, on account of our moral goodness, we must grow *selfish* in proportion as we grow virtuous, and be the more *interested*, the more benevolent we are. But of this there is certainly no danger, which he may easily see, if he will allow us to break through the ambiguity of words, and to put him in mind, that *self-love* is not *selfishness*. That kind of it especially, which is supposed to arise from our approbation of our own conduct, and to increase by our practice of moral good, must naturally incline us to continue in that practice, and to be the more beneficent, that we may perpetuate so just a foundation of our love and approbation of ourselves: Thus our virtue will be so far from being *fatal to itself* by strengthening our *self-love*, that our virtue will in return be strengthened by it; "Self-love thus push'd to social, to divine, Gives thee to make thy neighbour's blessing thine."* Finding thus our happiness in that of others; virtue and self-love will go hand in hand together, and mutually support each other. We are, therefore, secure enough from growing *selfish* and *interested*, by the practice and approbation of a *disinterested benevolence*; and now may the better go on to enquire, whether there is really any such thing in nature. To return then to chap. v.

Our author begins by telling us, that "the common and ordinary feelings of mankind, the senses and perceptions, that are uppermost in the human constitution, and most attended to, plainly direct to private good, and instruct each individual to provide for himself in the best manner he can."[1] Granting this, are there not other feelings too, almost as common, equally predominant in the human constitution, and constantly attended to, which as plainly direct to the good of others? Of this I need only mention one undeniable instance, the natural affection of parents for their children, which as strongly carries them to provide for the good of their offspring, as any other propensions do to provide for their own. This is a dictate of nature so obvious and so general, that it effectually overthrows the sole principle, upon which this whole *Essay* is founded, viz. *That men neither do, nor does nature or reason teach them, to pursue any other end, but every one his own private happiness.*

---

*   *Essay on man*, Ep. iv. [lines 353–54.]

---

1   Rutherforth, p. 73.

In consequence of this principle, the author here maintains, that all our approbation or love of virtue arises from a prospect of some advantage by it to ourselves; and in support of this he is so diffused, puts so many cases and suppositions, and views things in such various lights, that it would be impossible to go through the particulars, without writing a larger book than his own. But it will be less tedious to the reader, and less perplex him in the search of truth, if we give the substance of what is offered, and select all that seems of most weight, or of most importance to answer.

It has been usually urged by divines, in proof of the excellence of virtue, and of our natural perceptions of its worth, that even those, who do not practise it, give testimony to it by their approbation and love of it in others. But this author, with a great profusion* of words, and display of his eloquence, accounts for this love and approbation from his *favourite* principle; of which the following may suffice for a specimen.

"All that they approve (he says) in virtue or moral goodness, is the natural good, that it either produces, or is fit to produce;[1] and all their love arises from the share, which they suppose they should have in the happy effects of it, when others practise it.[2] Is not such a one the most fond of virtue, when he finds it in his friend or his partner, where he is the person, upon whom it is exercised the oftenest, and where he reaps the greatest advantages from it?"[3] And what is all this to the purpose? Very probably a man, who does not practise virtue himself, will be fonder of the *effects* of it, when exercised to his advantage, than he would be of the same *effects*, if others reaped the benefit of them: and this indeed must be placed to the account of his self-love, or desire of his own natural good. But notwithstanding this, his sentiments of the *virtue itself*, his approbation of the justice, the fidelity, the generosity of his friend or his partner, will be just the same, as if he considered those virtues abstractedly, or in any other instances, where he had no concern; for our natural approbation of virtue is quite distinct from, and independent of all consideration of the *effects* of it.

This appears evidently in that admiration and delight, which

---

* [Rutherforth], from p. 75, to 99.

---

1 Rutherforth, p. 75.
2 Rutherforth, p. 76.
3 Rutherforth, p. 76.

we are apt to feel, on hearing or reading of heroic disinterested actions, tho' done may ages ago, in distant countries, where our interest can have nothing to do; as has been often urged on this subject. Yet even this, according to our author,* is nothing but a reflection we make upon the delight it gave us, when virtue was practiced towards ourselves; for thus, he says, we may love virtue at a distance, or when it is exercised on others "just as we love roses in winter, or grapes whilst another is eating them. It is the pleasure, that we have in smelling the flower, or in tasting the fruit, when they come in our way, which makes us love them: And to say, that we love them, there is no necessity for actually feeling this pleasure: it is sufficient that we can reflect upon it, and know, that they will give us it. And thus when virtue is practised towards ourselves, it makes us happy, and we can reflect upon the delight it gave us, whilst another enjoys it."[1] We can so, if we have been made happy by the like virtues. But how does this account for that rapturous pleasure, which we feel on hearing of some generous heroic action, of which we never knew a resembling instance, or could possibly have been the objects of? If our approbation, love, and admiration of virtue depended on our experiencing the happy effects of it, how had the singularly eminent virtues we read of in the *Roman* history, passed through ages unapproved, unloved, and unadmired! For where is the man, who ever could reflect on the happy effects he had found of actions, resembling the generous virtues recorded there, particularly those of the brave *Decii*, and the intrepid *Regulus*?[2] Can any man call home the actions of those heroes to himself, and recollect the delight he found, when such were practised towards him? It is not to be imagined: Nor is it the happy *effects* of their virtues, that we admire. It is not *the good they produced, or were fitted to produce*: it is the generosity, the magnanimity of the actions themselves, that we esteem and love: the strict fidelity of the one, and the disinterested patriotism of both; and as it is impossible for us to have any view to our own advantage in such instances, our approbation and love must be no less disinterested, than were the virtues we contemplate.

And truly our author is so kind, as to give us leave to call it so, provided we will agree to call our love of grapes or roses

---

* [Rutherforth], p. 78.

---

1 *Ibid*.
2 Decii and Regulus refer to heroes of Ancient Roman history, who were notable for their acts of bravery and self-sacrifice in war.

disinterested too. "If any one thinks (says he)* that, to approve virtue, tho' on the account of the happiness, which it produces, whilst others practise it, should be called a disinterested approbation, because we approve it, whether we ourselves enjoy that happiness or not; he has my leave to call it so: But then it will be necessary for him, tho' our love of grapes or roses arises entirely from the pleasure, which they give us, to call this a disinterested affection too, because we love them as we do virtue, without actually enjoying the pleasure, which they are fitted to produce." But why must this be necessary? Or how will the comparison hold? As fond as this gentleman seems of it, by repeating it often for a parallel case, it goes entirely upon the mistake of supposing, that our approbation and love of virtue is *solely on account of the happiness it produces*, as our liking of fruits and flowers is only for the sake of the agreeable sensations they give. He may not, indeed, be sensible of this mistake, since he has no other notion of virtue; but I am persuaded he is not quite insensible, that our love and approbation of virtue is of a very different *kind* from our love of grapes or roses; nor does he venture to talk of our *approbation* of them, tho' he talks a great deal about I do not know what *happiness, that virtue affords, which may be taken in by any sense, or by all in their turns*; as if he designed to make virtue appear as much an object of our senses, as fruits or flowers are, that so our love of it may seem no more capable of being disinterested, than our love of grapes or roses can be. Yet (however he may *feel* or *smell* it out) he cannot sure be ignorant, that virtue is an object of the *understanding*; and that we may come to the knowledge of the worth and excellence of it, without having ever *tasted* or *felt* the effects of it; tho' we can have no idea at all of the value of grapes or roses, but by experiencing the agreeable sensations they raise in us; so that our love of them in winter, or when others are enjoying them, can indeed be nothing else but a *remembrance* of the pleasure they gave us, with a desire of repeating it, which can have no pretensions to be called a *disinterested affection* (if it be proper to call such likings *affections* at all). Whereas we can form an idea in our minds, either of virtue in general, a steady adherence to truth and right; or, in particular, of a just, a generous, or a grateful action, tho' we had never known any of them practised; and when we hear or read of virtuous characters, or of noble actions done a thousand years ago, we can love, approve, and admire the rectitude and magnanimity of them, and often feel a generous emulation of their excellence,

---

* [Rutherforth], p. 92.

without the least reflection of any advantage, that such virtues might bring to us. And this certainly has a better right (without this gentleman's good leave) to be called a *disinterested affection*, than the love of grapes or roses can pretend to.

Here he runs on again, for above six pages, in rejecting the argument commonly urged in favour of virtue, and to prove our natural approbation of it, *viz.* that even those, who do not practise it, will *confess*, that they cannot help admiring it, and that what they do is with the greatest reluctance; and where men condemn their own practices, there can be no room to suspect them of partiality. "But* there is great room (he says) to doubt their sincerity." And so gives us his conjectures of the several reasons they may have for pretending to love virtue, and to practise vice with reluctance, when they really feel no such thing; putting cases, in which he supposes all their reluctance must be† *an effect of what they fear from their vices, and what they might hope for, if they were virtuous.* "But‡ as long (says he) as the reluctance, which a man pretends to feel, when he is vicious, *is an allowed excuse for his being so*, it is no wonder, if all of this character make use of a plea, which will set them right at once in the opinion of the world, and which they think, for want of knowing their hearts, can never be overruled." I do not know what kind of casuists those are, who *allow* of this for an excuse. I have heard, indeed, of one person, a very noted one, who, in the account of his life written by himself, pleads, in excuse for doing a wrong thing, that he did it against his conscience: but I never heard that *this set him right in the opinion of the world*. It is, I think, the general opinion of the world, that acting against conscience rather aggravates than extenuates any man's guilt; and that therefore the vicious are more inclined to *conceal* the reluctance they feel, than to pretend to it when they feel it not. But as this is a fact, which cannot precisely be determined without *knowing their hearts*, (and I suppose our author has no more pretensions to that sort of knowledge than I have) we can only refer every man to his own breast, to observe, if in any instances, where he has deviated from the rules of virtue, he has not secretly approved the characters of those, whose conduct has been more regular. That this has been the case of all, who have had such an occasion of comparing themselves with others, I make not the least doubt; and the consciousness of every particular person of his own sentiments in

---

* [Rutherforth], p. 94.
† [Rutherforth], p. 99.
‡ [Rutherforth], p. 96.

favour of virtue, is a very probable ground of its being a generally received opinion, *that all men approve it*, even when they do not practise virtue.

I am persuaded, too, that this general approbation has a much more extensive influence on men's practice, than the author of the *Essay* supposes: And am much mistaken in the world, if (bad as it is) there are not great numbers in it, who do good, and generous, and grateful actions, without any kind of interested views. The author's* advice is right however, "to try what our approbation of virtue is owing to, and what use it can be of to us, by observing how far it engages us to be virtuous ourselves, if we love to be kind and generous ourselves, as much as we love to have others so." But why will he suppose that this is nobody's case? Why will he imagine, "that we† approve virtue in others *only* because it does us good, but *seldom* approve it well enough to practise it where it would hurt us? I might have said *never*," adds he, "unless some motives of happiness are thrown into the opposite scale," *&c.* And yet, in the very same page, he talks of our being in raptures, when we receive some signal favour from one, who *distresses himself to do us service*. I wonder of what species those generous beings are, who give occasion for such raptures! If they are a part of mankind, I suppose this gentleman has discovered some latent motive of their generosity, some remote view to their own advantage, which would abate much of our raptures, if we were as clear-sighted as he: but, till that appears, I must beg leave to conclude, that those at least, *who distress themselves to give assistance to others*, have a truly disinterested affection; and that therefore, all do not deserve the low and unworthy opinion he endeavours to give us of the whole species; contending to the end of this chapter, and indeed through the whole book, that there is no such thing as a disinterested affection among them.

Gratitude is the virtue he‡ has singled out, for what he calls *a favourite instance of a disinterested affection*; and here he tells us, that our loving or approving *gratitude in other men, when they are grateful to us, will never show our affection to be disinterested*. Who pretends, that it will? And yet in some cases it may be so, when no benefit can accrue to us, from the gratitude of those, whom we have obliged. But what does he think of gratitude in ourselves towards those, who have done us good offices? "Why this," he says, "is the most unfortunate instance, that could have been

---

* [Rutherforth], p. 90.
† [Rutherforth], p. 91.
‡ [Rutherforth], p. 100.

made choice of, for the proof of a disinterested affection for virtue: selfish regards are contained in the very notion of it. It is an affection towards a character considered as beneficial to us."[1] It is so, and I thought this sense of the word so well known, and so generally agreed in, that there was no need of any* "endeavours to show, that this name belongs to no other benevolent affection, or to settle the meaning of the word gratitude." Nor can I imagine to what purpose, (except to display the author's eloquence) eight or nine pages are employed in telling us, what affections are *not* gratitude; what views we may have of future benefits in being grateful for the past; and in what cases our gratitude would entirely cease. For who is ignorant, that humanity, benevolence, charity, forgiveness, *&c.* are *not gratitude*? Who knows not, that there may be joined with a grateful sense of past benefits an expectation of future favours? Or who doubts, that former kindnesses may be so entirely cancelled by greater injuries, that no ground for gratitude would remain? These are all unquestionable truths. But what is all this, and a great deal more of the same kind, to the purpose? If there is any such thing at all among mankind, as grateful sentiments, and kind returns for past benefits, where there is no possible expectation of future favours, then gratitude, so circumstantiated, is a very *proper instance of a disinterested affection*, though ten thousand *other things* should be raked together, which are not.

And that such sentiments are natural to us, even this author himself allows; for† putting the case, that we had been at any time in a very distant part of the world, where some of the inhabitants had treated us with extraordinary kindness and generosity; "we should," he says, "without doubt, feel some tender affections, when we were taking leave of a set of men, that we had been so much obliged to; and the sentiments of gratitude would remain, even after we were gone from them, and were settled at so great distance, as to put it out of their power ever to do us any further services." What then has he been all this while contending against? Is not gratitude, in such a case, an instance of *disinterested affection*, notwithstanding it is towards persons, considered as having been *beneficial to ourselves*? "But still," he tells us, "we might depend upon their constant friendship, kind memory, and

---

*   *Vid.* [Rutherforth's] *Essay* p. [101], 102, 103.
†   [Rutherforth], p. 107.

---

1   Rutherforth, pp. 101–102.

good offices, though we were never to see or hear the effects of them; and every time that we think of them, we might believe they were thinking of us."¹ These, it seems, are, in this nice gentleman's esteem, *selfish regards*; for in several other places he mentions, as *interested views*, our expecting, that those, to whom we are grateful for past favours, when it is no longer in their power to do us any services, should yet continue their good inclinations and good wishes for us; and this part of their character, he says, *is plainly the object of our gratitude*. Supposing it were so, this would not at all lessen the disinterestedness of it: a desire of the esteem, and love, and good wishes, of those whom we esteem, and love, and wish well to, when it has no farther aim, was never looked on as an interested or selfish view: it is a virtuous desire, which it would be wrong not to have.

That letter, from whence the author of the *Essay* has taken the few lines quoted above (instead of being any thing to his purpose) is a great instance of a pure and disinterested friendship;* and he might have found many among the familiar letters of that great genius and excellent man, sufficient to overthrow all the arguments of his book, against the reality of disinterested virtue: Not to insist on his generous friendship for persons *out of power, and out of credit*; his tender regards for his mother; his anxious concern for the continuance of her life, when she was of too great an age to be any way useful to him; the satisfaction he expresses in having an opportunity, by his cares and attendance, of returning part of the kind offices she had done him, and his fears of being too soon deprived of it; sentiments, which his heart was so full of, that they break out, on all occasions, to his intimates, in verse as well as prose. "Me let the tender office long engage, To rock the cradle of reposing age,"† *&c.* This solicitude "To keep a while one parent from the sky," with all his affectionate regards for her, (more than even religion required of him) give us such a proof of disinterested piety and gratitude, as is, I think, irresistible. Nor are there wanting other instances of a like nature, though not so shining, or so generally known, as the virtues of a character so illustrious.

---

* Mr. *Pope's* to Dr. *Atterbury.*

† *Epist. to Dr. Arb.* [*An epistle from Mr. Pope to Dr. Arbuthnot* (1734); lines 408–13.]

---

1 Rutherforth, p. 107. Rutherforth is here quoting from Pope's Letter to Dr. Atterbury.

Our author takes notice of one instance of disinterestedness, produced by the* noble moralist, *and without doubt*, says he, *more of the same sort may be met with.* "But the extravagancies, into which our affections hurry us, will only prove, that they are our masters, not that they are natural. The mixture of the kind and friendly, which, in the passion of love between the sexes, is sometimes so much superior to the affection of a vulgar sort, as to make even death itself be voluntarily embraced, for the sake of the person beloved," will no more demonstrate (continues he) that there are naturally in man any disinterestedly kind and friendly affections, than the death of a *Bruno*, a *Vanini*, or *Effendi*, will prove him to have a natural and disinterested love for *atheism*; or than the behaviour of *Felton* or a *Clement* will show, that nature implanted in man a disinterested desire of *doing mischief*.[1]

To all this I answer, that though our passions, our benevolent affections, our love of truth, and approbation of what appears to us right and fit, are natural, and implanted in us for good and useful purposes; yet the *application* of any of these, is not determined by nature, but is put in our own power, so that we may make either a right or a wrong use of them: It is our fault, if we suffer our passions or affections to be *our masters*: that indeed is not natural, tho' the affections themselves are so; for it is the province of reason to keep them in subjection, to regulate them, and to point out the proper application of them. Those voluntary sufferings of lovers, which the noble moralist speaks of, might be virtues or vices, according as the motives to them, were worthy or not worthy of such a sacrifice: But they certainly *demonstrate, that there are naturally in man disinterestedly kind and friendly affections*, which he may make either a wise, or an extravagant use of.

---

* Lord Shafts. Vol. ii. p. 105. [*Inquiry*, Book 2. Part 2, section 173; Earl of Shaftesbury (Anthony Ashley Cooper) (1671–1713), *An Inquiry Concerning Virtue, or Merit*, 2 vols. (1699). Shaftesbury was an early student of Locke's, who later rejected Locke's emphasis on rationality as a foundation for moral knowledge. Shaftesbury is most famously associated with his "moral sense" view, according to which morality arises from sentiment rather than reason.]

---

1 Rutherforth, pp. 111–12. In his notes on these pages, Rutherforth explains that these are all cases of people who died either for their beliefs or for their criminal acts. He concludes that since dying for a belief or a crime does not necessarily imply that these were somehow innate, the same can be said for the acts of disinterested benevolence which innatists cite in favour of their positions.

In like manner, our natural love of truth and approbation of virtue may be *misapplied,* if we have taken wrong measures in searching after truth, or formed our judgment of virtue by any other rules, than the nature of things, or the revealed will of God. This was the case of all those wretches, mentioned by our author, whose behaviour by no means shows us (as he* would suppose) *that piety and truth, or that virtue and truth, are not the same thing*; it only shows, that men may mistake error for truth, and vice for virtue. The resolute death of those atheists proves not, that there is in man a natural and disinterested *love for atheism*: it neither proves their *opinions* to be innate or true, but it strongly proves, that there is in man a disinterested attachment, for what appears to him to be truth: And that this affection may be misapplied, is no more an argument against its being naturally implanted in man, than the absurd use, which atheists have made of their *reason*, is an argument, that reason is not natural to man, or that it does not naturally lead him to the knowledge of an intelligent first cause of all beings.

The behaviour of a *Felton*, or a *Clement*, I do not take to be instances of any disinterested affection at all. The young friar was plainly a weak ignorant *enthusiast*, inflamed by the invectives of the preachers against *Henry* III of *France*, and instigated to murder him, by the doctrines then in vogue, that one might, with a good conscience, take away the life of a tyrant, as they represented that king to be: And no doubt the religious assassin expected (without stopping into purgatory) to be immediately transported to heaven for so meritorious an action.

Whether *Felton*, the murderer of the duke of *Buckingham*, was political or a religious enthusiast, is not so plain from what is known of his character; but his saying, that he had acted solely *from the impulse of his own conscience*, makes it probable, that he too expected a heavenly reward for having sacrificed his life, in doing what he judged an important service to his country.

These are no instances of *disinterestedness*, but, on the contrary, of highly *interested* prospects, upon *false notions of piety and virtue*: Mistakes, which, I suppose, no one will deny, that man may fall into, notwithstanding any principles naturally implanted in him; since all allow he has it in his power, either to suffer them to run wild, or to cultivate and improve them; and therefore, it can never be said, as this author suggests, "That everything is piety and virtue in a man, which he has persuaded himself to look upon in

---

* [Rutherforth's] *Essay*, p. 112.

that light."¹ Nor will it "excuse the persons concerned in the *Irish* rebellion, the massacre of St. *Bartholomew, &c.*"* that they were persuaded destroying heretics was *doing* God *good service.* These, too, were religious enthusiasts, who had departed from all proper rules, by which they should have judged of their duty, to follow their guides with an *implicit faith.* They ought to have known better, *what spirit they were of*; they ought to have known, that God had forbid them *to do evil, that good may come of it*; they should not have suffered themselves to be persuaded, that what was contrary to the common sentiments of humanity, and to that universal rule of equity, *doing unto all men, as we would they should do unto us,* could be acceptable to God. His written word, and their own natural notions, left them *without excuse,* in giving the sacred names of *piety and virtue,* to the most infamous treachery, and the most savage barbarity.

I do not know how far such instances as these may affect the principles of those moralists, who found virtue *solely* on benevolent affections, and an *instinctive* sense of right and wrong; for if these may be worn out, or unattended to, or misguided, virtue must be left on a very precarious foundation, which I leave them to defend as well as they can. I am only concerned to maintain, that a disinterested benevolence and approbation of virtue are *natural* to man, and given him as proper excitements to good actions; that tho' these may be misapplied or misguided, he has it in his power to regulate them, by the obvious *relations and nature of things*; (for I take our consciousness of right and wrong to be the result of some perception, that every rational mind necessarily has of the essential difference between good and evil) and therefore, when we are careful not to be misled from these natural perceptions of the understanding, the *moral sense,* arising from thence, has a real right to influence our actions, is a proper *cause or ground of obligation.* However, I allow, that since it may be extinguished, or misguided, it is too precarious to be esteemed the *sole* cause or foundation of moral obligation. And indeed I see no reason, why any *one* principle should be looked on as such, since there are certainly several principles in the nature of man, which all concur to direct him to the practice of virtue: And if each of these were allowed a share in *obliging* him to it, this would no way weaken the force, or lessen the impor-

---

*   *Vid.* [Rutherforth's] *Essay* p. 113.

---

1 Rutherforth, p. 112.

tance of any other principle, but rather contribute to strengthen it.

I do not know what idea some late writers can have of *moral obligation*, that they are so zealous for excluding every principle from being in any degree a ground or foundation of it, except their favourite one, a prospect of future rewards and punishments. But the author of the *Essay on Virtue* (who has distinguished himself among them) seems to think, that the *cause* of obligation (as his term is) should be something in a manner irresistible; for the reason he gives* why an instinctive approbation of virtue cannot *be made the cause of moral obligation*, is, that "this instinct is so much too weak to restrain us, that we can, with a sense of the beauties of virtue upon our mind, and under the full influence of our approbation of it, not only neglect to comply with its dictates, but even act directly against them." But if this be a good reason for excluding our approbation of virtue, from being *a cause of moral obligation*, I am afraid the same reason will exclude every other principle from being so too; for I know of none strong enough to restrain free agents, when they give a loose to their passions and appetites, instead of attending to the obligations they are under of subduing them. Future retributions are allowed by all to be considerations of great importance, and generally most effectual to influence the bulk of mankind; yet it is notorious, that great numbers, with a full conviction upon their minds of the reality of the sanctions of God's laws, *not only neglect to comply with their dictates, but even act directly against them*. So that if our author's reasoning hold, here would be an end at once of all moral obligation.

But rather than set mankind free from every obligation, because none is strong enough to force them, I beg leave to conclude, that it is not the *strength* of any principle, but the *tendency* of it, and the *right* it has to influence men's practice, that makes it a true ground of moral obligation. And that the perception we have of the essential difference of things, with the fitnesses and unfitnesses resulting from thence, and our consciousness of right and wrong, have a *tendency* to direct us to virtue, and a *right* to influence our practice, seems to me as clear and certain, as it is, that we are reasonable beings, and moral agents: and that therefore they are both *true causes or grounds of moral obligation*. For, "By obligation I understand, such a perception of an inducement to act, or to forbear acting, as forces an agent to stand self-condemned, if he does not conform to it." A definition, which I

---

* [Rutherforth], p. 114.

think, all the contending parties on this subject might agree in; for no stronger restraint can be laid upon a *free agent*, even by the commands of God, and the sanctions of his laws, than that of forcing him to stand *self-condemned*, if he chooses to hazard the consequences of disobeying them. So that if this definition were acquiesced in, there could no dispute remain, unless it be, whether we can counteract our plain perceptions of good and evil, fit and unfit, right and wrong, without standing self-condemned? Which perhaps would scarce bear a question.

The three or four last pages of this chapter are a train of *sophisms*, founded upon an equivocal use of the terms *reluctance*, *affection*, *approbation*, *&c*. "If (says he) the* supposed natural *approbation*, from whence the unwillingness to give up virtue is said to arise, was all that obliged us to practise it, we should, upon *the same principles, be as much obliged to be vicious*; for no vicious man ever gives up vice without reluctance: and such a reluctance must, in one case as well as in the other, be a mark of his naturally *approving* what he parts with so unwillingly." Poor sophistry! is there no such thing then as reluctance of inclination? No difference between a reluctance to part with what we *like*, and a reluctance to part with what we approve? A man, who gives up his *vices*, does *not approve*, tho' he may love them; a man, who gives up his *virtue*, may approve, tho' he does *not love it*. The reluctance on one side proceeds from *an affection* to practices, which he perceives to be wrong; the reluctance on the other, from perceiving practices to be *right*, for which he has *no affection*. Are these the *same principles*? Or can they have an equal *right of obliging us*? No matter for that, approbation is affection, or affection approbation; a reluctance of the judging faculty, and a reluctance of the sensual appetites, the same thing, whenever this gentleman's argument requires it. But let these things be rightly distinguished, and all his *entangling queries* are resolved. To those, therefore, I shall only answer in general; if our natural conscience, moral sense, or whatever that faculty in us may be called, which judges of our actions, and approves or condemns them, if this is in its own nature *superior* to mere appetite, and propensions; then a reason will appear, why we should give the preference to our approbation of virtue, rather than to our sensual inclinations; why we ought to restrain these, whilst it is our duty to improve the other. And without looking farther, we may find a reason in the *approbation* itself, why it should be esteemed a *true*, tho' not the sole *cause of our obligation to virtue*.

---

* [Rutherforth], p. 114.

Remarks on Chap. vi.

It is painful talk for a plain searcher after truth, to have to do with an author skilled in all arts of wrangling in the schools; which may be of use there, to try the sagacity of young students, in detecting the sophisms, cavils, and fallacies of an opponent; but can only serve to puzzle and mislead an ingenuous reader, who expects to be instructed by fair reasoning and solid argument; to which if the author before us had confined himself, his book would have been reduced to a much less compass, and his readers been less perplexed in going through it.

The great point to be proved in this chapter is, that *no eternal and necessary differences, no fitness or unfitness of things, can be the cause of moral obligation.* The two authors,* whom in this he chiefly opposes, have established, upon immutable foundations, the obligation of all reasonable beings to act agreeably to the essential differences, nature, relations, and fitness of things; and this with great simplicity, and direct argument, free from all the bewildering arts. But the author of the *Essay* has attacked them in a very different manner; fallacies, cavils, a multitude of puzzling questions, wrong suppositions, and putting unfamiliar cases, are the arms he makes use of; and against such random shots, what possibility is there of making any regular defence? We must look about us, and turn and return as well as we may.

He† begins with taking notice of a concession those authors have made, of the necessity of calling in the hopes of a future state, to support men in the practice of virtue, when it would expose them to death or misery here; which he thinks gives him great advantage against them. But I pass it over now, because *this single point*, upon which he supposes *the whole dispute might very safely be rested*, will soon come more than once in our way again. And we have here in the meantime a notable argument to encounter, by which he begins his "*endeavours to prove,* that the reasons for practising virtue, which flow from the differences and relations of things, are not only too precarious to deserve the title of obligation, but farther, that they afford us *no reason at all* for being virtuous." Let us attend to these worthy *endeavours.*

"There is, without dispute (says our author‡) a natural difference between one thing and another: good and evil, or happiness and misery are certainly not the same thing." I believe, indeed, no

---

* Dr. *Clarke,* and Mr. *Balguy.*
† [Rutherforth], p. 119.
‡ [Rutherforth], p. 120.

body ever disputed this. "And since moral good or virtue consists in doing good to others, or in taking care not to make them miserable; and moral evil or vice in the contrary; one of these must differ as much from the other, as happiness does from misery." Indisputable again. "But from this difference, there cannot arise any obligation to the practice of virtue; for to say, that moral good or virtue is our duty, because it differs naturally and essentially from vice, is to make it our duty for such a reason, as would equally have proved the very reverse: vice or moral evil must be as much our duty upon the same principle, since it differs naturally and essentially from moral good: All that can be gathered from this difference is, that between virtue and vice there is room for choice." Excellent! But pray, who ever gave for a reason, that moral good or virtue is our duty, barely *because it differs naturally and essentially from vice*? It is not *because it differs* from vice, but because their natural difference is such, as makes one fit to be chosen, and not the other; which is a very different proposition. Certain fitnesses and unfitnesses arise from the essential difference between virtue and vice, which makes it our duty to practise one, and avoid the other. But does this gentleman really think, that nothing more is meant by the natural and essential difference between happiness and misery, or between moral good and evil, but that they are not the same things? If he does, he must suppose the great writer he contends against, to have trifled egregiously in opposing Mr. *Hobbes*'s principles,[1] by insisting on the immutable nature and essential difference of moral good and evil; for even *Hobbes* himself, absurd as his principles were, was never absurd enough to maintain, that just and unjust, fidelity and treachery, killing an innocent person, and saving his life, were *the same things*. That which he maintained was, that none of those actions, which are called morally good or evil, were in their own nature *better or worse* than another, till they made so by *positive institutions*. What then must his opposers mean by asserting the natural and essen-

---

1 Thomas Hobbes (1588–1679), a materialist philosopher, Hobbes famously asserted a strong brand of empiricism, according to which experience, or sensation, is the definitive justification for our ideas about the world. Hobbes concluded that there can be no unseen, or spiritual, forces in nature. In ethics, he espoused a constructivist view of morality according to which, broadly speaking, human reason creates moral concepts. His works include *De Corpore* (1655) and *De Homine* (1658). Hobbes was villified in his time as an atheist, for his strong materialism. This reputation of Hobbes's explains Cockburn's dismissal of his views, in the next line, as "absurd."

tial difference of good and evil, right and wrong (if they meant any thing to the purpose) but that one of these was, *in its own nature*, antecedent to all positive appointment, better, more valuable, or fitter to be done, than its contrary? And that they did mean this, is plain from the whole tenor of their reasoning. If by the natural and essential difference between happiness and misery, this author really means nothing more than that they are *not the same thing*, then, by his own argument, *as this gives no preference of one to the other, it cannot oblige us to either*. He would do well then to tell us, what it is that obliges us to choose happiness rather than misery; for I fear it will be difficult to find it out, if it be not the *natural difference*, or that *which distinguishes it* from misery. For what is the *natural* difference of happiness from misery, but that the first is suitable to our nature, desirable, and fit to be chosen: misery, on the contrary, unsuitable, hateful, and unfit to be chosen? And this is the very case, the only meaning to the purpose, of the natural and essential difference of right and wrong, virtue and vice, or moral good and evil: one of these is *in its own nature*, or in *that which distinguishes* it from its opposite, better, more suitable to a reasonable being, and fitter to be chosen than the other.* If virtue (as this author owns) must differ as

---

* Upon this subject, the great author of *the Divine Legation* having said, that the contenders for the natural essential difference of things have *mistaken it for the moral difference*; I answered in some remarks formerly published, "That they plainly saw these were distinct things, but they saw too, that one was so dependent on the other, that when they had clearly demonstrated the former, they needed not give themselves much trouble to prove the latter." This I really then took to be the case of the writers, who maintain the natural and essential difference of things: but the fallacious argument of the *Essay* writer having given me occasion to consider this matter farther, I find there was more ground for that great author's observation, than I at that time imagined. The truth is, those writers scarce take any notice at all of what may be strictly called *the natural difference* of things, if by that is only meant, that virtue and vice, justice and injustice, fidelity and treachery, *&c.* are *not the same things*: this, I presume, they could not mistake for a moral difference, but it is a truth so obvious to every one, that it would have been trifling to have solemnly asserted, and formally proved, what nobody pretended to deny. Their meaning therefore must be, that there is naturally and essentially such a difference in things, as made one preferable, or fitter to be chosen than another; which is much the same as to say, that *moral good and evil are such in their own nature*, without any positive appointment. This is well known to be their doctrine; and if they called this a *natural* difference, a little attention may convince any one, that this implies in it a *moral*

much from vice, as happiness does from misery; then their *difference* not only acquaints us, that between them *there is room for choice*, but plainly directs us where that choice ought to be placed; informs us, that virtue, as well as happiness, is fitter to be chosen than vice or misery; and till he can show us in what that *natural difference* consists between happiness and misery, virtue and vice, *which gives no preference of one to the other*, this formidable argument, by which he thinks we have just now seen, that the essential difference of good and evil *can be no cause of obligation*, can no more oblige us to virtue than to vice, and that therefore *we may be sure there is some fallacy in the argument*; this will itself appear to be but a mere fallacy, and the natural difference of things, the natural preferableness of virtue to vice, with the fitnesses arising from thence, remain an unshaken *ground or cause of moral obligation*.

The fallacy our author imputes to a* *favourite* writer upon this subject, consists in his using *good to be done*, and *reasonable to be done*, as expressions of the same signification, on which he expostulates as follows: "And if because we must grant, that virtue, from the very nature of it, is good to be done, it was therefore reasonable to be done, and so our duty, *&c.* But good to be done† signifies either good for him who does it, or good for others: and this ambiguous meaning of the words seems to have been made too much use of. For as everybody will allow, that what makes him happy, who does it, is fit to be done and reasonable; and because it will be readily granted farther, that virtue is good to be done, it is concluded, that virtue must therefore be fit and reasonable. Whereas in granting, that virtue is good to be done, we do not mean, that it is in its own nature good for him who does it, but good for others: for if we go no farther than the nature of it, then this is the only sense, in which virtue appears self-evidently to be good." Thus far our author.

But he might have known, that the *favourite* writer, referred to, dealt in no such ambiguities, or trifling propositions; that he never thought of such a thing as *good to be done*, which yet was *not good for him who does it*; of virtue being in its own nature self-evidently good, though not good for the doer; that is to say, *virtue consisting in doing good to others* is in its own nature self-evidently *good for others*. He talked not at this rate indeed; this would have

---

    difference; i.e., that one is fitter to be chosen by an agent than the other: the want of which attention may be an excuse for the fallacious consequence drawn from that expression, by the author of the *Essay on Virtue*.
*   Dr. *Clarke*.
†   [Rutherforth], p. 121, [122].

been strange language to him, who thought, that the practice of virtue, or good to be done, was without any ambiguity *good for him who does it*, as it is more suitable to a reasonable being, more perfective of his nature, and makes him more approved to his own mind than the practice of vice: he thought, too, that acting agreeably to our own nature, and to the several relations we stand in to other beings (in which, according to his doctrine, the entire nature of virtue of moral good consists) was *fit and reasonable*, therefore good to be done, good in him that does it, *and so our duty*. Nay, even according to this author's own notion of virtue, imperfect as it is, is not *doing good to others* a good action in him, who does it? Is he not a better man than one, who does nothing but mischief? Supposing then all consequences to the *agent* perfectly *equal*, that he was neither to be a *gainer* nor a *loser* by his virtue; would it not in that case be more *fit and reasonable* to make all in his power happy, rather than to make them as miserable as he could? Surely no one can think otherwise, that has not thrown off all sentiments of humanity. And if what is *fit and reasonable* is our *duty*, as this author seems here to own, I hope he will own too, that the practice of virtue may be *fit and reasonable, and so our duty*, in cases, where we can do much good without hurting ourselves, though we had no prospect of any particular advantage by it.

However we are told, that those writers, who found the original obligation to virtue on the reason and nature, and fitness of things, antecedent to all positive appointment, and to all expectation of reward or punishment; do yet own necessity of the belief of a future state, that God will take care, that we shall, upon the whole, be no losers by our virtue, to support the practice of it in the world; and that in extraordinary cases, it would be unreasonable to expect, that men, by adhering to virtue, should part with their lives, or even all the comforts of life, if thereby they eternally deprive themselves of all possibility of receiving any advantage from that adherence. This the author of the *Essay* thinks is* giving up their whole cause; "is plainly not so much supporting this sort of obligation, as introducing another quite distinct from it: the will of the Supreme Being is called in, not to strengthen an obligation, which we should have been under without it, but to produce an obligation, where there was none before; and to make the practice of virtue reasonable, where it would not have been so otherwise." But this is quite misrepresenting their sense, as well as the truth of the case: the obligation to virtue arises always and

---

* [Rutherforth], p. 119, 127.

invariably from the reason, nature, and fitness of things: the practice of virtue, that is, acting agreeably to justice, equity, goodness, and truth, must always be fit and reasonable. Yet in such a world as this, men may be, in some extraordinary cases, so circumstanced, that, by strictly adhering to what they unavoidably judge to be their duty, they must bring upon themselves such sufferings, as it would scarce be possible for them to support themselves under, without a regard to the providence of God, and a full persuasion, that he will not allow his creatures to be finally losers by steadily practising those virtues, which the nature he has given them requires from them, and which therefore must be approved by him. How is this *calling in the will of the supreme being, to produce an obligation where there was none before?* Is not sole ground of hoping for a future recompense plainly fixed on that perception, which we unavoidably have of a prior obligation? If we did not perceive the practice of virtue to be fit, and reasonable, and our duty, and that its natural tendency is to produce happiness; upon what ground could we expect (without revelation) that God should interpose to make virtue and happiness finally inseparable? But if virtue is acknowledged to be the natural duty of mankind, or a duty arising from their very nature, and designed their chief good; then, from the frequent impediments it will meet with, and the various sufferings, that sometimes attend it *here*, the strongest argument may be deduced, that natural reason can discover, for the certainty of a *future state*: so that calling in this hope for the support of suffering virtue necessarily presupposes our obligation to practise it; presupposes it *fit and reasonable in itself to be done* since otherwise we could have no ground to expect a recompense for it.

With this view Dr. *Clarke* urges the necessity of the belief of a future state, to support the practice of virtue in such a world as this, in that very* Discourse, where *he was more immediately engaged in the defence of his darling scheme of morality* (as the author of the *Essay* calls it) and not, as is† suggested, *when his thoughts were turned another way.* For that great master of reasoning well knew, that *his scheme,* and a *prospect of future rewards and punishments,* are, by placing the obligations of morality *antecedent to that prospect,* the stronger supports of each other. But to go on with our author.

---

* Evidence of Natural and Revealed Religion. [Clarke, *A Discourse concerning the Unchangeable Obligations of Natural Religion, and the Truth and Certainty of the Christian Revelation* (1706).]

† *Vide* [Rutherforth's], *Essay,* p. 122.

"I see not therefore (says he) the great use of this *fanciful* account of our duty, supposing it could be defended: For if in the more exalted instances we must have recourse to the will of God, and can allow it in them to be a proper foundation to act upon; why may not we submit to it, and entertain the same opinion of it in the lower instances? Why is this the only rational source of obligation, in cases of the greatest importance; but a wrong and unreasonable one in cases, where we meet with few or no temptations to be otherwise than virtuous?"[1] I am sorry to find an account of our duty deduced from the essential difference of good and evil, and the immutable nature and relations of things, called by a grave divine and philosopher, *a fanciful account*; but I am at a loss to know, whose *fancies* he is here opposing: For it is certain the writers he had mentioned have no concern in them; they have always allowed *the will of God*, which is ever directed by the reason and truth of *things, to be a proper foundation to act upon*, in all instances high or low: yet they have never said, that this is the *only* rational source of obligation, even in cases of the greatest importance; much less that *it is a wrong and unreasonable one* in any case. Let those, whose *fancies* these are (if our author knows where to find them) be answerable for them.

But perhaps *the will of God* is put here for the *sanctions of his laws* (fallacies and ambiguities being not unusual with this author): Yet even in that case, he is out in his reasoning; for though the writers he professes to oppose, allow *future rewards and punishments* to be considerations of great importance, and highly necessary to keep the generality of mankind to the practice of virtue; (so that he may, if he pleases, call them *a proper foundation to act upon*) yet they are never allowed by those authors, to be *the source of moral obligation*, or that which makes virtue to be our duty. The *duty* is ever supposed *prior* to all consideration of them, though without that support men might not be able or willing to perform it in extraordinary cases; but *in all cases*, the duty arises from the reason, and nature, and fitness of things; for by these the declared will of God is itself directed.

But our author sees not the great use of this *fanciful* account of our duty, *if in the more exalted instances we must have recourse to the will of God*. He has not, it seems, considered a very obvious use of it in one case, *viz.* where the will of God is not expressly revealed. A great part of mankind have no other rule to govern

---

1 Rutherforth, p. 128.

their actions by, but what they must deduce from the nature and relations of things, and their own unavoidable perceptions of good and evil, right and wrong. These, by a due use of their faculties, may lead them to know the will of their creator, and to a probable expectation of a *future state*, if they suffer *here* by doing what they perceive to be right and fit. This is one great use of the scheme he calls *fanciful*. But what need of it, he may say, where the will of God is known? Why here again it is of excellent use, to convince the mind of the reasonableness, the fitness, and rectitude of all the commands of God. The man, who sees, that they are founded on the essential difference of good and evil; and that they require nothing of him but what was his duty to do as a reasonable being, though it had not been commanded; must, in all likelihood, be better disposed to acquiesce in the will of God, and to acknowledge the goodness and equity of future retributions, than he, who considers God's commands as arbitrary things, which he would have had no obligation to perform, if they had not been required; and who thinks his only business here is to pursue his own happiness: for why might not he have been left to seek happiness directly, by gratifying his most pressing inclinations and appetites? Why must he go such a roundabout way to his end, as to suppress his own natural desires, and force himself to do good to others, when he has no natural disposition to benevolence, and neither of these would have been *fit or reasonable*, if they had not been commanded? This proceeding must seem a little tyrannical to such a one, and these sentiments upon it be the most natural product of our new *darling selfish scheme of morality*.

I must therefore say, in my turn, I see not the reason, or use, of the great zeal some late writers have shown to establish it. If mankind are by nature so *selfish* as these gentlemen suppose, and if religion requires them to be divested of that disposition, or to act contrary to it; why do they labour so much to increase it, by persuading them, that nature and reason teach every one to pursue nothing but his own happiness; and that it would not be fit or reasonable to have the least regard to the good of others, if we were not ourselves to be gainers by it? This seems not to be the readiest way to promote the practice of virtue or true religion, in the world; for moral obligation and true religion are *internal* principles, that affect the conscience, which *external* motives can never do. Hopes of reward, or fears of punishment, may indeed excite to good actions, or restrain from evil; but *of themselves*, without a sense of duty arising either from the fitness of acting suitably to the nature, which God has given us, or of obedience to his will, they can never make a virtuous or a religious man. Let it be considered then of what service it can be to religion, to decry, as *fanciful*, and void of all obligation, a principle, by which, as St. Paul says, *those, who have not the law, are a law unto themselves*; which, where the will of God is known, necessarily coincides with it, and which equally carries our views to a future state, and upon surer grounds, than the scheme of those, who allow *no cause of duty or obligation,* no not the will of God itself, without a prospect of rewards and punishments. Those gentlemen would do well to consider too, how wantonly they set loose, not only Atheists, but all mankind, who have ever been without the knowledge of God's revealed will, and the sanctions of his laws, from owing any duty to him, or to their fellow creatures; and whether this is not contrary to that express declaration of the Apostle, just now quoted.

The author of the *Essay* having endeavoured to prove, by the fallacious argument we have lately examined, that the *natural difference* of things produces no obligation to the practice of virtue; comes next to consider,* "Whether it does not produce such a fitness or unfitness, in the application of different things one to another, as will make some sorts of behaviour evidently wrong, and such as reason will disallow; others right, such as reason cannot but approve?" Whether, for instance (in the words of a judicious writer)[1] "To give pain *without cause* to a sensible creature is not an action self-evidently wrong, as being directly repugnant to the nature of the object, and the circumstances of the agent?" One would think this a question, that could hardly bear disputing: But our author has found means to dispute it through sixteen pages, by all the arts of puzzling without convincing. Chicane, sophistry, captious questions, arguing upon wrong suppositions, or a false sense of words, are the sure means to perplex a plain reasoner, unused to wrangle; who, though he knows the *direct* road to truth well enough, may be at a loss how to come at it by the windings of a maze of words. This author is so fearful† of our being misled by a *doubtful* signification of the words, *agreeable or repugnant to nature*, that he has taken care to fix such a

---

* [Rutherforth], p. 123.
† *Ibid.* [Rutherforth, p. 123.]

---

1 John Balguy, "The Foundation of Moral Goodness" in *A Collection of Tracts, Moral and Theological* (1734), p. 74.

meaning to them, as the author he opposes could not possibly intend: "I cannot grant (says he) that an action, which gives pain to a sensible being, is *repugnant to nature*, if by this is meant, that such an action uses it otherwise than its nature has *fitted it to be used*: For nature, which gave it perception, made it as *fit* (by which he means as capable) to receive pain as to receive pleasure." Now could he suppose any writer of common sense to mean, that to give pain to a sensible being is wrong, because such an action uses it otherwise than its nature has made it *capable* of being used? For how could pain be given to any being, which nature had not made capable of receiving it? or, in our author's new phrase, *fitted it to be so used*, by which that he means *made it capable of being so used*, is plain thro' his whole argument; nay a little lower he gives us his sense in that very expression. After having told us, that giving poison to a man is using him as nature has *fitted* him to be used, since the poison is as sure to kill him as wholesome food would have been to nourish him; he goes on at the same rate of chicaning thus: "He is *capable* indeed of happiness, but then he is capable of misery too; and he who makes him miserable, acts up as much to the nature of things, as he does who makes him happy; for the aversion to misery, of those beings, that have perception, is as *natural* as their desire of happiness, and he who gives them pain, because they have an aversion to it, has a reason in nature for what he does, no less than he who gives them pleasure because they have a mind to it."[1] What manifest sophistry is all this? How well it shows what work an artist can make with a false or ambiguous sense of words! At this rate of *wrangling* (for I would not wrong the author by supposing he designed it for reasoning) allowing his sense, no kind of usage, no infliction of the greatest evils, sensible beings are *capable* of, can be *repugnant to their nature*; because, as he affects to express it, nature has *fitted them for that sort of treatment*; so that pleasure and pain, happiness and misery, life and death, being equally *natural* to them, must of consequence be equally *agreeable to their nature*, that is, they are made capable of either. But have not all *fair reasoners* hitherto meant, by any thing being *agreeable to the nature of a sensible being*, that it tends either to the happiness, the perfection, or the preservation of it; and by *repugnant to its nature*, the direct contrary? He, who poisons a man, or makes him miserable, finds indeed a ground or reason in nature for the *possibility* of his action, for nature has made him *capable* of being killed, or being

---

1 Rutherforth, pp. 124–25.

miserable; but such a treatment is not the less self-evidently *repugnant to the nature of the object*, in the commonly understood and allowed sense of those words, as destructive of its being, or its happiness.

We have next a train of* questions, that may puzzle better heads than mine to frame answers to them, being either formed upon wrong suppositions, that lead us from the purpose, or aiming at nobody knows what. Let us attend to some of them. "Who are those sensible beings, that are to be humoured in their inclinations? To whom is it self-evidently wrong to give pain because they dislike it? Are not the agents sensible beings as well as the objects? And must it not therefore be self-evidently wrong for the agents to give themselves pain?" No doubt it is, if they have no reasonable cause for it; but I believe we are seldom in danger of that. But to go on: "Nay, is it not self-evidently right upon these principles, to give themselves pleasure? I mean, to make themselves happy. What then is to be done, when we can make our selves happy by being vicious; or must submit to pain, by persevering in our virtue? Are we obliged in these circumstances, to neglect virtue and to pursue vice? If not, why should we give a preference to the fitness between happiness and our fellow-creatures, rather than to the same fitness, between happiness and ourselves? Why may we make an unfit application of misery to a sensible being in our own case, in order to avoid making it where others are concerned?"—Truly, I cannot guess what the author aims at here, but must answer at random; that I know of no *fitness* in making either ourselves, or our fellow-creatures happy, by being vicious; nor of any *unfit application* in giving them, or ourselves pain, in order to preserve their virtue or our own: this is not giving pain *without cause*, for here is a very important cause for it.

The next enquiry is: "Are we to judge of the importance of these fitnesses, or unfitnesses, by the *quantity* of happiness and misery, which a sensible being will feel from our behaviour, and so to look upon it as a duty to make that application, which will produce the greater happiness, and avoid that, which will produce the greater misery? But the approved judgment of mankind does not form itself upon these principles."[1] No, certainly, nor do I know whose *judgments* are concerned in these

---

* [Rutherforth], p. 125.

---

1 Rutherforth, p. 125.

enquiries: for, according to the scheme our author should here be opposing, duty, or moral fitnesses, were never pretended to be measured by mathematical proportions; but by the suitableness of actions to the circumstances of the agent and the object. All the queries, therefore, and conclusions, made upon that *wrong supposition*, are nothing to the purpose, with regard to that scheme, or to any other purpose, that I can find out; but some of them are not a little surprising, in respect of his own principles. "Suppose (he says) a man should do himself more good than he does others harm by his vice, is he at liberty to be vicious in these circumstances? If he is not, then balancing the quantity of misery, produced by an unfit application, against the quantity of happiness, that results from a fit one, is not the method, by which we determine what our duty is: But if he is at liberty, then how poor a principle of obligation must this be, which will recommend virtue to us only where it is not against our interest, and will discourage vice only where we can get but little by it?"[1] How poor a principle indeed! but this seems an unlucky observation, from an author, who has writ a large volume to prove, *that interest is the sole cause of obligation*; and I would advise him to apply it where it will be more proper. *The excellence and worth of virtue* may, upon *that* principle, be (as he speaks) *greatest of all, when it advances our interest the most*;[2] but upon the principles, which were to be confuted in this chapter (though he often seems to forget them) the *excellence of virtue* consists in the *rectitude* of it, and is neither greater nor less when it *advances our interests*, or when it *does not*.

The author of the *Essay** seems to suppose, that "what he has urged against their opinion, who contend, that fitness of application is a motive, which obliges to virtue, will show, that it is not a rational motive in any case, nor indeed any motive at all." But growing a little diffident, he adds: "Or if this has not been made appear already," (we have seen at what rate it has been made appear, for his arguments are all of a piece) "let them *consider farther*, why it should be less a breach of duty to give pain to brutes than to our own species. What causes pain, is as disagreeable to their nature as it is to ours: And if this unfitness of application is not self-evidently wrong, then neither is that so, which gives pain to our fellow-creatures." This is a case, that may have

---

*   [Rutherforth], p. 128.

---

1   Rutherforth, pp. 126–27.
2   Rutherforth, p. 127.

some difficulty in it, even with fair minds, who sincerely seek truth; and therefore is indeed worth *considering*.

If we regard ourselves only as *sensible* beings, the brutes are upon a level with us; and in that case it must appear as wrong to give them pain, as to give it to any of our own species: But as reasonable beings, we are manifestly superior to them; and though this implies no right to give them pain *without a cause*, which must in all cases be self-evidently wrong; yet from that superiority, and the differences between their nature and ours, a cause may arise, that will make it fit and reasonable to treat them in *another manner*, than would be fit from any of us to our fellow-creatures. The general practice of mankind, of sustaining their lives by animal food, except a few philosophers, who scrupled it upon a fond notion of the transmigration of human souls into the bodies of brutes; this almost universal practice must be derived, either from an original grant of the great Creator (who has an undoubted right to dispose of the lives of all his creatures as he thinks fit) or else from the agreement of it with the common sense of mankind, and their observations on the nature of things. They would soon perceive themselves to be the chief inhabitants of this earth; that there were no other beings here capable of living in society, or entering into mutual compacts; that all *men* being equal by nature, it was reasonable, that every one should do unto others what he would have them do unto him; but that *brutes* being incapable of such reciprocal obligations, it was impossible to live upon the square with them: And as they are manifestly inferior to man, and yet are endued with many faculties, that may be made useful to him, it might well be concluded, that such of them, as could be fitted for his purposes, were designed by nature, or, to speak more properly, by the God of nature, for his service. It was obvious likewise to observe, that a large part of the animal creation do, *by natural instinct*, feed upon others of a different species, that, in some respects, are their inferiors; and since the author of that instinct thoroughly knows the nature of all beings, it must be supposed, that, on some account or other, the most proper means of supporting the lives of such animals is by other living creatures of a *lower rank*; and that therefore the thing cannot be *unfit* in itself, or contrary to nature. This was sufficient to satisfy men, if animal food was the most nourishing and strengthening for them, that it must be fit and reasonable, and that they had the permission of their Creator, for the support of their own lives, to take away the life of creatures so much *inferior* to them, and of so much less importance. And now let our author consider, whether a reason can be found,* *of exactly of the same sort,* to vindicate us in giving pain to, or in taking the life of, our fellow-creatures; and whether this, though it should appear *fit and reasonable, with respect to brutes,* may not yet, contrary to his conclusion, be *self-evidently wrong, with respect to our own species.*

We need not wonder, that a writer, who could undertake to deny, as we have seen, *that giving pain to a sensible being is repugnant to the nature of the object*; should carry on his opposition to the same author, by denying, that it is *contrary to the nature of the agent,* which may not seem so glaringly odd. The argument he supposes, which is to prove, that vice *is repugnant to reason,* he gives us, as it is stated, "by the most candid, the clearest, and most judicious writer, that ever undertook the defence of this scheme of morality."[1] And it were to be wished he had been as just to the reasoning, as he is here to the *character* of that fine writer. He has set down the argument at large, but, according to my designed brevity, I shall only take so much of it, as is necessary to show it in its whole strength.

"We† are certainly informed by our senses, that pain is natural evil: here is therefore a plain and perpetual reason against the infliction of it, when no stronger intervenes to make it requisite.‡ To give pain to a sensible being must be wrong in a rational or moral agent, having no cause or reason to give pain, if it be morally unfit. And that it is morally unfit, seems to me as plain and evident as any proposition can be. It is contrary to the nature and the truth of things; it is contrary to the nature of the object; it is contrary to the nature and circumstances of the agent; because he being rational must act unnaturally, whenever he acts unreasonably; and he must act unreasonably, when he acts *both without and contrary to reason.* Now he is supposed to have no reason for giving pain, and yet must see a good reason for not giving it; for where there is no reason for pain, there is always a good reason against it, arising from the nature of the thing itself." This, I confess, seems to me an unanswerable demonstration, that to give pain, a known evil, having no cause or reason to give it, *is contrary to the nature of a rational agent*; for what can be more

---

* Vide [Rutherforth's] *Essay,* p. 129.
† Balguy's *Tracts,* p. 75.
‡ [Balguy, *Tracts*], p. 122.

---

1 Rutherforth, p. 130.

unnatural in such a being, than to act *both without and contrary to reason*? But how does the author of the *Essay* confute this argument? Why, just at the usual rate; he wrangles, and cavils, and objects to every thing, but neither proves nor disproves anything.* First, he lays hold of the expression of acting *without reason*; but to act without reason, he tells us, is not in all cases, contrary to our duty, as in choosing one, between two things, quite indifferent, or preferring white wine to red, only for whim: who (says he) would think it a violation of his duty to get up and walk, when he might have sat still? And what is all this to the purpose? If in trifles or things quite indifferent, where reason has nothing to do, there is no crime in acting without reason; does it follow, that in cases of importance, as in the instance of inflicting a known evil, where reason ought to interpose, there will be no violation of duty in acting *without reason?* But the writer he opposes had urged farther, that an agent, in giving *causeless* pain to a sensible creature, acts unreasonably and therefore unnaturally, since he acts *both without and contrary to reason*. This our author takes notice of too; this, he says, *is indeed alleged*. And what does he allege against it? Truly nothing, though this was the main point to be disproved. But that writer having before said, that *pain being a natural evil, there is a plain and perpetual reason against the infliction of it, when no stronger intervenes to make it requisite*; he runs off from the principal point to ask: "And what† is that stronger reason, which may intervene? Does it depend upon *the interest of the agent*;" he is sure to fix upon what he knows is not the case; and here he could not but know, that, according to the principles he is opposing, *the interest of the agent* can never be urged as a reason for giving pain, or in any way injuring a fellow-creature; because this is contrary to the fitness of things, contrary to that relation of equality, which subsists between them. This is a reason, which could only be allowed in *Hobbes's state of nature* where everyone might be doing mischief to another for his own interest, till all were destroyed: But let the judge, who condemns a criminal, the surgeon who cuts off a limb, or the prudent parent, who corrects his child, be asked what it is that makes it fit and reasonable in them to give pain to a sensible creature? Their motives will acquaint him (if he wants to be informed) that the safety of the public, of the life, or the virtue of the object, and such like, is *that stronger reason, which may intervene*, and which in no case depends upon *the interest of the agent*. But our author

---

* [Rutherforth's] *Essay*, p. 132.
† [Rutherforth], p. 133.

seems to delight in putting *wrong suppositions*, only to show his art in objecting against them, whilst he fights without an adversary. Well then; "If that stronger reason *does not* depend upon the interest of the agent; then tell me (says he) why the agent, by neglecting to give a pleasure to himself, or by choosing to give pain to himself, does not act as irrationally as by giving pain to others?"[1] I believe no body denies, that this would be irrational in any agent, unless some *stronger reason intervenes to make it requisite* to forbear pleasure, or to give himself pain. But so he goes on, repeating the same kind of expostulations, and the questions we had a little before, about the agent's having perception as well as the objects: "Why is not it a duty to give pain to them, if by that means he can avoid suffering it himself? And why is it not irrational to give pain to brutes? Is it because the advantages we receive from their pain is a stronger reason, which intervenes? Then why is not this reason from interest, which keeps us clear of any crime in killing or in hurting them, sufficient to make the same behaviour towards our own species neither irrational nor wrong?"[2] This gentleman seems to have no just notion of the scheme he opposes, by making suppositions, and queries, quite inconsistent with *the nature, relations, and fitness of things*; and indeed he gives frequent grounds to apprehend, that he does not know the true meaning of those terms. But all the questions here, which are only repetitions, have been considered* already, so far as their aim could be guessed at, and I hope sufficient satisfaction given, particularly with respect to that *difference* of the nature of brutes from ours, which may make the same behaviour fit and reasonable towards them, that would be irrational and wrong towards our own species, who are all by nature equal. But I find we shall have occasion given us hereafter to consider this subject farther; yet here I would observe, that to give pain unnecessarily, even to brutes, out of a cruel humour, or wantonly only for sport, is contrary to nature and reason, and morally *unfit*, tho' perhaps not so much attended to as it ought to be.

We have next a heap of† cavils at particular parts of the argument he was to confute; putting imaginary senses upon words and propositions, when the true sense was the most obvious; then

---

* In p. 53, 56–57 of these *Remarks*.
† [Rutherforth], from p. 134 to 138.

---

1 Rutherforth, p. 133.
2 Rutherforth, p. 134.

wrangling against his own fancies, and repeating a great deal of what we had before, about nature having *fitted* sensible beings to receive pain as well as pleasure, &c. which would be tiresome to the reader to go over again, or to examine his cavils minutely: and indeed it is needless, for there is not so much as an attempt to confute the argument, by which the writer he opposes had proved, that *to give pain to a sensible creature, without cause, is contrary to the nature of a rational agent*. He only tells us, that he does not perceive the self-evidence of this proposition, and that the demonstration, which follows, does not make it much clearer to him, *viz. Whatever is contrary to the nature, or truth of things, is wrong: such an action, as gives pain to a sensible object, without cause, is contrary to the nature of things, as has been just proved*. "But what (says our author) had been just proved? That such an action is contrary to the nature of the sensible being, which feels it, not that it is contrary to the nature of the rational agent, which produces it; for this latter point was to be made good by the demonstration."[1] Here he seems to be mistaken; this latter point was made good before; nor was the demonstration intended for a new proof of it. But the judicious writer having enlarged upon his argument, and urged the *glaring disagreement*, which a rational agent must perceive between such an action *coming from him*, and such an object; in case his proposition should not be strictly self-evident, puts the proofs he had given of it before, into the closer form of a syllogism; a method, which certainly has nothing in it unworthy of an *ingenuous writer*. But it was not to be expected, that our author should go back for proofs, which he had at first slipped over unnoticed: it was a more compendious way to[*] affirm roundly, that "When this writer says, he had just proved such an action to be contrary to the nature of things, he means, that it is contrary to the nature of the *object*; and that *this in truth was all that he had proved*." But it does not follow (continues he) "that every action is a breach of duty in a rational agent, by which he gives pain to others. To have supported such a conclusion, it ought to have been shown, that it is as *contrary to the nature of the agent to give it*, as it *confessedly* is to that of the patient to receive it." And, pray, what was the whole purpose of the argument we have been considering, but to show this? Whether it has been sufficiently shown, must be left to the judgment of the reader, who

---

[*] [Rutherforth], p. 138.

---

1 Rutherforth, p. 137.

has the argument before him. One would think there needed no great skill in logic to prove, that it is contrary to the nature of a rational agent to act *unreasonably*: the art lies in evading proofs, and not seeming to see such, as cannot be confuted. However, let it be observed, that our author is here at last so sincere as to own, that giving pain to a sensible being *is confessedly contrary to the nature of the patient who receives it*; notwithstanding all his cavils and objections to perplex a proposition, which otherwise, by a plain understanding, might have been thought self-evident.

And now, since we are still likely to ramble and wrangle on for a while, lest the reader should be at a loss to know what we are about, it may not be amiss to put him in mind, that the design of the chapter we are upon, is to confute that scheme of morality, which deduces our obligation to the practice of virtue, from the nature, relations, and fitness of things; and therefore he is to consider all the cavils he meets with, as having somehow or other a view to that end. But truly I am afraid, the very next, that occurs, will be found to have no view at all, unless the mere pleasure of disputing.

The same judicious writer, whom we have been just now defending, not having the fear of a cavilling answer before his eyes, had said, that* there is an agreement between the ideas of *bounty and gratitude, that they tally to each other with great exactness*; omitting to particularise that bounty, which a man's self had been the object of. But though he sometimes uses a general expression, probably for brevity's sake, and because his adversary had used it; yet in that very place, he much† oftener speaks in the more limited terms, of the suitableness of gratitude to the mind of *a person obliged*; of receiving benefits being a good reason why the *receiver* should be grateful; that a man ought to be grateful to *his* benefactors being equivalent to a self-evident proposition, *&c* all which our author must know, and therefore could not think any other *bounty* was meant here, than that, which the grateful person had been the object of; besides, that gratitude is always understood to relate to no other bounty or benefits, but what has been conferred on a man's self. I cannot guess, therefore, to what purpose he lays hold on this expression, to argue against nobody:‡ "That it is not the agreement between the notions of gratitude and bounty (meaning bounty in general) which obliges

---

* Balg. Tracts, p. 109. ["The Second Part of the Foundation of Moral Goodness" in *A Collection of Tracts, Moral and Theological* (1734).]
† *Ibid* p. 110, 112, 114.
‡ [Rutherforth's] *Essay*, p. 139.

us to be grateful; for then we should have been as much obliged to be grateful towards the benefactor of another person, as towards our own, since the fitness of these two notions to each other would be the same in both cases;" with more of the like nature, which I pass over as quite insignificant. Might he not, without all this cavilling, even as well have begun where he ends? which is by observing, that if any fitness obliges us to be grateful, when we have received a favour, it must be *an agreement between such a behaviour, and the relation we stand in to our benefactor.* This will, no doubt, be allowed him, and he may, if he pleases, observe too, that an agreement between the ideas of gratitude, and of bounty, or benefits received, is the very same thing in other words; for what is this, but an agreement between the ideas of a suitable *behaviour* in the person obliged, and of the *relation* he stands in to his benefactor? Well; but if gratitude is our duty, because it is *agreeable* to certain relations; "from hence," he says, "it would follow, that every behaviour, which is *expressive of* (he should have said *agreeable to*) the relations we bear, must be our duty."[1] We grant it, and what then? Why then our author has an argument at hand to prove, that *this rule will oblige to vice as much as to virtue*; and cut off at once all pretensions to make virtue consist in acting agreeably to relations. This would be news indeed, and what the reader may think must be worthy his attention, if he is not, by this time, enough acquainted with him to suspect some fallacy. Let us see what we can make of it.

"If,"* says he, "this agreement was the true reason, why our behaviour is fit and right; then it must, in every instance, be fit and right to act agreeably to our relations, and wrong to counteract them. But the relation between a tyrant and his vassals is as clear, as that between a king and his subjects; and either of them are such, as may be *expressed* by behaviour. Is it therefore the duty of a tyrant to behave like a tyrant? If it is, then relations may indeed oblige, but they oblige to vice as much as to virtue: if it is not, then there may be a fitness between behaviour and *character*, or behaviour may be agreeable to relations, and yet at the same time be wrong: and therefore fit, in this sense, does not mean the same as right, and it would be false conclusion, that an action is right, because it has this fitness, or is expressive of the character and relation of him, who does it." It would be a false

---

* [Rutherforth], p. 140.

---

1 Rutherforth, p. 140.

conclusion indeed; for an action may be very *wrong* (and perhaps have no fitness in it) that is *expressive of the character* of him, who does it. But why does this author change his terms, when he pretends to answer, and give us such, as are never made use of by any of the moralists he opposes? We apprehended a fallacy, and this is the very same, which I took notice of once before. *Character* is put here, as if it signified the same with *relation*; and *expressive of*, for suitable or agreeable to it; but I must beg leave to tell him, that an action may be agreeable to a man's *character*, or *expressive* of it, that is very unsuitable to all the *relations* he stands in to other beings: when a tyrant behaves like a tyrant, he acts agreeably to his own character, but very unsuitably to the fitness of things, or to the relation between him and his vassals. To them he is related as *a man*, and as *a governor*; by the first relation he is obliged to that equitable behaviour, which men, being all equal by nature, have a right to from one another, doing unto them what, in the same circumstances, he would have had them do unto him. By the second relation he is obliged to protect and defend them from all injuries and oppressions. In becoming a tyrant he has violated all the duties flowing from those relations, but the relations still subsist; and what new relations has he acquired? That of an injurer and oppressor. Now if all relations oblige to act agreeably to them, the question here will be, what behaviour is suitable to this relation. Is it the duty of a tyrant to continue to injure and oppress? That cannot be, for it is contrary to all the *previous relations* he was engaged in, and which he cannot divest himself of. How then must he act suitably to this *new relation*? Truly I know of nothing so suitable, as to get out of it as fast as he can, by redressing and repairing all the injuries he has done, as far as it lies in his power: this is the only duty, that can be incumbent upon one, who is engaged in relations, *that arise from his vices*.

And here if I should say (what every good man will say) "that* such relations as are expressed by vices, ought not to be engaged in;" how would this be *giving up the cause*, as our author pretends? Why he tells us, if a man may engage in some relations, but may not engage in others, "the notion of crime and duty must be previous to these relations, and so cannot be owing to them." What a consequence is this! May not the *notion* of crime and duty resulting from all possible relations, be previous to engaging in those relations, and yet the crime or duty be owing to its agreement or disagreement with them? The *notion of gratitude*, as due

---

* [Rutherforth's] *Essay*, p. 142.

to a benefactor (the particular virtue our author chooses to instance in) may certainly be previous to engaging in the relation of *persons obliged*; but the *duty* can be owing to nothing else but the fitness of acting agreeably to that relation.

We have here a good deal, but little to the purpose, about the different significations of the word *fit*: it may signify decent and proper, or right and reasonable; and then we are asked, "How does it follow, that gratitude is a duty, because it is *fit* and *right* only in one sense, when what is a duty is fit and right only in another? If either gratitude was self-evidently decent and proper, right and reasonable; or if whatever behaviour is conformable to any relation, that we bear to mankind, was apparently a duty; then, and not till then, the conclusion would be rightly made: but the former of these is the very point in question; the latter has been shown not to be true."[1] That gratitude is *self-evidently decent and proper, right and reasonable*, one would think should be a point quite out of question; for what disposition of mind can possibly be thought of so decent, proper, right, and reasonable, as *gratitude to a benefactor?* It is indeed too plain to admit of any proof, nor can any one, who understands the terms, make the least doubt of it. Gratitude then must be *fit* and right, not only in *one sense*, but *fit* in all the senses, which this author has imagined to perplex the meaning of that word: and since the fallacies of his reasoning about acting agreeably to relations have, I presume, been clearly removed, *the conclusion* he would evade must appear to be *rightly made; viz.* That the *duty* not only of gratitude, but of all other virtues, *arises from the fitness and relations of things*. For, from what has been said, a behaviour *conformable to any relation we bear to mankind*, rightly understood, must be *apparently a duty*; and the arguments, by which he pretends, that this *has been shown not to be true*, will be found no other than an artful piece of sophistry, by the help of a fallacious use of terms, and putting a false sense on *the duty of acting agreeably to relations*.

Nay, notwithstanding all this gentleman's art in contending against so plain a principle, as that it must be our duty to act agreeably to the several relations we bear to other beings; he sometimes appears sensible himself, that virtue consists in this conformity. "If," says he,* "a man asks what his duty is, who knows beforehand that virtue in general is; he should be directed

---

* [Rutherforth], p. 143.

1 Rutherforth, p. 142.

to consider what good his circumstances point out to him to be done: here *all his different relations are to be examined.*" And even when he seems afraid of being thought to have asserted here something, which he had opposed before, he cannot explain his sentiment away; "when* I say," continues he, "the relations, that we bear to those about us, will teach us what virtue is to men in our circumstances, I do not mean, that any sort of relations are the *mark or characteristic of virtue* (which if any body means, I do not know who can understand) but only that, from a view of our several relations, we may learn to practise virtue." And pray how can we learn to practise virtue from that view, unless virtue consists in acting agreeably to those relations? But if our author should allow this point, it would still be a question with him, whether it is our *duty* to be virtuous.

"After all," says he, "which these relations teach us, the great question is still unanswered; why are we obliged to be virtuous? Why is it our duty to do good, and to avoid doing harm?"[1] This would seem a strange question to a plain well-meaning man, who had been accustomed to look upon *virtue* and *duty* as the same thing, and to think, that doing good, and avoiding to do harm, were practices, that carry their reason with them: to tell such a man, that actions suitable to his nature, circumstances and relations, are *virtuous* actions, would be the same thing as to tell him they are his *duty*. But our new system of morality has not only taught us to distinguish between *duty* and *virtue*, but would have us learn too, that neither the nature, reason, relations, or fitness of things, from whence virtue arises, can make it our duty to be virtuous. Virtue, according to these moralists, is a very good thing, that is, to those, who are the *objects* of it; but is quite indifferent, has no goodness or worth in it to the *agent*, until he is secure to be a gainer by it; and then, and not till then, it becomes his *duty*.

In support of this doctrine, the author of the *Essay* goes on in his way of proving, *that fitnesses arising from relations produce no obligation.* To make this appear, he chooses an instance, frequently urged on the other side, which he gives us in the words of Dr. *Clarke*: "It is as certainly fit, that men should honour and worship, obey and imitate God, rather than the contrary, as it is certainly true, that they have an entire dependence upon him; and not only

---

* [Rutherforth], p. 144.

---

1 Rutherforth, p. 143.

so, but also that his will is as certainly and unalterably just, and equitable, in giving his commands, as his power is irresistible in requiring submission to it."[1] The fitness therefore (as our author remarks) "of worshipping God, is owing to our dependence upon him, and to the justice and equity of his commands." Rightly observed. And yet in the very next line he* supposes this fitness to consist *only in its being expressive of the relation between the creature and the creator*, though there is no mention here of that relation at all; but from this supposition he takes occasion to urge, that "such a fitness has been shown in other instances to produce no obligation; and in this instance," he says, "it will appear so, to as great advantage as in any of the rest." By what *fallacy* this was pretended to be shown, has been so lately considered, that the reader may easily recollect it. But we have here a fairer and more plausible argument, which proceeds thus: "For would not this relation subsist as well between the evil principle of the *Manichees* and his creatures, as between the good and gracious God of the *Christians* and his? And yet very few can think it a duty to worship a malevolent creator; they in particular certainly thought otherwise, who, to make out the duty of worship, added the consideration of God's commands being just and equitable. But if every fitness of behaviour to express a relation makes a duty, why is not it a duty to worship our creator, whether he is just and good, or unjust and cruel? Will nothing but benevolence in him give our worship such a fitness, as to make it a duty? Then that behaviour, which has in it conformity to relations, is not always decent, proper, and right. But does not this very instance show us what makes an action fit in such a manner as to be proper and right? It is fit to honour and obey a benevolent creator only. And what is a benevolent creator? Is not it such a one, as provides for the good and happiness of his creatures? Therefore, as far as we are persuaded, that it will be the better for us to obey such a master, so far it is fit, so far it is right, and our duty to obey him."[2] This is the substance of the argument, though I have taken the liberty to shorten it a little, and must now beg leave to reply.

Creation is the ground of so many benefits to such a being as man, that we have been accustomed to consider creation itself as

---

* [Rutherforth], p. 146.

---

1 Rutherforth, p. 146.
2 Rutherforth, p. 146, 147, 148.

the chief of them, and to deduce all the duties we owe the deity from the relation of a creature to its creator. But strictly speaking, existence is *of itself* no benefit at all, without regard to the *manner* of it; and if it were attended with inevitable misery, would be the greatest of injuries. Could we suppose a creator to have brought creatures into being, on purpose to make them miserable, nothing could be due from such creatures to their creator, but hatred and detestation; not only on account of the evil he had done them, but on account of the malignity of his own nature, his having no regard to rectitude, justice, or equity. Worship could not be due to such a creator: he might compel indeed to obedience and *external* worship; but the true worship of the mind, honour, veneration, and love, he could not force, nor would it be in their power to give, where the object was so unworthy of it. To make out therefore the duty of worship and free obedience, it is absolutely necessary to add to the relation of a creator that of a *benefactor*; and likewise to consider him as a being of perfect rectitude, whose commands must all be just and equitable. So that it is undeniably true, that *it is fit to honour and obey a benevolent creator only*. But notwithstanding this concession, the conclusions our author would draw from it will not be allowed him: it does not follow, *that a behaviour, which has in it conformity to relations, is not always proper and right*. It only follows, that the same behaviour, which *is* conformable to the relation of a *benevolent* creator, and therefore fit, proper, and right, would *not* be conformable to the relation of a *malevolent* creator, and therefore neither fit, proper, nor right. Creation considered of itself, abstractedly from the nature and manner of existence of the beings created, produces no *moral* relation, and consequently no fitness of behaviour resulting from it: the relation and fitness arise from the nature and *manner* of the creature's existence. The relation therefore between the evil principle of the *Manichees* and his creatures, (whom we must suppose created to misery) would not be *the same*, as that between the good and gracious God of the *Christians* and his: one is the relation of creatures highly benefited, the other of creatures deeply injured: consequently *the same behaviour* could not be suitable to both relations, but the different behaviour conformable to each would always be proper and right. Neither can I agree to the other conclusion our author would draw from the fitness, *to honour and obey a benevolent creator only*: therefore, says he, as far as we are persuaded, that *it will be the better for us* to obey such a master, so far it is fit or proper, so far it is right; and our duty to obey him. The duty of honouring and obeying a benevolent creator, arises, as has been observed, both from the perfection of his nature, and the benefits he has bestowed upon his creatures. If he is a being worthy of honour and veneration, it must be fit and right to pay him that worship, which is due to his perfections: if he has given us many faculties, and valuable enjoyments, gratitude and obedience would be fit, right, and our duty, in return of those benefits we have received, independently of any persuasion, that this *will be the better for us*. Supposing our creator had given us no assurance of a future state, can it be said, that we should be under no obligations to him, for all the blessings of our present existence? Or can it be made appear, that no returns are proper, fit, or due, for favours received, unless we are persuaded, that more are to follow? It is sufficient, that we are certain from the rectitude of his nature, that our divine benefactor will never deal otherwise with us than is just and equitable. This undoubtedly gives him a right to our worship and obedience, both in acknowledgement of his superior excellence, and of all the benefits we are at present possessed of, though we should have no expectation of *bettering* our condition by it.

Our author tells us,[*] he shall trouble the reader with examining only one more of those writer's arguments he is here opposing; but it is one, says he, which has as many ambiguities in it, as any they make use of. The ambiguities must be then of his own making, by imagining senses the authors never thought of; for none ever was freer from them than that[†] plain and fair reasoner he here quotes, whose words are these: "That the same reason of things, with regard to which, the will of God always, and necessarily does determine itself to act in constant conformity to the eternal rules of justice, equity, goodness, and truth, ought also constantly to determine the wills of all subordinate rational beings to govern all their actions by the same rules, is very evident." The reasons given for this, our author has not thought fit to examine, and, as if none had been given, answers by asking, "But what obliges us to make that the rule of our actions which God has been pleased to make the rule of his? Why is it our duty to follow the same law, *that he from the beginning hath set himself to work by*, if the reason of that law should either be unknown to us, or be such as we are no way concerned in?"[1] If this gentleman

---

[*] [Rutherforth's] *Essay*, p. 148.
[†] Dr. *Clarke*.

---

1 Rutherforth, p. 148.

had considered *on what grounds* we are assured, that the will of God always determines itself to act in conformity to the eternal rules of justice, equity, *&c* he would have seen, that *the reason of that law, which God from the beginning hath set himself to work by*, can neither be *unknown to us*, nor be such, as we are *no way concerned in*. Let him consider, that the common administrations of providence can give us no certainty of the perfect rectitude of God's government, but would rather furnish us with objections against it. It is from the moral perfections of the deity, which are deducible from his natural attributes, that this must be demonstrated. Now we can have no knowledge, that those are moral perfections, which we ascribe to the deity, but from our own ideas of the essential difference of good and evil, right and wrong, and of the agreement of justice, equity, goodness, and truth, with the reason and nature of things; from whence we conclude, that acting in conformity to them must be *fittest* and best for a reasonable being, and that therefore God himself makes this the invariable rule of all his actions. From this brief deduction it will be easy to see, that *the reason* of that law, *which he hath set himself to work by*, cannot be *unknown* to rational beings, if they make a right use of their faculties; and that it is such as they must have *a very great concern in*: for the very same arguments, which I have but just hinted at, as they serve to convince us, that God *does* always act in conformity to the rules of equity, goodness, and truth, must show us likewise, that all subordinate rational beings *ought* constantly to govern their actions by the same rules, as most suitable to the nature of intelligent and moral agents, to the perceptions of their own minds, and to the reason and relations of things; as well as most conformable to that perfect pattern, which God himself has set us.

To this last reason our author objects:* "This is putting obligation upon a very different footing from what was intended; it is deducing it from the authority of God's example, not from the reasons and relations of things." But in this he is mistaken; it is not the *authority* of God's example, but the *perfection of the pattern*, that obliges us to imitate him. We are obliged to govern our actions by the same rules, to which the will of God is always conformed, because they are such, as must oblige all reasonable beings, whom he has made so far like himself, as to be capable of distinguishing good and evil, and of choosing one and refusing the other. And since we are sure that God does this in the most perfect manner, knowing with the greatest exactness all the dif-

---
* [Rutherforth], p. 149.

ferent natures, circumstances, and relations of things; therefore, so far as we can trace him in the wisdom, goodness, and rectitude of this conduct towards his creatures, so far we are to set his example before us for our imitation; as one, who would acquire any art, endeavours to imitate the most perfect matter in that art, which, I presume, is never called acting upon *the authority of the example*.

But our author goes on in objecting: "And indeed," continues he, "unless these reasons and relations are otherwise *explained* than we commonly find them, it will be difficult to show, that our behaviour is even agreeable to them, when we practise the virtue of benevolence in imitation of the goodness of God: For if the relations between a creature and its creator are different from those between beings of the same kind, the same conduct cannot well suit with both, or be *expressive* of relations so very unlike. If doing good to his creatures suits with the notion of a creator, one would think, that the same behaviour could not *express* the relation, which a creature bears to those of his own species."[1] I don't know what explanation this gentleman requires; but he seems indeed, both by his former arguments, and the present, and by the terms he uses, not very well to understand, what is meant by acting *agreeably to the reasons and relations of things*. The same *rule* of behaviour may be suitable to all intelligent beings, though the very same behaviour is not: acting in conformity to the rules of justice, goodness, and truth, must be *suitable* to all relations, (I do not say *expressive* of them, not knowing what that unusual phrase may import) but the application of these rules, in different circumstances and relations, may require very different actions. When God gives rain and sunshine in their seasons, he acts agreeably to the relation of a benevolent creator to his creatures. In this we cannot imitate the *action* of God; but when we bestow part of the possessions he has given us, to relieve the distresses of our fellow-creatures, in this we imitate the *goodness* of God, act agreeably to that reason and nature of things, with regard to which his will is always determined; yet suitably to our own circumstances, and to that relation we bear to those of our own species, I hope this language will not be altogether unintelligible to the author of the *Essay on Virtue*; and that he will excuse my not using the peculiarities of expression, which he has brought into this subject; some of which I have dropped, even in quoting him, because I think the accustomed terms of the authors he

---

1 Rutherforth, p. 149.

opposes, more *expressive* of their sense, without fallacy or ambiguity, and I have no delight in wrangling.

The next argument we meet with, is in opposition to the reason given for concluding, that God always acts agreeably to goodness, justice, and truth; and that we ought to govern our actions by the same rule. This, it is urged, is best and fittest to be done, and that the will of God, being under the guidance of infinite wisdom, cannot but choose to do what is *fittest and best to be done*. These propositions have been largely proved, both from the essential difference and necessary relations of things, and from the natural attributes of God. Yet our author has thought fit to contend against them (as if no such proofs had been offered) in the following manner: "That God should* govern the world by the rules of justice, goodness, and truth, is, without all dispute, most agreeable to the nature of his creatures, and therefore it may, *in respect of them*, be called best and fittest: but as far as infinite wisdom is concerned in the guidance of his will, he must be unerringly directed to do what is *best and fittest for him to do*, or what is most agreeable to *his own nature*." And is not this the very thing, which the great writer,† he pretends here to oppose, has clearly and strongly proved, *viz.* that acting in constant conformity to those eternal rules, as it is best, upon the whole, for the government of the creatures, is absolutely *best and fittest for God to do* and most agreeable to his own nature? But our author goes on: "So that after all, this question remains to be determined; Is it most agreeable to the nature of God to do that, which it is most agreeable to the nature of his creatures to desire he should do?" Then he determines the question himself. "If he is a benevolent being, it is; if he is a malevolent one, it is not: And thus (says he) what is called a demonstration of the goodness of God, has, from an ambiguity in the words *best and fittest*, the appearance of one; but leaves us just where we set out, and teaches us no more than this, that his wisdom will direct him to act according to the rules of goodness, if he is good, but to act

---

* [Rutherforth] *Essay*, p. 151.

† *Clarke, Boyle's* Lectures. [Clarke's *A Demonstration of the Being and Attributes of God* and *A Discourse concerning the Unchangeable Obligations of Natural Religion, and the Truth and Certainty of the Christian Revelation* were originally presented as lectures for the Boyle lecture series, a series of talks funded by Sir Robert Boyle in the interests of resolving religious issues arising from the theoretical assertions of the new mechanistic science. Clarke presented his lectures in 1704 and 1705, respectively.]

otherwise, if he is not."[1] What would this gentleman be at? Who is it, that teaches us no more than this, that *if God is good*, he will act according to the rules of goodness? Where are we to find that ambiguous use of the words *best and fittest*, which has given us only an appearance of what is called a demonstration of the goodness of God? And by whom was his question left undetermined, about the manner, that is most agreeable *to the nature of God* to deal with his creatures? I really don't know what to make of all this, but am very certain, that the writer, whose arguments he pretends to be here considering, has no concern in any one word of it.* He has not left it doubtful, whether God is a benevolent or a malevolent being, having plainly demonstrated the goodness, and all the other moral perfections of the supreme being, *a priori*, from his natural attributes; he has shown, that it is most agreeable to *the nature of a reasonable being*, always to act according to the reason of the thing, and the truth of the case; and wherever he speaks of acting in conformity to the eternal rules of equity, goodness, and truth, as best and fittest to be done, his plain and obvious meaning constantly is, *best and fittest for the doer*. If there is any ambiguity in the words, it must have been occasioned since by those, who have applied them to an unusual and very trifling sense: the practice of virtue, they say, or doing good, is best and fittest only for those, who are the objects of it, those, to whom the good is done; that is, *it is good and fit for people to have good done to them*. A very instructive proposition! This set of moralists can have no notion, it seems, how the practice of virtue, or rectitude of action, can be at all fit or good for the doer. What then do they mean by *goodness?* If it is anything more than a mere abstract idea, there must be some *subject* of it; and who does it belong to? Not to the objects of it, I suppose, those, to whom good is done: it must belong to the agent then, and if it is not good *for* him, I hope it will be allowed, at least, to be good *in* him. However, the author of the *Essay*, we find, has at last been *taught*, that *if God is good, his wisdom will direct him to act according to the rules of goodness*. And by what means, I pray, are we taught this? Is it not by *perceiving*, that it is fittest and best for a wise and good being, to act in constant conformity to the most perfect rule of equity, goodness, and truth? There is no other way to learn it that I know of: Yet our author,

---

* See *Clarke*, *Boyle*'s Lectures.

1 Rutherforth, p. 151.

unwilling to perceive this, goes on, as if still *untaught* it, saying: "And if we do not know what infinite wisdom can discover, in doing good, which should make it best and fittest for the doer of it."[1] What would he know more, than that infinite wisdom discovers *rectitude of action*, or acting by the most perfect rules, to be absolutely fittest and best for an intelligent and moral agent? He would know, I presume, *why this is fit, when the agent can have no advantage by it*. To which I can only answer, that it is itself absolute good, and therefore worthy the choice of such a being. If he does not see this, if he sees no goodness in doing good, nothing better in doing right than in doing wrong, nothing fitter in making creatures happy than in making them miserable; better and fitter, I mean in the *doer* of it; if he *will* see nothing of all this, I can no more convince him of it, than I could prove, that there is daylight in the world when the sun shines, to a man, who with his eyes open should deny it. But I beg the author's pardon for interrupting him, who proceeds thus: "However sure we may be, that it is best and fittest for the infinitely wise God, by seeing, that he always *does good*; however sure we may be by what we feel in ourselves, that it is best and fittest for those, to whom it is done; yet when out of duty we imitate God, we are virtuous upon no other principle but that of an implicit conformity to his example. This, if he does not require it, would be no better than enthusiasm in us: If he does require it, but does not design to make us happy for obeying his authority, it would be tyranny in him: But if he does both expect it, and intend to reward us for it, then is this the very principle of duty, that I would endeavour to establish."[2]

The knowledge, that God requires us to imitate him, and intends to reward us for it, is unquestionably a very solid principle of duty: But supposing this not to be known, suppose we knew nothing more of the matter, but that God is a good and wise being, and is always doing good to his creatures; if from thence we should conclude, that since this is fittest and best for supreme wisdom, it must be fit reasonable, and therefore the duty of all subordinate beings, who are capable of distinguishing good and evil, to imitate their great benefactor, by doing all the good they can to their fellow-creatures, agreeably to their several circumstances and relations; where, I beseech you, would be the *enthusiasm* of this?

---

1 Rutherforth, p. 151.
2 Rutherforth, p. 152.

On the other hand, supposing God had *required* of all his reasonable creatures, to imitate him in his goodness and equitable dealings towards them, by constantly observing the rule of equity, and by doing good to their fellow-creatures as occasions offer; without acquainting them of any designed reward for their conduct; where would be the *tyranny* of this? If they were conscious, that his commands were such, as their own minds could not but approve, as tending to promote the good of the whole, and consequently of every individual, where would be the hardship put upon them? Might not such creatures say, when they had done all, *we are unprofitable servants, we have done what was our duty to do*. And how it would be tyranny in God to require a conduct, which is right and fit in itself, and necessary for the natural good of the system, though no positive rewards were appointed for it, I confess I cannot see. We do not reckon it tyranny in a magistrate to require a strict observance of his laws, if they are visibly calculated to promote the public good: this is commonly thought a sufficient reason for obeying his authority, and even for punishing those, who do not pay obedience to it, though no particular reward is assigned for those that do. And why would not the same reason acquit the supreme governor of the world from tyranny, in requiring all mankind to imitate him, by conforming all their actions to the rules of equity, goodness, and truth, upon no other consideration, than that this conduct is the fittest to procure the welfare of the whole, and of every particular, if strictly adhered to? Nay would not this consideration alone be sufficient to make every good man think the practice of virtue to be his duty, that he might contribute his share towards the natural and moral good of the society, to which he belongs, though he had no views beyond his present existence?

Extraordinary cases may indeed be supposed, where virtue may expose a man to great sufferings, even for the sake of his virtue; and then it is not to be expected, that he could persevere in it, without the support which natural religion might afford him, of a full persuasion, that God would not allow him to be finally a loser, by a conduct, which he had made him unavoidably judge to be his duty. But these cases are in fact very rare, and, in the general course of things, virtue certainly bids fairer for that measure of happiness, that is to be attained in this life, than vice can do. The tumultuous pleasures, which the intemperate and the debauchee are transported with, attended as they are with the disorder of their faculties, and the anxiety and dangers to which they are exposed, by breaking in upon the honour and peace of families; cannot, sure, by a sound mind, be thought preferable to that calm delight, that solid lasting satisfaction, which the virtuous man enjoys without alloy. And yet this set of moralists reason, as if all the natural advantages were on the other side, as if vice was *in itself* far more eligible than virtue; since, according to them nothing can make it fit or reasonable, or be any motive to practise virtue; it would be enthusiasm in man, and tyranny in God, to expect it in imitation of him, without an immense reward; whilst *vice*, it should seem, may be reasonably followed for its native charms, if no punishment was to ensue. A discovery, which I could wish had been left to the *minute philosophers*. 'Tis surprising to find the author of the *Essay on Virtue* perpetually linking *virtue and misery, vice and happiness* together, as if they were the same things, or at least constantly so united in this world: And yet he has himself* given us a description of very considerable advantages in being virtuous; and many inconveniencies to be feared from being vicious; sufficient, I should have thought, to have determined our choice in favour of virtue, if nothing more than the natural consequences of both were to be considered. What need of any bribe to follow her, *whose ways are ways of pleasantness, and all her paths are peace?*

Brief Remarks *on* Chap. vii., viii. *and* ix.

The author of the *Essay on Virtue*, having hitherto exerted his arts, in attempting to demolish the schemes of others, which yet, I presume, remain unhurt, begins now to establish his own; and in the four following chapters endeavours to prove, that nature and reason teach us to pursue nothing but our own happiness; and that we can be under no obligation to practise virtue, till we are first secure, that it will make us happy. Chap. vii. is wholly employed in showing, *that all men seek happiness*; a point I intend not dispute with him; but cannot pass by an observation he there makes,† "That there is in all of us a great unwillingness to confess, that the principal end, which we have in view, is to make ourselves happy: that all mankind are taught alike, either by fear or shame, to conceal the motives, which influence their behaviour, and to deny, that they have any design of promoting their own happiness at all." I don't know among what sort of people this author has made his remarks; but by all my observation, I

---

* [Rutherforth's] *Essay*, p. 230.
† [Rutherforth], p. 154, 155.

cannot find, that mankind have learnt any such lesson. Men neither pretend to be regardless of their own interest, nor expect, that others should be so of theirs. Many, indeed, profess a disinterested pursuit of the public good, and some perhaps not very sincerely: but if any one should pretend, that he had a great desire to promote the happiness of others, but had no concern at all for his own; he would be laughed at for so unnatural an exclusion, rather than admitted for his disinterested benevolence. It is, I think, allowed by all, that every man's *first* care should be for his own good. *Charity begins at home*, is a maxim, not only of *fact*, but of *right*, implying, that it ought to do so. But then, if charity *ends* at home too, this indeed men are unwilling and ashamed to confess, and with very good reason, first, because it is not true, that men are generally unconcerned about everybody's happiness but their own; and next, because it is a very blameable selfishness, where this is the case. Yet unwilling as mankind are to confess this, a few late moralists have (nobody knows how or why) got the better of all disinterested *professions*, and own, without either *fear* or *shame*, that they would not stir a foot, or give themselves the least trouble, to do the greatest good to their country, their friends, or nearest relations, unless they were sure of being gainers by it themselves. And let them keep to themselves the honour of their prudent resolution, I am persuaded, mankind will not readily acquiesce in a principle so contrary to their natural feelings and propensions: as long as there are any such things as affectionate parents and children, brotherly love, generous friendships, or public spirit, in the world, 'till these are no more, mankind will assert *a natural disinterested benevolence*; and yet they will confess, *that nature teaches every man to pursue his own happiness*. These things are by no means inconsistent, and notwithstanding all the pains some writers take to separate them they will very frequently be united in the same breast. There need not our author's* comprehensive views of the means, by which "the good of each particular is closely connected with that of all mankind." Men *feel* their own happiness so involved with, and dependent on that of others, that they pursue both together, even without reflecting on the connection.

And in the same manner they practise virtue in every other instance, without considering whether it will make them happy: they find something in it fit and right, worthy of their approbation and choice, something which they cannot counteract, without standing self-condemned. If it does not make them

---

* *Ibid.*

happy, they find it at least a *sine qua non*: nothing can (whilst they continue reasonable beings) make them happy without it. It is a fundamental error in this set of writers, to place the *whole* happiness of man in *sensible* good, which is what they always appear to mean by *natural good*: this may make a considerable *part* of our happiness as we are sensible beings; but sure there is some different kind of happiness belongs to us as *reasonable* beings; for what gratification can reason find in any of the pleasures of sense? Our superior faculties must have a good *proper* to them, some object, which they can rest in as an ultimate end. And what objects can be imagined so suitable to our reasoning and elective powers, as *truth and virtue?* Why may not these be allowed a right to our pursuit, as parts of the natural happiness of rational beings, even upon the grand principle of this *Essay, that men are obliged to pursue nothing but their own happiness?*

Chap. viii. leads through the various opinions of the old philosophers, in order to show, that they all agree in making happiness, or self-good, the ultimate end of action; against which I have nothing to object. But when the learned author was thus engaged, and found among that wiser part of mankind, that reason teaches us to pursue self-good, or our own happiness; 'tis strange he should not learn from them another truth, which reason taught them too, that *virtue is the good of a reasonable being.* The *Stoics* would indeed have carried him too far, for *sensible beings* ought not to overlook *sensible good*; and that this gentleman must allow was their case: whether they were wrapped up in admiration of moral good for its *self-excellence,* or as their only *natural good,* it was still in regard of *sensible good,* and was so understood by the ingenious* writer he disagrees with on that point. But this only by the way.

The *Peripatetics*[1] kept more within the bounds of nature and truth; who by maintaining, that virtue is our *greatest good,* and yet allowing the advantages of body and fortune to be good too, and the want of them an evil, might have helped our author to see

---

* See [Rutherforth's] *Essay*, p. 208. [Rutherforth is answering Balguy on this point.]

---

1 *Peripatetics* is a term referring to adherents of Aristotle's philosophy. The term literally means "to walk around," and it describes the style in which lectures were conducted at Arisotle's school, the Lyceum. Aristotle taught while walking around the quadrangle that made up the grounds of the school, followed by his students.

(with the better lights he now enjoys) that virtue may be an essential part of the happiness of such a *compound* creature as man, necessary to the perfection of his nature, and therefore his duty, though it should not be sufficient to make him completely happy in the present state of things, where the sensible part of him is liable to many evils, which it is not in his power to secure himself from, either by the practice of virtue, or by any other course of action.

But far from seeing this, our author having in chap. ix rambled through all the various disappointments, that men will meet with in the pursuit of happiness without a guide; concludes, that virtue cannot be their happiness, and consequently not their duty, since it does not secure them from many external calamities, by which they may be very miserable, notwithstanding the most perfect rectitude of their conduct. I need not be particular on this chapter, which has more of declamation than argument in it, or opposes principles, that I have no concern to support. But it would be doing the author wrong to pass by, unnoticed, a specimen he there gives of his usual art of disputation.

Some writers having said, that the happiness of all beings consists in the perfection of their nature; and that a rational being is most perfect, and consequently most happy, when its actions are perfectly rational. Our author applies* this to a *mechanic*, who works by the exact rules of mathematical reasoning; and a *mariner*, who navigates his ship with perfect art; who, if acting rationally was their sovereign good, must, he says, be happy whilst they thus act, though one should be under the torture of the stone, and the other find, that, in spite of all his skill and labour, he must be wrecked within sight of the harbour. As if any moralist, in speaking of the perfection and happiness of a *moral being*, could be supposed to mean, by *acting rationally*, any other kind of actions than such as are of a *moral nature*. Yet upon this fallacy he triumphs, as if he had defeated his adversary, and proved, that man's happiness cannot consist in *acting rationally*, tho' he makes not least mention there of the *practice of virtue*, the only sense of that expression, which any moralist (even a freethinking one) could intend: And in that sense man's happiness might consist in *acting rationally, i.e. virtuously*, though it did not in the sense of rightly navigating a ship, or making a watch by the exactest mathematical rules. But this was only to show his art in managing *ambiguities*; for, to give him his due, he labours abundantly elsewhere to prove, that virtue cannot be the happiness of

---

* [Rutherforth], p. 220.

man. This is one of the great designs of chap. ix which in general is to convince us, that we want a guide to teach us what our happiness, and what our duty is. On this I shall take the liberty to expostulate a little, and so leave it.

No *Christian* can be insensible of his advantages in having an infallible guide, to teach him plainly the way he should choose, and the end, to which it leads: but what must those do, who happen to be set out upon the journey of life where no such guide is to be had? They can only consider what course of action their nature directs them to, as most likely to bring them safely to the end they were designed for. If in this search they should observe, with the author of the *Essay*, that virtue cannot secure them from various external calamities, by which they may be very miserable; should they then resolve to quit virtue and pursue vice, that I presume would no better secure them from any of those accidents, which he has reckoned up as allays to the virtuous man's happiness; or, if they aim at riches, power, or honours, these would still be liable to the same objection: even these, how successfully soever pursued, could not exempt them from suffering by the tortures of a gout or stone, the disloyalty of a wife, or the misbehaviour of children. What then is to be done? Must they pursue none of these things, since they may be miserable in the full possession of them all? Or is virtue only to be deserted on that account? This would sure be too partial a judgment, and yet this seems to be our author's conclusion, for he does not direct men to pursue virtue as they do other desirable objects, to get all the good by it they can, and take their chance of the evils, that may attend it; but tells them plainly, that nothing can make it fit or reasonable for them to practise virtue, unless they are certain it will make them happy: Not all the natural advantages it bids fair for, not the usefulness of it to mankind, nor the suitableness we perceive in it to a rational nature; not even the hopes we may deduce from thence, that it may be itself, or lead us to our *final good*; though he* observes that, in all other pursuits, men constantly act upon bare *probability*; nothing less, it seems, than *certainty* of the event can reasonably determine men to the pursuit of virtue; which is not to be had without an express revelation.

However the philosophers he has been lately travelling with, were necessitated to go on in their journey, without any other guide but nature and reason, to teach them what their happiness, or what their duty was; and those *Gentiles*, of whom St. *Paul* says, *these having not the law, are a law unto themselves*, were in the same

---

* [Rutherforth], p. 235.

case; yet some of them found out, that virtue was their *duty*, and others judged it to be their *sovereign good*. Had our author lived with them, he would, no doubt, have assured them, that they were all mistaken; that nature and reason taught them to pursue nothing but their own happiness; that virtue is plainly not their happiness, and therefore it could not be their duty to pursue it, since it cannot secure them from being miserable by bodily pains, and other calamities in this life, and they had no certainty of being rewarded for it in another. These are the principles he labours through the whole *Essay* to establish; and therefore, we may presume them to be the doctrine he would have taught the *Peripatetics*, and those *Gentiles* St. *Paul* speaks of; in whose name I take the liberty to offer what probably would have been their sentiments upon it.

We would readily, say they, pursue whatever is most likely to procure us happiness; but if we look for it in the goods of body and fortune, a small reflection will serve to inform us, that our sovereign good is not to be found among them; and that whatever degree of good may be in them, it is in no man's power to secure to himself the possession of them. Virtue we perceive to be a good of a superior kind to any of these, more agreeable to the nature of a rational being, more perfective of it, and the only good, which man has in his own power. This therefore we think must be our *greatest good*, and that which nature and reason teach us to pursue. Virtue, it is true, will not prevent our being exposed to pain, and many calamities incident to man; but neither will any other conduct of life secure us from these. The supreme governor of the world seems to have reserved to himself the disposal of all *external* good and evil, which he dispenses when and where, and in what measure he sees fit, so that no man can ascertan to himself any portion of the one, nor by the greatest caution avoid the other. Virtue is the only good, which he has put in our power to acquire, without danger of disappointment, if we are steady in the pursuit of it. This, therefore, we conclude, must be the part he has allotted us: the nature he has given us requires it; the judgment of our minds unavoidably approves it, and condemns us, if we neglect it; we find from it *self-approving joy*, which nothing else can give, and which is our only support under afflictions. By thus consulting nature, we are assured, that the practice of virtue is acceptable to the author of nature; that it is the end he has formed and fitted us for; and if it fails of making us happy here, this gives us great ground to hope, that there will be some future state of things, where we shall find our account in it, and ample amends be made to those, who have suffered by adhering to what we must perceive to be our duty, since the very frame of our nature directs us to it.

If it should be objected, that the moral reflections of the philosophers did not lead them to the knowledge of a *future state*; this is very well accounted for by the great author of *The Divine Legation*, from their strong attachment to their false *metaphysics*. But that did not hinder them from seeing, that virtue was so agreeable to their nature, that it must be, though they know not how, the greatest good of a reasonable being. And I appeal to the common sense of mankind, whether the foregoing reflections are not more just and suitable to unprejudiced persons, under the influence on *natural religion*, than any author's scheme could suggest.

He would do well to consider to what purpose our wise creator (who certainly does nothing in vain) has bestowed on man, a judgment to discern the essential differences of things, with a consciousness of right and wrong, if he did not design, by our natural reflections, to lead us to the knowledge of our duty? These faculties are utterly useless, if they are not directions to us, what course of action the author of our nature has fitted us for, and requires of us. We could, *without them*, have been taught, that if we obey the revealed will of God here, he will make us happy hereafter; and if those, who have never been taught this, cannot, *with them*, discover, that virtue is their duty; then God has formed all mankind with perceptions and faculties adapted to moral things, of which (according to our author's scheme) a great part of them have *no need*, and the other part can have *no use*.

The design of chap. x is to show, that virtue becomes our duty, when revelation has informed us that God will make us finally happy for it in a life after this. But first the author leads us to consider, whether we can discover the will of God in this particular, by our own reasoning upon what we see now. And here he runs into various views and reflections on the works of creation, in order to observe, that the creator had, in all of them, the happiness of his creatures in view. But it is not our business to pursue him through his large excursions; it is sufficient, if we attend him, when in his way he touches upon the principal subject.

The first return I meet with of this kind, is after having* observed the influence, which the moral world has upon the good of the natural world, "That the practice of virtue is the only

---

* [Rutherforth's] *Essay*, p. [246–47.]

channel, through which God conveys his blessings, in the ordinary course of providence, to many of his creatures; that through our neglect, what was ordained for good, may fail of accomplishing it, and, by our perverseness, the best institutions may be made to produce evil. Thus," adds he, "in one sense, the virtuous act agreeably to the will of God, for they comply with that rule, by which he wills to act himself." One would think the most natural conclusion, that could be drawn from this observation, should be, that man was designed by his creator, to practise virtue, in order to carry on the gracious course of his providence. But quite the contrary; it is only made here to introduce the old questions, "Are we* obliged to pursue the same end, that he pursues? Is the law, which he expects we should obey, the same, that he has set himself to work by? Though we may be sure, from the constitution of things, that the practice of virtue is doing what God wills to do *himself*; can we from thence conclude, that this practice is doing what he wills *we* should do? Such a conduct may be the law of *his* nature, without being the law of *ours*," &c. I have† before given an answer to his queries of this kind, and shall only add now, that if the law, which God has *set to himself to work by*, were of an *arbitrary* nature, depending merely on his *will*, and changeable at pleasure, there might be room for such doubts as these: we could not in that case know by what law God governed his own actions, nor consequently, whether he expected, that we should observe the same: but since the law, to which he constantly conforms, is immutable, and founded on the nature of things; it cannot be peculiar to the divine nature, but must necessarily oblige all reasonable beings; and therefore we may be certain, that God expects we should guide our actions by the same rule, that he directs his: having made us such creatures as we are, he could give us no other law, but the law of virtue, as some of the writers on that side have themselves asserted.

However, our author stops not long here, but runs immediately off to another point, which seems to have no connection with that we have just left. "Man," he says, "is sometimes vain and partial enough to imagine, that the care and favours of his creator are confined to him alone."[1] This serves to introduce a beautiful description from our late great poet, of the care, by

---

* [Rutherforth], p. 248.
† See p. 71 of these *Remarks*.

---

1 Rutherforth, p. 248.

which God and man provide for the brute creation: A passage designed, I suppose, to relieve his readers; for I see not, that it is any way else to his purpose. He takes indeed occasion from it, to renew his former expostulations in favour of brutes, with large additions; and though we have already considered their case, we will not refuse it a review, since it is laid again before us.

Having shown us, in the poet's fine words, that God has worked for the good of all his creatures; our author expostulates thus: "Will* any one say, after this view of things, that we are therefore obliged to be virtuous because God is good? Does reason assure us, that what he does in the natural world, is the measure of that behaviour which he requires from us in the moral one? I would ask, why our duty does not, upon these principles, extend to brutes, as well as to men. If you go on with this reasoning, you will find yourself forced to confess, that our duties reach as far as the relations and fitness of things would have carried them; and that our obligations towards all sensible beings whatsoever, are exactly the same with those towards mankind. For if you prove from God's having worked for the good of man, that he could have no design in creating us but our happiness, you may prove by the same argument, that he could have no design but the happiness of brutes in creating them: and then you must conclude, that the behaviour, which tends to prevent their misery, and to promote their happiness, is what God requires of us, and will reward us for. Why is not it, therefore, as criminal to warm ourselves with the *fleece of our sheep*, as with the *fleece of the fatherless*: Why is killing a man one the blackest crimes, but to kill an ox no crime at all?" Though I am not disposed to *allow*, much less to *prove*, that God *could* have no design in the creation, but the happiness of his creatures; yet as there is no occasion to dispute that point here, and I deny not, that God has worked for the good of all his creatures; let us suppose the truth of the principle, and consider what will follow from thence, and from our being obliged to act for the same end, and by the same rule that God does. "We shall be forced to confess (our author says) that our duties reach as far as the relations and fitness of things would have carried them; and that our obligations towards all sensible beings are exactly the same with those towards mankind."[1] *Exactly the same!* How so, unless our relation to them all is exactly

---

* [Rutherforth's] *Essay*, p. [249], 250–51.

---

1 Rutherforth, p. 251.

the same? What is meant here by *our duties reaching as far as relations and fitness would carry them*, I really do not know. But I hope it does not mean so absurd a thing, as that brutes stand in the same relation to us, that mankind are in to one another; or that the fitness of things requires exactly the same behaviour towards irrational beings, as towards those that are rational. These are suppositions so evidently false, that I would not suppose they could be intended. But (as our author argues) God has worked for the good of *brutes* as well as for the good of *man*, and therefore if we are obliged to act for the same end that God does, "Why* ought we not to have the same regard, in every instance, for the happiness of the creatures below us, as we have for the interests of those, which are placed in the same rank with ourselves?" If we have the same regard for the creatures *below us* that God has, I hope it will be thought sufficient; and I believe it will be pretty difficult to show, that God has had an *equal* regard for their welfare in *every instance*, as for that of mankind, though we may conclude, he has done for them as well as for us, what is best upon the whole. It is evident enough, that the uses we make of them is really to their advantage; they are much better provided for, and even those we kill are longer lived, than they could have been without our protection, or if we did not lay up winter stores for them. This the beautiful passage our author has quoted, might have instructed him in, of which the following lines are a part, and which he much mistakes, if he thinks it in favour of his argument: "Man cares for all: to birds he gives his woods, To beasts his pastures, and to fish his floods. That very life his learned hunger craves he saves from famine, from the savage saves; Nay feasts the animal he dooms his feast, And till he ends the being makes it blest."[1]

Thus we see it is by our means, that *God provides* for a great part of the lower rank of creatures, which, if we had no occasion for them, would be far less happy than they are. Our common creator, in giving to brutes faculties, that would be useless, if we did not employ them, and to man a capacity of discerning and training them up to the purposes they are fitted for, has plainly shown, that he intended them for our service; and this makes it our duty to be careful of their interests, as far as is consistent with

---

* [Rutherforth], p. 250.

---

1 Rutherforth is here quoting Alexander Pope's *Essay on Man*, Epistle III, lines 57–66.

our own. In making them our food, we are directed by a pattern, which God himself has set us; for *natural instinct* is the work of God: by that he has licensed several species of animals to feed upon others, whom they excel either in strength, or swiftness, or cunning; and certainly man excels the highest rank of brutes, by so much a greater proportion than they can exceed one another in, as may well entitle him to the like privilege. If we make slaves of some of them, they are generally treated with much less hardship than those wretched slaves of our own species, who differ from their masters in nothing but complexion. And for such of the beasts, as are employed by sportsmen, it is well known, that they are frequently used with more tenderness and care than the rational part of the family. Thus in designing the brutes for the service of mankind, God has provided better, upon the whole, for their happiness, than if they had been left to themselves.

And now, *will any one say, after this view of things*, that, "if the* end, which God works for, is the measure, by which he expects we should regulate our conduct, we must find out different sorts of food, of clothing, and of diversions from what are in use at present." There is certainly no kind of reason to doubt, that *one* end, which God had in view, in the creation of brutes, was their usefulness to man, to feed, to clothe, and to assist him in his labours. As for his *diversions*, I have not much to say; let those, who, for sport's sake only, divert themselves by giving *needless* pain to sensible beings, acquit their conduct of immorality if they can; I am no advocate of theirs.

But this I must say, that supposing men were ever so much in the wrong as to their usage of inferior creatures, or that their practice could not be shown to be consistent with the principles, which the author of the *Essay* opposes; this would only prove, that men may mistake in the application of their principles, and by too great a partiality for their own species, not extend their duties so far, as the fitness of things, and the end of God in the creation, would have carried them; but it would by no means follow, from such mistakes, either that the principles themselves are *not the rule of our duty*, or *not agreeable to the sense of mankind*; as this gentleman supposes. So that he has bestowed a vast profusion of words, and laid a mighty stress upon an argument, which, if granted him, would conclude nothing for his purpose. However, as he had the objection, the answer, and replies in his own management, which he has taken care should be such as he might best deal with, it would be hard, if he could not bring them to

---

* [Rutherforth's] *Essay*, p. 234. [This discussion is found on pp. 254–55.]

what conclusion he pleased. "Thus," says he,* "the only method of showing, why brutes may be treated in a different manner from men, will bring us to the very conclusion, that I wanted to establish." And what is that? Why, that "we do not use to determine what God requires of us by knowing what he does himself, but by knowing what he will make us happy for." But I presume it has now been shown, that our treating the brutes in a different manner from men, is founded on reason, and the nature of things, on the appointments of God, the pattern he has set us, and the ends he designed them for, distinct from all consideration of his rewarding or not rewarding us for it.

Once more we are happily returned to the principal subject, which we will now pursue to the end, without running after any digressions we may meet with. "The will of God (argues† our author) declared to us at first by our nature and constitution, and suggested to us again by the voice of reason, cannot differ from that will, by which he governs the world: and as the former directs us to pursue happiness, the latter cannot be supposed to direct us to pursue virtue, till we know, whether it will make us happy or miserable; for before we can tell what course he would have us follow, it is necessary we should be satisfied, that it leads to the end, which he has taught us constantly to endeavour after." Very well; but if the will of God, by the voice of nature and reason, directs us to pursue *virtue* as well as happiness, a direction, which the wisest of the *Heathens* well understood, then what will become of this fine reasoning? However, let us go on with it: "So that instead of saying God requires us to be virtuous, therefore he will make us happy for it; we should reason the other way, and should have some grounds for believing, that he designs to make us happy for our virtue hereafter, before we can determine, that he requires us to practise it, when it makes us miserable at present."[1] Poor virtue always appears, to this gentleman, joined with misery! But even if that was the case, what possible grounds can we have (supposing no revelation) for believing, that God designs to make us happy for our virtue hereafter, without a clear perception, that virtue is the law of our nature, and that therefore it must be the will of him, who gave us that nature? This once acknowledged, it may be reasonably inferred, that whatever we

---

* [Rutherforth's] *Essay*, p. 258.
† [Rutherforth], p. 259.

---

1 Rutherforth, p. 260.

suffer for it here, will be recompensed hereafter. But take away this natural judgment of the human mind, this sense of right and wrong, of moral good and evil, and of our duty to practise one, and avoid the other; take away this, and you deprive mankind of the strongest proof, that reason can discover, of a future state of rewards and punishments; which is no small objection against this author's *inverted* scheme, that seems to turn religion and morality topsy-turvy, with the wrong end uppermost, and the seamy-side without.

He cannot see any force in a proof, which is founded on a supposition, that men may perceive virtue to be their duty from its agreeableness to nature and reason; nay, he often argues* as if no such proof had been offered. "Why," says he,† "do we hear of an unequal distribution of things, of suffering virtue, and of prosperous vice? Is the justice of God at all concerned to make men happy for what he did not require of them? Can they be entitled to any future recompence for having made themselves miserable by their adherence to virtue, if it was matter of their own free choice, and what they might have let alone; if nature did not persuade it, nor reason dictate it, nor God command it." I do not know what this reasoning tends to confute, except the author's own principles; for certainly those, from whom *we hear of an unequal distribution of things*, as matter of complaint, or a ground for future expectations, have either proved beforehand, or thought it clear enough to be taken for granted, that virtue was *not* a matter of free choice, and what they might have let alone: they plainly saw, that *nature did persuade, and reason dictate, and God, by the voice of both, require it*. Upon this ground it is, that we hear of *suffering virtue*, and of *prosperous vice*, as the general complaint of mankind, till it leads them to the hope of more equitable distributions in a future state. But this gentleman must needs invert the common order of our natural reflections, and begin where they used to end.

"Teach me," says he,‡ "that my creator will hereafter put me in possession of my final good, upon condition I behave, whilst I am here, so as to please him; and then, *from the nature of things*, I can satisfy myself, that virtue is my duty." And why cannot he satisfy himself of this, as well before he is taught what his creator intends to do with him, as after? *The nature of things*, from which he owns he can satisfy himself, that virtue is his duty, is, I

---

* See [Rutherforth], pp. 268–69.
† [Rutherforth], p. 266.
‡ [Rutherforth], p. 267.

presume, just the same, before he knows, that God will recompense him according to his behaviour here, as it is when he knows this. Why then will he not *first* deduce his duty from thence, that he may, with a better grace, enquire after a reward? But whatever end he thinks fit to begin at, this is a plain concession, *that we may know from the nature of things, that virtue is our duty.* Now how preposterous is it to direct men to learn *what God will do with them hereafter*, which he has *not* taught them, (I mean where there is no revelation) and not to allow them to learn *what he requires them to do here*, which he *has* taught them by the nature of things, and the dictates of their own minds, that having not the law they may be *a law unto themselves?*

But what can be expected from an author, whose head is so turned with the notion, "That we are incapable of being obliged to anything without a view to our own happiness," as to be capable of saying,* that "even God's authority will have little weight, where our compliance with it does not forward the pursuit of our ultimate end; for the cause of our obligation to practise virtue is not so much his will to have us practise it, as his will to make us happy for it." Modest and pious! The maintainers of this doctrine, we see, are for making a sure bargain. Let their duty appear ever so plain in the nature of things, or let God command as he pleases, what is that to them? Not a foot will they stir, till they are certain what they are to get by it. Sentiments very suitable to the principles, from which they are deduced, *viz.* That every man's own happiness is the only end he is obliged to pursue; that moral good is no part of that end; and that there is nothing in the nature of it, or in the nature of man, that can oblige him to pursue it, till God has assured him, that he will make him happy for it. These are principles, which run through the whole *Essay on Virtue*, and are the foundation of a great many wrong conclusions, and false reasonings, diffused through every part of it. A minute examination of these would be a tedious and unnecessary labour: they must fall with the principles they are founded on, which need only be set in a just light to show their deficiency.

To suppose a system of *social* beings, that is, beings fitted to live together, to have a mutual dependence, and their happiness to be unavoidably interwoven with each other's; and yet that every one of them, as if made for himself alone, was designed *solely* to pursue his own private happiness, is a *contradictory idea*. Again, how absurd is it to suppose *moral agents*, that is, beings

---

* [Rutherforth], p. 260.

capable of perceiving good and evil, right and wrong, and of choosing or refusing either; yet quite unconcerned about them, having no consciousness of any obligation to pursue moral good, as any good to them, or to trouble themselves, whether they choose right or wrong? Once more, if there is nothing in the nature of virtue or moral good, that can oblige us to choose it, then there is no essential difference between moral good and moral evil: justice and fidelity are no better than fraud and treachery, till God has assured us, that he will reward one, and punish the other; so that we have the exploded principles of the *Leviathan*[1] revived in a new dress.

But if virtue has no essential worth or preferableness to vice, that can oblige us to choose it, and the will of God is not the cause of our obligation to practise it, as is here maintained; I fear the principles of this *Essay* will fall very short of proving virtue to be our *duty* at all. The promises of a reward will make it our *interest* indeed; but interest and duty are very different things, which ought not to be confounded. The first is an *external* motive, that can only affect us as sensible beings; but duty becomes us as *moral agents*, and must arise from a consciousness, either of the fitness and rectitude of an action, or of the obedience due to an authority commanding it. Where neither of these is, there can be no foundation for duty; and since both these principles are excluded by the author of the *Essay on Virtue*, all that can be collected from the principle he has so much laboured to establish, is, that though neither the law of nature, nor reason, nor the will of God, can make it our *duty* to be virtuous, he has made it our *interest*, by promising to make us happy for it.

And now I would ask the author of the *Essay* whether in making this promise, he supposes God to have had chiefly in view sensible good, or moral good, the happiness, or the virtue, of his creatures? If he says (as upon his principles, I think, he must say) that God's chief design was to make his creatures happy; then certainly he cannot suppose, that God will make any of them miserable for the neglect of virtue, which he esteems of inferior consideration. And what a fine encouragement is here to libertines, who imagine they may find their happiness in their vices! for though God commands them to be virtuous, he cannot, they may think, be very angry with them for preferring happiness, which he is supposed himself to prefer to virtue. But if, to avoid this, our author should choose to say, either that the chief design of God

---

1 Thomas Hobbes, *Leviathan* (1651).

was to make men virtuous, or that virtue is so necessary to the happiness he designed them for, that one is not attainable without the other; then I must have leave to conclude, that in either case God must have originally designed man to pursue virtue, either as the *end*, for which he was created, or a *necessary means* to that end. And if so, whatever doubts this author may suggest, about our being obliged to pursue *the same end, that God pursues* (which, by the way, he has not attempted to disprove, nor given any answer to the reasons alleged for that obligation) certainly no one can pretend to doubt, that we are obliged to pursue *the end*, or *the necessary means to that end, for which God created us, and to which he has fitted our nature*. Now by whatever means this can be discovered, it must *oblige* us to the practice of virtue, though there was no explicit command or reward appointed for it.

I hope nothing has been said in these papers, that can be fairly construed in favour of the prejudices, which the author of the *Characteristics* expresses against any regard to future retributions.[1] Nobody, I am persuaded, can have a deeper sense, than I have, of God's goodness and condescension in assisting our weakness by such assurances, and appointing, for our imperfect performances, the reward of an *exceeding weight of glory*. Yet I am sorry so just cause of offence should have been given to the disciples of that noble author, by running into the other extreme, as is done in this *Essay*, and by the preceding writers on the interested scheme. There seems to me something strangely absurd in the notion, that God designed the reward of our duty should be the *sole motive* to it. Who can doubt, that it will be more acceptable to him, who *requireth truth in the inward parts*, if we acquit ourselves of our several duties to him, to our neighbour, and to ourselves, from an awful sense of the homage due to him, from a consciousness of the fitness of promoting the welfare of our fellow-creatures; and of subjecting our passions and appetites to reason; with an humble acknowledgment of God's goodness, in designing to reward *unprofitable servants, who had done what was their duty to do?* Under the influence of these principles, who would not appear before his judge at the last day, with more assurance, than if he could only plead, that he had done what God had required of him, and had directed others so to do, because he had promised to make them happy, for what other-

---

1 Cockburn is here referring to Shaftesbury's work *Characteristics of men, manners, opinions, times* (1711).

wise they need not have thought themselves obliged to perform? For my own part, were it my case, I should greatly fear to be answered, *inasmuch as you did it not in regard to goodness, truth, and righteousness, you did it not in regard to me.*

In the three last chapters of the *Essay*, the author proposes to show, that all the revelations, that have been made to mankind (which he divides into three periods) enforced their obedience to the will of God, by the promises of happiness *in a life after this*. The first of these periods is that before the law of *Moses* was given, which beginning with the state of innocence, he, at first setting out, contradicts himself, by* supposing the promise made to *Adam* to enforce his obedience, was the continuance of the happiness he then enjoyed in *Paradise*, and *not that of a life after this*. The second period is whilst the law of *Moses* subsisted; and here he engages a *volunteer* in the unaccountable opposition to a noble design of turning the objections of *infidels* against *Moses*, to proofs of his *Divine Legation*; and to a curious dissertation, which sets the command to *Abraham*, of sacrificing his son, in such a light, as dispels all the difficulties it was environed with; either of which, one would think, none but unbelievers could have any concern to oppose. It is certainly of no consequence to the design of *The Essay on Virtue*, whether obedience was enforced under the *Mosaic* dispensation, by the hopes of a future life, or by the promises of temporal happiness only; for if the promises of God to make men happy, are the sole ground or cause of duty, as it is the whole purpose of the *Essay* to maintain, they are equally such, whether they respect this life or another; and therefore the author had no call here to declare for the opposition. Neither is it of any more consequence to the cause I am defending; for whether the sanctions of God's laws are temporal or eternal, it is equally true, that they are *not* the proper cause or ground of duty. Moral obligation must arise from the reason and nature of things, not from *external motives*, whether present or future. It is therefore no more incumbent upon me, than it was upon the author of the *Essay*, to enter into that debate; and I have less inclination to go a volunteering. This part of the work should have been wholly unnoticed by me, had not an extraordinary† passage called upon me to give the reader a further opportunity of considering, whether this author's definition of virtue can be a true one, or agreeable to the common sense of mankind, in consequence of which he has advanced the following odd, and, I believe, singular notions:

---

* [Rutherforth], p. 248.
† [Rutherforth], Chap. xi. p. 281.

"If virtue," says he, "was from the very nature of it, from its own beauty and excellence, the ultimate end of man, then virtue itself suffered no damage by the fall, and man suffered but little. For though we became mortal and unhappy, yet virtue still retained the same charms, that it had before; and we lost nothing, that was of any consequence; so inconsistent is this scheme of morality with the *Mosaic* history of man's origin and fall; so vain, if it was true, would be the penalty inflicted upon man for his disobedience! The haughty *Stoic* would have smiled at the empty threats of his creator, and would in his own heart, have triumphed at the thoughts of losing nothing, which he cared for. What is it to him, that his life is to be full of pain and sorrow, who does not desire any thing but virtue?" Again, "What if man lost his happiness, not by parting with his virtue, but transgressing a positive command? If his happiness, before he disobeyed that command, consisted in being virtuous, as disobeying that command would have left him in possession of his virtue, it is impossible it should have deprived him of his happiness."[1] "Virtue itself," he says, "suffered no damage by the fall; virtue still retained the same charms, that it had before."[2] This may be allowed of virtue in the *abstract*, which is nothing to the purpose; for it is not the *idea*, but the *practice* of virtue, in which happiness is supposed to consist. But who ever thought, till now, that virtue in the *concrete*, that *Adam's* virtue, *suffered no damage by the fall?* Or had this disobedience *left him in possession of his virtue?* Had the haughty *Stoic* been as well acquainted with his creator, and the advantages of the state of innocence as *Adam* was, he would have been conscious, that disobeying even a *positive* command of his great benefactor, was a moral evil, which he could not be guilty of without departing from his virtue; for the *Stoic's* notion of virtue (as this author very well knows) was not that partial and imperfect one, to which his definition has restrained it. *Fitness, rectitude, agreeableness to nature, to relations, &c* were, in their language, the characteristics of virtue; and every one of these must be violated in the disobeying the known will of God, though in an instance, which, *of itself*, might have no immorality in it. So that the *Stoic* could never have dreamt of man's possessing his virtue when he lost his innocence. Instead of smiling at his creator's sentence, as *empty threats*, he would then have perceived, that amidst the calamities, to which he was going to be exposed, virtue would

---

1 Rutherforth, p. 285, 286.
2 Rutherforth, p. 281.

be no more so uniformly practised, or with such perfection, as to make his happiness complete; yet that this did not hinder virtue from being still his *duty*, still self-eligible, and the greatest good a reasonable nature can be capable of.

For want of knowing the *Mosaic history of the fall*, the *Stoics* were indeed a little too self-sufficient: otherwise their scheme of morality was no ways *inconsistent* with that history; for it is by the steady practice of virtue, that man must recover, as far as in him lies, the happiness he lost by deviating from that principal of moral virtues, the obedience due to his beneficent creator. How little consistent with that history, or true in itself, our author's scheme of morality must be, who supposes man to have retained his virtue, when he knowingly disobeyed the command of his God, is, I think, pretty apparent. He seems to have given us here an instance of the justness of an observation of his own, p. 64 where he says, "This is the great danger of using words, even after we have defined them, in a sense different from their common one; that when we have found out consequences, which are true, whilst the words are used in our own sense, we are very apt to think them true too in their more usual acceptation." Now it may perhaps be true, that *Adam* retained his virtue, in this author's sense of the term virtue: but whether this is agreeable to the common notions of mankind, or whether (to use his own words) "it will be unfair to extend this consequence to virtue, in the sense, which *common use* has given it,"[1] let the judicious reader judge.

And now I promise myself I shall have his leave to conclude, that the *Essay on Virtue* has neither given us a just account of what the nature of virtue consists in, nor assigned the true grounds of our obligation to practise it, since all *internal* motives are excluded. He may remember, that I have shown all the author's arguments, against any obligation arising from the essential difference and relations of things, to be mere *sophisms*; and I persuade myself, that not a few will, by consulting their own breasts, and their observations of nature, agree with me, that in denying to mankind all *disinterested benevolence*, and to the duties of religion or virtue any foundation but the *prospect of a reward*; he highly injures and dishonours both.

This last point I have greatly at heart, it seeming to me essential to true virtue, and sincere religion, that they proceed from *a consciousness of what is fit and right*, and, on that account, *accept-*

---

[1] Rutherforth, p. 64.

able to God. Without this, whatever good works may be done, or external worship and obedience may be paid to the governor of the world, they will never make a virtuous or religious man. God certainly requires us to act from an *internal* principle, *to approve things that are excellent, Phil.* i. 10. What else can be meant by worshiping him *in spirit and in truth,* by being subject *not only for wrath, but also for conscience sake? Rom.* xiii. 5.

And now we are appealing to Scripture, it is of importance to observe, that in delivering particular precepts, the inspired writers frequently refer us to the example of God, *forgiving one another even as God, for Christ's sake, has forgiven you,* Eph. iv. 32. *If God so loved us; we ought also to love one another,* 1 St. John iv. 11. Or to the reason of the thing; *Speak everyone truth with his neighbour, for we are members one of another,* Eph. iv. 25. And this sufficiently shows, that those principles, which the *Essay* most strenuously labours to exclude, the *imitation of God, and the relations of things,* are true grounds of *duty or obligation*; tho' enforced, as became a divine commission, by the authority of God, and the sanctions of his laws.

Before I take leave of Dr. *Rutherforth,* I would desire him to observe, that there is an insuperable difficulty which attends the doctrine he is so zealous to establish; which I do not find has been obviated or answered by any of those moralists, who found all obligation to the practice of virtue, solely on the promise of God to make us happy for it. I suppose it is agreed on all hands, that whatever part of mankind have, in any ages of the world, lived under *the law of nature,* they were accountable to God, and will be punished at the last judgment for their immoralities, or their neglect of moral virtue. Now this certainly supposes them under some obligation to practise it; for how can persons be accountable, or justly punishable, where there is no duty, no obligation incumbent upon them? Either therefore these authors must conclude, that those, who have known no other law but that of nature, will *not* be punished at the last judgment for the most immoral lives; which is contrary to the general opinion of the *Christian* world, and leaves the Heathens in a *safer* condition than those, who have had the benefit of revelation. Or else they must allow, that *duty arises* from that perception, which we have of the essential moral difference and fitness of things, *that law, which God has written in our hearts.* They must allow, that he expects we should attend to it, should consider it as flowing from the nature of such beings as we are; and consequently the will of him, who gave us that nature. Upon this principle, and upon this only, it may be reasonably concluded, that *Heathens*, and even *Atheists*, are justly punishable for the neglect of moral virtue. But if, according to the principles of the *Essay*, *virtue was not their duty*, for want of knowing, that God designed to make them happy for it; I see not how the author can do less than set them free from *punishment*, for the neglect of what, by his doctrine, they could not be under any obligation to pursue. Or if, rather than yield them such an advantage, he will choose the other part of the dilemma, the public may be willing to accept so easy a refutation of his elaborate *Essay*.

Appendix: Selections from Cockburn's Correspondence[1]

1. From Salisbury, 9 December 1701, Cockburn to Thomas Burnet of Kenmay[2]

Sir,

I fear you begin to accuse me in your thoughts, of forgetting an absent friend, so long it is since you had reason to expect to hear from me: but I assure you, this delay was not for want of the regard I owe to you, or inclination to show it. And yet I cannot say, it was absolutely for want of time; though whenever I allotted any to write to you, some unexpected company or business has prevented me; and I have so few hours at my command, that I am unwilling to interrupt my constant employment in those I am sure of; which I wholly give to some solid study, and have just finished the *Vindication* you know I designed in answer to the *Remarks* I had from you for that end; though I am conscious, so noble a cause deserves a better advocate.[3] But I found the adversary so weak, I could not doubt of vanquishing him with justice on my side, though I should fail to place the truths I maintain, in all the lustre they are capable of; for which I have not been wanting in care, to the best of my judgment, and yet I am more afraid of appearing before him I defend, than of the public censure; and chiefly, for the honour I bear to him, resolve to conceal myself. A woman's name would give a prejudice against a work of this nature; and truth and reason have less force, when the person, who defends them, is prejudged against. I depend

---

[1] What follows is a selection from the correspondence included in Thomas Birch's edition of *The Works of Mrs. Catharine Cockburn* (1751). Birch's edition generally gives month, date and year for each letter; however, some letters have incomplete dating. I have provided the full information wherever possible.

[2] Thomas Burnet of Kemnay Scotland, a friend of Cockburn's and a relative of Bishop Gilbert Burnet. Anne Kelley, notes in her biography of Cockburn that although Thomas Birch, the editor of Cockburn's *Works*, misidentifies her correspondent as *George* Burnet. Kelley also notes that Thomas Burnet was a correspondent of Locke's. (Anne Kelley, *Catharine Trotter* [Aldershot, Hampshire, England: Ashgate, 2002] 4).

[3] Cockburn here refers to her defence of Locke against Thomas Burnet's series of pamphlets (see Introduction, pp. 22-23).

upon your secrecy, and that you will not break it for anyone, without my consent; but am irresolute, whether to present it with my name to Mr. *A—* or not. I am most inclined to do so, and have some thoughts of addressing it to him; but of both desire your advice. I fear I must trust some bookseller, but know not whom; nor how to have it exactly corrected, if I do it not myself; but am sure I shall miss you when in town, where I think to be a little after *Christmas*: but my relations will not part with me before.
[...]
Your very humble servant.

2. From London, 8 August 1704, Cockburn to Thomas Burnet of Kenmay

Sir,
[...] I should willingly send you my *Defence of Mr. Locke*, if I knew how it might be conveyed to you; and am much obliged to your desire of making me known to a person of so much worth, as Mr. *Leibniz*,[1] whose remarks, I believe, will have little relation to what I have written on that *Essay*, being designed, I suppose, as a philosopher, and not as a divine; for I cannot think any unprejudiced and judicious person can find anything in Mr. *Locke's* principles, prejudicial to, or defective in the true grounds of morality and religion; on which account alone, I have endeavoured to vindicate the *Essay*. I am told Mr. *Toland* (who I think is now at *Hanover*) has, in a book of his lately published, mentioned that *Defence* with much commendation,[2] and as written by a woman;

---

1 G.W. Leibniz (1646–1716), a rationalist philosopher famous for his view that the universe is composed of perceptive entities called monads, which all move in harmony with one another. His works include the *Discourse on Metaphysics* (1686) and the *Monadology* (1714).

2 John Toland (1670–1722) was a theologian most famous for his work *Christianity not Mysterious* (1696). In this work, he uses Locke's epistemology to argue for the ultimate rationality of religion, a view which characterizes the heretical position of Deism. In particular, Toland argued that no religious doctrine (e.g., the trinity) should be a mystery to human reason. Cockburn is here referring to Toland's work, *Letters to Serena* (1704), in which he writes "... *you may find a Lady not personally known to me, who is absolute Mistress of the most abstracted speculations in the Metaphysics, and who with an easy Turn of Style and Argument has defended Mr.* Locke's Essay of Human Understanding *against the letters of an Eminent Divine*" (Toland, *Letters to Serena* [Reprint; New York, Garland, 1976] Preface).

yet I cannot join with you in desiring to have it translated, that (in my opinion) not being fit for a thing of such a nature. [...]
Sir,
Your real friend,
and humble Servant,
C.T.

3. From London, 19 February 1705, Cockburn to Thomas Burnet of Kenmay

Sir,
[...] I was very sensibly touched with the news of Mr. *Locke's* death: all the particulars I hear of it are, that he retained his perfect senses to the last, spoke with the same composedness and indifference on affairs, as usual. His discourse was much on the different views a dying man has of worldly things; and that nothing gives him any satisfaction, but the reflection of what good he has done in his life. Lady *Masham*[1] went to his chamber to speak to him on some business, which when he had answered in the same manner he was accustomed to speak, he desired her to leave the room, and immediately after she was gone, turned about, and died. I wish to know on what particular subjects that Lady wrote to Mr. *Leibniz*; but whatever they were, I wonder you should suspect any other hand than her own in it. It is not to be doubted, that women are as capable of penetrating into the grounds of things, and reasoning justly, as men are, who certainly have no advantage of us, but in their opportunities of knowledge. And as Lady *Masham* is allowed by everybody to have great natural endowments, she has taken pains to improve them; and no doubt profited much by a long intimate society with so extraordinary a man as Mr. *Locke*. So that I see no reason to suspect a woman of her character would pretend to write anything, that was not entirely her own. I pray be more equitable to

---

1 Damarais Cudworth, Lady Masham (1659–1708). She published two works in her lifetime: *A Discourse concerning the Love of God* (1696) and *Occasional Thoughts in Reference to a Virtuous or Christian Life* (1705). In these works, she applies a broadly Lockean epistemology to the concepts of morality and religious belief, concluding that rationality is integral to the proper understanding of each. She argued that in the interests of moral and religious understanding, a proper education for women as well as men must be instituted. She also had a philosophical correspondence with Leibniz. She was a very close friend of John Locke's.

her sex, than the generality of yours are; who, when anything is written by a woman, that they cannot deny their approbation to, are sure to rob us of the glory of it, by concluding it is not her own; or at least, that she had some assistance, which has been said in many instances to my knowledge unjustly. [...]
Sir,
Your most humble Servant,
C.T.

4. From Aberdeen, 6 December 1731, Cockburn to her niece, Mrs. Anne Hepburn

Dear Niece,
[...] There is [a] passage in [*Clarke's*] sermon of *loving God*, which, knowing your regard to his judgment, I am willing to send, because it is directly opposite to an assertion in the discourse on the *Divine Rectitude*,[1] by which the author endeavours to confirm his notion of reducing all the moral attributes of God to the rectitude of his nature, and ascribing all his dealings with his creatures to that, rather than to the distinct attributes of justice, goodness, &c. You may remember he says something to this purpose: That the virtue of a man, who does acts of justice or goodness, merely from a principle of right reason, is greater than his, who does them from the benevolence of his nature; and the more opposition his nature gives to such actions, the more exalted his virtue is in performing them. You may perhaps recollect the words* better than I; but that, I think, is his meaning. To which the following words of Dr. *Clarke* seem entirely contrary, *viz.* "Virtue becomes more perfect, when it is made easy by love,

---

* The words of Mr. Balguy in this *Divine Rectitude*, p. 9, 10, edit. London 1731, 8vo. are as follows: "When a man is born with an affectionate disposition and high degrees of benevolence, this, in itself, is not moral but natural goodness, or goodness of nature, as we justly call it. If we suppose another person with lower affections, and the same abilities, equally beneficent, we plainly perceive the moral merit of the former to be less, in proportion to the betterness of his natural disposition. If we suppose a third, without any natural affection at all, producing, from a principle of reason and duty an equal quantity of beneficence, it is manifest, that his moral worth would exceed that of the two former in proportion to the excellence of his principle."

---

1   John Balguy (1686–1748), a rationalist moral theorist and defender of *Clarke's* ethical doctrines.

and by habitual practise incorporated, as it were, into a man's very nature and temper: for so the Scripture represents angels as rejoicing and delighting to perform their Lord's pleasure." This is certainly a more amiable idea of virtue; and I cannot but think a more just one; though the other notion may be in some sense true, it requiring a great strength of virtue to act against a violent bent of nature. However, this can have no place in the divine being, of whose essential goodness we may have proofs from reason, as well as from Scripture, where his love and benevolence to his creatures are frequently urged to excite our gratitude and imitation. [...]

I am, with much esteem, dear Niece, your sincere friend, and affectionate Aunt,
C. Cockburn.

5. From 6 October 1732, Cockburn to her niece

I will not suppose my dear niece has made any misconstructions of my long silence, since she may be well assured, I have neither indifference enough for her, to neglect her willingly; nor ill nature enough, to design a retaliation of her former delays. The hindrances you have found in your intentions or inclinations of writing may furnish you with excuses for me, to whom you ought in reason to give more allowance.

Sundays being privileged from the needle, I have found time of late to read three short pamphlets in answer to *Christianity as old as the Creation*, by Dr. *Burnet*,[1] which, they say, are the best, that have been written on a subject, that has, for some time, employed all pens and heads; the only question being now, believer? or not believer? It seems, that the author's chief argument is, that God gave man all the laws, that are necessary for him at the creation; and that nothing can be necessary now, which was not so then; and, consequently, no law can be a matter of revelation, which is not contained in the law of nature; and reason is sufficient to discover them. To this Dr. *Burnet's* chief answer is, that if man had continued in the state he was created in, the same laws would have been sufficient for him. But different circumstances require a different treatment. Man was created perfect, but is now very

---

1 *Christianity as old as Creation* by Matthew Tindal (d. 1733) was another famous work espousing Deism—the view that the truths of religion must be known via reason, independently of revelation. Thomas Burnet, author of the *Remarks*, wrote in response to Tindal's work.

imperfect; which change of circumstances revelation all along supposes, and supplies a remedy for; and it is plain by experience, that not one man in a million, or, perhaps, not one man in the world, can now, with any certainty, discover his whole duty, by the light of reason, without the help of revelation; which, indeed, the *Deists* are obliged to for all their fine schemes. I send you this account, because infidels are now so busy, that all, who think, should furnish themselves with the best antidotes they can against their poison. [...]

6. From 17 February 1741, Cockburn to her niece

Dear Niece,
[...] I can give you no other account, in a letter, of the papers I once mentioned, than that they are remarks on some writers in the controversy concerning the foundation of moral virtue and moral obligation, and in opposition to those, who found them solely on the will of God, or the sanctions of rewards and punishments. One of them, I am so hardy as to oppose, is the translator of the Archbishop *King's Origin of Evil*.[1] Another person of great name, and author of the *Divine Legation of Moses*;[2] a work I have great value for, and, I assure you, a high esteem of both those authors, though I differ from them in that point. My design at first was only to strike light into my own thoughts, by remarks on the subject; but your uncle proposed to print them, and my son has sent for them to put into a friend's hands at *London*; so that if they should come to be published, you shall have one of

---

1 Edmund Law (1686–1761), Bishop of Carlisle, befriended Daniel Waterland (a critic of Clarke) as a student at Cambridge. His first work was the translation of William King's *An Essay on the Origin of Evil* from its original Latin. Law not only translated this work, but appended voluminous footnotes to the text, in which he presents his voluntaristic morality and his view of moral obligation as arising solely from hedonistic considerations. Cockburn's work *Remarks upon some Writers* (included in this volume) takes critical aim at Law's views. He was a devotee to Locke and in 1777 he published a four volume edition of Locke's works.
2 William Warburton (1698–1779) was a well-known theologian of the period whose *Divine Legation* is a refutation of Deism. Warburton was so impressed with Cockburn's discussion of his work in her *Remarks upon Some Writers* that he published and prefaced her subsequent work *Remarks upon Dr. Rutherforth's* Essay (both of these works are included in this volume).

the books: but I am in some fear of trusting the manuscript by sea, having no copy. [...]

7. From 12 June 1744, Cockburn to her niece

Dear Niece,
[...] I read the *World unmasked*[1] twice as you did, and found a good deal of agreeable amusement in it, but not a whit the more instruction, or solid satisfaction upon a second reading. If his aim was to show, that every man's conscience sincerely attended to would prove an unerring guide, why so much mysteriousness? Why such dark and roundabout ways, to inculcate so plain a proposition? (Though by the way I think it a very false one.) How are we to know, when we have found his *true*? Which is I know not what, distinct from all particular truths. I like an author, who shows, that he has a clear idea of his subject, and that he honestly intends to convey his thoughts to his readers, by expressing himself intelligibly, without endeavouring to puzzle or amaze. Otherwise, I am apt to suspect, either that he does not know himself what he aims at, or does not design his readers should. If I have any guess at your favourite's aim, it is to draw people from adhering to any particular church, and to be *Christians* at large, which was not to be plainly spoken out. This is indeed running from bigotry to another extreme. Those, who embrace this scheme, must lay aside all positive ordinances, though sure they are too expressly commanded for any sincere *Christian* to think they may be safely neglected: and what need is there of it? Cannot we join in communion with a church, that holds all the essentials of *Christianity*, and which we think has the fewest corruptions of it; and comply with its customs in indifferent matters, without adopting any bigotry for trifles on the one hand, or aversion to them on the other? We may silently judge for ourselves, and live free from party heats, and bigotry, in communion with bigots. As to the doctrine of redemption by *Jesus Christ*, rejecting that may well give offence to judicious *Christians*, since it is plainly and frequently delivered in Scripture: but I

---

1 Marie Huber (1695–1753), a Swiss deist, author of *The world unmask'd; or, The philosopher the greatest cheat; in twenty-four dialogues ... In which true virtue is distinguished from what usually bears the name or resemblance of it. To which is added, The state of souls separated from their bodies ... in answer to a treatise, entitled, An enquiry into Origenism* (translated from French; London, 1736). This work was published anonymously, which explains Cockburn's mistaken reference to its author as a man.

confess the general way of explaining it is so little agreeable to reason, that it may as justly give offence to considering men. For my part, I could never assent to the common notions about it; yet for all that I never doubted, but that a doctrine, which is the very foundation of *Christianity*, must be consistent with reason, and the divine rectitude, if rightly understood; and though I rejected some explications of it, I saw both the obligation and the comfort of believing the truth of the thing. Dr. *Clarke* went as far as most in removing the difficulties; but I have lately met with *An Essay on Redemption*,[1] that has given me great satisfaction, and, I think, obviates all the objections of unbelievers. I wish you could get the reading of it: it is the second part of *Divine Rectitude*, by the author of the first, Mr. *Balguy*. I read the fourteen letters with pleasure, and remember they gave me a pleasing idea of the whole creation being happy at last: but alas! when I came to consider the grounds of his proofs from reason and Scripture, I found them very defective. His arguments from Scripture have been extremely well answered some time ago, in the *History of the Works of the Learned*;[2] and there are several considerations in Archbishop *King's Origin of Evil*, which show, how reasonably it may be concluded, that free creatures, designed for immortality, will be continued the whole extent of their duration, in that state, which is the natural consequence of their own choice. Indeed this seems more agreeable to rectitude, and the nature of things, than that the good and the wicked should be at last equally happy, and equally in favour with God. But this is a subject too copious for a letter. I shall only add with respect to Scripture, that though it is very true, that *everlasting, &c* is sometimes to be understood in a limited sense; yet reason, and all the rules of interpretation must assure us, that such terms are to be taken in the same sense, when spoken of the *miseries* of a future state, as when applied to the *happiness* of it; so that, if one is temporary, the other must be so likewise.

I come now to Lord *Shaftesbury*,[3] who perhaps was a good

---

1   Balguy, *Essay on Redemption* (1741).
2   An English literary periodical, in which Cockburn's own work, *Remarks upon some Writers*, was published in 1743.
3   Third Earl of Shaftesbury, Anthony Ashley Cooper (1671–1713). An influential philosopher of the period who was at one time a student of Locke. He eventually became one of Locke's most vociferous critics. He is generally credited as the founder of the "moral sense," or "sentimentalist" school of thought, owing to his view that moral rules are known not by reason alone, but by a feeling or sentiment that shapes our understanding of right and wrong.

Christian, when he published the sermons you speak of, and wrote so like a divine; for no doubt his education led him that way. He was Mr. *Locke's* pupil, and seems to have taken a prejudice against him at the same time, that he fell out with revelation. I do not know from whence his prejudices arose; but if it was from the violences, divisions, or degeneracy of *Christians*, surely a man of his penetration might have known mankind well enough to conclude, that the best religion in such hands must be mingled with the passions, frailties, and mistakes of men; and should not have thought it reasonable to condemn the purest principles, for the sake of practices entirely opposite to them. Could he know the world, and think, that morality, and by consequence the good of his country, would be less advanced by the belief of *Christianity*, (even with his hard thoughts of its teachers) than by no religion at all? Without which it has never been thought practicable in any age, or country, to keep up any tolerable order in society. If, instead of that, he proposed to bring the bulk of mankind to a love of virtue for its beauty, and excellencies, and to give them all his own refined taste; he might as well (as a great author says) have proposed to make them all lords. But supposing he was not so firm a believer, as one could wish, you tell me, *that* will admit of a great deal of excuse in Dr. *Butler's* opinion;[1] for he says some people's trial in this probation state may spring chiefly from difficulties in speculation. I do not remember that passage in the *Analogy*, but I dare almost venture to answer for the doctor, that he no more meant it for an excuse of infidelity, than he would have meant it an excuse for vice, if he had said, that most people's trial in this state came from the difficulties of practice; and I doubt not you will find he had some other aim in view, if you read him again, and consider the occasion, or the use he makes of that observation. Perhaps it was to warn those, whose trials lie that way, to arm against them; as those, whose trials are in points of practice, ought to arm on that side: or he might design to show, as Dr. *Clarke* somewhere does, how faith comes to be accounted a virtue, and unbelief a vice, which some pretend are not in our own power. Dr. *Clarke* asserts, that the right or wrong disposition of mind, which leads to the one or the other, is in our own power:

---

[1] Joseph Butler (1692–1752) was a well-known moralist who held that moral decisions regarding right and wrong must arise from a proper hierarchical ordering of sentiment, self-interest, benevolence, and conscience. The work to which Cockburn here refers is *Analogy of Religion, Natural and Revealed, to the Constitution and Nature* (1736).

it is the business of reason and virtue to cultivate or correct them: we ought to bring our minds to a sincere desire of knowing the truth, and a readiness to receive it upon such evidence, as the nature of the thing will admit. That skeptical turn of mind, which you speak of as an apology for infidelity, is that very wrong turn, which it is the province of reason to correct; for it can never lead to truth, and nothing can be more unworthy a rational creature, than to be always wavering and doubting about every thing. I should be loath to suspect you of being a sceptic, for it is a very unhappy, as well as faulty turn of mind; but I do not know what to think of your saying, that *most things are involved in a vast uncertainty*. What things do you mean? The truth of the *Christian* revelation is, in my opinion, established upon as strong and convincing proofs, as the nature of such a dispensation can admit. The essentials of it are plain enough to a sincere enquirer, and we are not obliged to concern ourselves about disputable matters. But I will say no more on a subject, which perhaps you have only engaged in to vindicate your admired writers; and I do not know, whether you can forgive my taking so much freedom with them, though you may be assured I mean well. If anything I have said, can help you to judge more impartially of them, I shall not think my pains ill bestowed; and if your inquisitive mind would turn from authors, that strike the imagination, and puzzle the understanding, to such, as establish solid truths, in a clear and rational manner, you would find your account in it. And contributing to it in any measure would yield a great satisfaction to me, who love you sincerely, and am
Your faithful friend and servant, *&c.*
C. Cockburn

8. From 20 November 1744, Cockburn to her niece

Dear Niece,
[…] When you read my *Remarks* again, you will observe, that I place morality solely and entirely on the *nature, relations, and fitness of things*; for I cannot conceive how any other principle can have the least share in the foundation of virtue. But perhaps you meant our *obligation* to the *practice* of moral virtue, which is a distinct consideration; and that I do indeed place upon a threefold bottom, the fitnesses of things, the moral sense, (not a blind instinct) and the will of God: but *interest* is no part of the ground of moral obligation in my judgment; for what has that to do with conscience? And yet I think my scheme is in no danger of running

into wildness or absurdities; for what is there of either, in practicing what our nature directs us to approve as fit and right? Or in obeying God, on account of the relation we stand in to him, and a desire of being acceptable to him? The sanctions of his laws are, no doubt, of great importance, and in many cases necessary incitements to a steady performance of our duty; but they are not the *ground* of our duty, which must be prior to all consideration of them: and a man, who should conform to the laws of virtue, *merely* with a view to rewards and punishments, would not, according to my notions, be either a virtuous or a religious man. In this I am nearer to an agreement with Lord *Shaftesbury*, than you seem to be; though, in other respects, I think his scheme very defective. [...]
Your affectionate aunt
C. Cockburn.

9. From 2 October 1747, Cockburn to her niece

Dear Niece,
We were all uneasy at your long silence, till we received your letters dated in *May* and *June*, which did not come to our hands till the beginning of *September*, when your uncle got them at *Newcastle*. I know I am much in arrear to you; but my health is so precarious, that no account can be laid on my part of the correspondence. What with the cough, and while I was free from that, a violent disorder on one side of my head, with an extravagant toothache, I have had no respite all this fine summer, and have not been able to write once to my son, since he went last abroad, till the middle of last month. This by way of excuse for my not being punctual in my answers to you. I shall now begin with your last letter, and then, if I have time and paper to spare, may look back on some things in your former.

You say, "the ground of moral obligation seems a very perplexed subject. But you should think the essential difference, the moral sense, and the will of God, do all perfectly coincide." I make no doubt they do; but how will this disentangle the perplexity? Since most of Dr. *Clarke's* opposers allow none of these to be grounds of obligation at all, founding it solely on a prospect of future rewards; which (as I have observed) discharges all men from being obliged to the practice of virtue, who either do not know, or do not believe, the sanctions of God's laws. How contrary is this to Dr. *Butler's* doctrine, as well as mine! "Neither, you say, are you sensible of any inconsistency between Lord *Shaftesbury's* scheme and mine." How this comes in, I do not know, for I never opposed that Lord's scheme, nor do I precisely remember what it is; for when I read him, I had no view to the controversy I have been of late engaged in: but if he founds *virtue* on the *moral sense* as I think he does, his scheme and mine can by no means agree; for I found virtue solely on the essential difference, nature, and relations of things, not on any instincts; though I allow the moral sense its due weight in point of obligation. It is so long since I read anything of Lord *Shaftesbury's*, that I have forgotten, whether I saw the letters you mention; but I remember something of his speaking slightingly of Mr. *Locke's Essay*, as if there was little use in knowing from whence we have our ideas, in which he is surely much mistaken; but he is thought to be prejudiced against that great philosopher, for his strong attachment to *Christianity*. Perhaps you may think I am agreed with him, in his dislike of having any regard to future retributions, in the practice of virtue: but I assure you, I am very far from it, though I contend against those, who have run into the other extreme, and would have us regard nothing else.

"As to human nature's being *capable* of disinterestedness, you make no doubt but it *may* be so with care and cultivation, *&c.*" Strange! that your two favourite authors should have so little influence on your opinions. Both Lord *Shaftesbury*, and Dr. *Butler*, strongly assert a *natural* disposition in mankind to benevolence; an instance of which, brought from the first, I have supported in my *Remarks*; and the Doctor has a whole sermon tending to show, that benevolence is as much a part of our nature as self-love, and no more inconsistent with it than any other affection is. And he more than *seems* to think, that man cannot divest himself of self-love; for he all along supposes *that* to be a fixed principle, given him to direct him to private good, as the other is to direct him to public good; and he says, that men's acting often contrary to the last is no proof, that there is no such thing; for they as often act contrary to true self-love. But you entirely mistake the question, which is not, how much or how little disinterested benevolence is practiced in the world; but whether that, which there is of it, proceeds from an artificial *association* of ideas, or from a disposition to delight in the good of others, *implanted in the nature of man*? And that, which you bring as an objection against this disinterested benevolence, is the strongest proof of it; for that affection for their offspring must be *natural*, which the most *selfish tempers* cannot divest themselves of. Indeed I wonder how you come to imagine, that there is little real benevolence in the world; for I think you may have observed a good deal of it, even in the small place where you are. Pray what is all the concern among you for the sufferings of your country, when you do not share in it yourselves, but disinterested benevolence? What *deceitful appearance* was there in Major *Petrie's* kind intentions for your son? Or in the brotherly affection of the *Barclays*? And what deceit in the friendship between you and your cousin *Kitty*? I could give many more particular instances, but let us return to your letter.

You next bring some passages by Dr. *Butler*, as if you thought them something from my sentiments; I do not know why, for I have said nothing inconsistent with any of them. That I am no enemy of self-love, appears sufficiently from page 21,* &c of my *Remarks*, and I assure you there is not a sentence of that author's, that I would not readily subscribe to, so perfectly I am satisfied with the whole tenor of his doctrine. And if in reading him and me, you would rather consider the drift and design of what we say, than particular expressions, I believe you would more clearly understand both our principles, that you seem to do. In that sermon you mention, in order to explain the text, and to justify the apostle's assertion, that all other commandments are comprehended in this, *Thou shalt love thy neighbour as thyself*, the Doctor shows how the *most common* virtues of mankind may be traced up to benevolence: but then he talks of cautions, restrictions, and exceptions, which might require to be considered, on which he has a large note. In all this I perfectly agree with him. No doubt the social virtues are all included in the love of our neighbour, and the self-duties *may in practice* be reduced to it, though perhaps they rarely are. But how you come to think, that I brought *Silverton's* case *to contradict that opinion*,[1] I cannot guess. Had I differed ever so much from it, I could have no occasion to oppose it, when I was remarking on an author, who asserts the very reverse, that *all benevolence may be traced up to self-love*. But I was then upon a quite different point, *viz*. to show, that by Dr. *Rutherforth's* definition of virtue, *that*

---

* P. 19 of the present edition.

---

1 She refers here to the case of the rich miser, which she uses to illustrate the point, in her *Remarks upon ... Dr. Rutherforth's* Essay, that actions tending to overall good ends do not necessarily conform to the definition of a virtuous act (in particular, to the definition of virtue derived from moral fitness theory). See p. 155 of the present edition.

quality in our actions, by which they are fitted to do good to others, and to prevent their harm, is not a just one; for there may be actions *fitted to do good, &c.* which yet are not virtues; and for this I instanced in *Silverton's* case. His was an action fitted to do good to a great many, and to prevent their harm; and yet upon the whole, would not be esteemed a virtuous action. Now, unless you think his was a virtuous action, you cannot differ from me, for this is all I have said about it. I have not pretended to guess at his *motives*, not knowing his heart; and if I had, it would have been nothing to my purpose, which was to show, that practical virtue consists in acting agreeably to the nature, relations, and fitness of things. If you would read my *Remarks* with a proper attention, I doubt not you would be better acquainted with my opinions. You may observe, that when I speak of desiring the happiness of others, it is upon a supposition, that this does not interfere with our own. I always consider man as a sensible being; but I contend, that there are principles in his nature, that direct him to regard what is right and fit, and to desire the good of others; and that these are therefore proper grounds of obligation, as well as his natural desire of his own good. This is partly in answer to something in a former letter of yours, about allowing interest a share in the obligations of a sensible being, which I always do. But I have not done with your last letter yet, though my paper is at an end. What shall I say to the rest? [...]

[...] You ask me, who it is, that calls the moral sense *a blind instinct*, for you are sure Mr. *Hutcheson*[1] does not. But *that* is understood to be Mr. *Hutcheson's* meaning by all, who have written upon it, and I do not hear, that he contradicts it. Indeed, an *instinctive approbation of virtue, &c* can have no other meaning, for all instincts are figuratively said to be blind, that is, they act without judgment by a kind of *Taste*; and therefore you see I several times express a doubt, whether the *moral sense* and *conscience* are the same thing. If they are the same principle or faculty in us, I think, at least, they are different ideas of it, and I take care to show, that by *conscience* I do not mean a *blind instinct*. [...]
Your affectionate aunt,
C. Cockburn

---

1 Francis Hutcheson (1694–1746) was an influential moral philosopher, who held that human beings are naturally disposed towards acts of benevolence, or virtue. Human response to virtue, according to Hutcheson, is regulated by the "moral sense, a perceptual faculty which produces feelings of approbation upon the perception of benevolent acts." See Introduction, pp. 21-22.

10. From 29 September 1748, Cockburn to her niece

Dear Niece,
Once more it has pleased God to enable me to begin a letter to you (as for finishing I will not yet answer). A tedious winter had brought me in deep arrears with all my correspondents: it was *June* before I could write at all, but I have at last cleared off my debts, and now come to acknowledge yours of *Aug.* 14, since I find my last has not discouraged you from writing to me again, notwithstanding the perverseness of my politics, and the freedoms I took upon your inattentive reading.

I am glad you now apprehend my arguments better, and have come to some agreement with me on moral points. The objections you make against a *disinterested benevolence*, are, I believe, owing to your not being thoroughly acquainted with the scheme of those, whom the advocates for it oppose, which makes you not see the drift of our reasoning. You say, our concern for our offspring has much of an *instinctive* nature in it. Why, that is the very thing, which we contend for, and which they deny. They pretend, that all the appearance of benevolence, that is in the world, is owing to an early associating the *idea* of doing good to others, with that of our own interest. We on the contrary maintain, that God has planted in man a natural disposition to delight in the good of others, quite independent of any consideration of his own, and particularly a strong propension to seek the good of his offspring. You say, we consider them much as part of ourselves: and what can be a greater proof of the strength of our affection? They are really no more a part of ourselves, than any other of our species are. What then makes us consider them as such? Why because we have so great a natural benevolence for them, that we cannot be happy, if they are not so; that is, we love them as well as we do ourselves: and what is this but a disinterested benevolence? Your objections prove what you argue against: but why have you a quarrel with the world? I dare say you have none with the thing. It is certain, self-love may be joined with benevolence; and I know no harm in it, nor any necessity of determining the goodness or badness of actions, by the epithets you dislike. I do not know whom you oppose here. All we contend for is, that God has given to man such a disposition to benevolence, as should lead him to virtue; should teach him, that he was designed to seek the good of others, as well as his own; and that self-love, or an artificial association of ideas, are not the sole ground of our benevolence, or the proper foundation of virtuous practice, as the gentlemen of the interested scheme maintain.¹ And if you can read Dr. *Butler* with attention, and doubt of this, I shall much wonder: or, without any reading at all, if you but consult the movements of your own heart towards those you love, or pity, or for whom you have any good will.

Here I have had a long interruption for letters of importance, and will not now go on with the rest of your letter, for fear I should not have time or room to consider Lord *Shaftesbury's*,* which is indeed a curiosity. Nothing can more strongly show the force of prejudice, even in thinking men, than his mistakes of what Mr. *Locke* has said, and the false consequences he draws from what he has denied. How ridiculously does he run upon his denying innate ideas! about the time of their entering, the idea of woman, *&c* and learning all from our catechism, as if Mr. *Locke* had denied, that any appetites, affections, or propensities were *natural* to man; or that being adult, he would naturally have the ideas of virtue, and of God, if he made use of his faculties; not *necessarily* indeed, if he neglected to use them; for to that neglect it is, that he imputes the ignorance of those barbarian nations, with whom Lord *Shaftesbury* rambles so wildly, though Mr. *Locke's* chief proofs, that the *Idea of God is not innate*, are taken from the different and contrary nations of those, who have an idea of God; he mentions indeed, some wild people, who are said to have none. But Lord *Shaftesbury* says, "he poorly plays upon the word *innate*: the word, though less used is *connatural*." That is, he would suppose Mr. *Locke* to deny what he does not deny, for connatural is not the same sense with innate, nor is the expression so clear and determinate. But enough of this, let us come to the terrible accusation, that "it was Mr. *Locke*, that struck at all fundamentals, threw all order and virtue out of the world, made the very ideas of these *unnatural*; that, according to him, virtue has no other measure, law, or rule, than fashion and custom. God, indeed, is a perfect free agent in his sense; that is, free to

---

* *Letters written by a noble Lord to a young man at the university.* Let. viii. p. 39-41, Edit. 1716. [Shaftesbury, *Several Letters Written by a Noble Lord to a Young Man at the University* (1716).]

---

1 The "interested scheme" refers generally to the view that moral obligation arises from hedonistic considerations regarding the agent's personal happiness. Some versions of hedonism or egoism also account for moral concepts as arising from an association the mind makes between several ideas—on this type of account morality is a human construct.

anything, that is however ill: for if he wills it, it will be made good; virtue may be vice, and vice virtue in its turn, if he pleases, and thus neither right nor wrong are anything in themselves." *&c.* Now, dear niece, saving your noble Lord's honour, this is all utterly false: whether mistake or misrepresentation, I cannot say, but not one word of it is Mr. *Locke's* sense. They are Mr. *Hobbes's*[1] principles indeed, and he has his followers in this age; but Mr. *Locke* was far from going in the same tract. I wish I had you here with his *Essay,* to convince you of it; for it will be difficult to quote enough from him to clear him, and to show you on what slight grounds this slander has been raised; but I must do something towards it. First then, Mr. *Locke* asserts, that "morality might be ranked among the sciences capable of demonstration." Now this would be impossible, if it depended on *will,* if virtue may be vice, and vice virtue in its turn, if God pleases. Secondly, he grounds the demonstration on the nature (not the will) of God, and the nature of man; and, thirdly, he frequently speaks of the eternal and unalterable nature of virtue and vice, as things *in themselves* right or wrong; which is directly contrary to what Lord *Shaftesbury* taxes him with. But what has he said to give any colour for this accusation? Why, he has observed, that the *name* of virtue and vice has been given, at different times and places, to different things, as the customs, fashions, or interest of men have prevailed. This is the whole of it. He is so far from making these the measure or rule of virtue, that he there says, "the name of virtue and vice are everywhere supposed to stand for things, in their own nature, right or wrong; and when they really do so, they so far coincide with the law of nature, the only true touchstone of moral rectitude." And a great deal more of the eternal and unalterable nature of right and wrong, of virtue and vice, he says in that very place, enough to make his Lordship quite inexcusable. Yet I must own to you, I am not myself satisfied upon a review of what Mr. *Locke* has said on moral relations. His plan led him to

---

[1] Thomas Hobbes (1588–1679) was a materialist philosopher who famously asserted a strong brand of empiricism, according to which experience, or sensation, is the definitive justification for our ideas about the world. Hobbes concluded that there can be no unseen, or spiritual, forces in nature. In ethics, he espoused a constructivist view of morality according to which, broadly speaking, human reason creates moral concepts. His works include *De Corpore* (1655) *and De Homine* (1658). Hobbes was villified in his time as an atheist and the dismissal of views associated with Hobbes, such as we see here in Cockburn, was commonplace. See Introduction, pp. 18-19.

consider them only with reference to the present constitution of things; and though he is very free from the charge of making the nature of morality uncertain, I fear he has given occasion to the interested scheme so much in fashion of late, but carried, I dare say, far beyond what he intended.

You see, I have left myself little room to answer the rest of your letter; but, what is worse, my disorders, which disable me from writing, begin to come upon me, so that if I can do no more before your uncle sends his letter away, this must suffice to show you my willingness to continue our correspondence, and that I am,
Dear niece, your affectionate aunt, and sincere friend,
C. Cockburn.

11. From March 1747, Cockburn to unidentified correspondent[1]

Rev. Sir,
My disapprobation can be of little consequence to one, who sees much farther into Mr. *Locke's* designs, than I can pretend to. I confess I was never sagacious enough to discover notions and views of his, which he did not declare, nor can I find in all his works the least ground to conclude, that he had reserves on account of what he judged the world could then bear, so freely he attacked the most inveterate prejudices of the learned. As to an association of ideas, he seems wholly to have confined his thoughts to that wrong one of ideas, that have no connection in nature to which he gives the harsh term of madness, the source of the most obstinate prejudices in philosophy and religion, and of all the odd and fantastical likings and aversions, that may be observed among mankind. But I think he gives not the least hint of our owning to the same source our most reasonable, and such as we call natural affections, *&c* though he speaks of ideas connected by nature, which it is the business of reason to keep so united. Innate practical principles surely, sir, are very different things from appetites, propensities, affections, *&c.* These, I presume, may be left in us, when the others are plucked up, and

---

[1] It can be inferred from what she says below, and in the next letter of August 1748, that she is writing to Edmund Law, the translator of King's *Origin of Evil*, whose notes she critiques in her *Remarks upon some Writers*.

allowed to be natural, not wholly owing to the chance of our association of ideas. [...]
Rev. Sir, your obliged and most humble servant,
C. Cockburn

12. From August 1748, Cockburn to unidentified correspondent

Rev. Sir,
[...] I saw a book, last year, on the origin of the human appetites and affections, which derives them all from *an association of ideas*; and I concluded it was that, which you expected would soon appear from a gentleman at *Bath*, though I confess I thought it neither worthy of you, nor of the character of that gentleman; and I am since informed, that it was published by a clergyman of Lincoln, from some MSS stolen from Dr. *Hartley*. He has attacked three passages of my *Remarks* on your notes, weakly enough, I think; and I had drawn up a defence of them; but hearing the author's character, I thought it not worth my while to engage with him. He talks, in my opinion, very poorly about eternal relations, eternal truths, and abstract ideas, as if they had no reality in the nature of things, but were whimsies, which any man may form a thousand of a day in his own brain. Such reasons must mistake the doctrine of eternal relations, truths, *&c* which are whimsies indeed, if they are not conformable to the ideas of the eternal mind.

You speak, sir, of "a difficulty, which you apprehend remains, and will remain unanswered by the advocates for abstract fitnesses." Excuse me from entering into the particulars, and give me leave only to say, that I believe they think reason rightly exercised is a sufficient supply for all the wants of the human mind, without presupposing a *sense*; and that, as reason increases, it is the proper director of all the passions, appetites, and affections, which are found there, before reason can act, or any association of ideas be made. And after all, sir, what is an association of ideas, but right or wrong reasoning? Or at least must not the understanding determine, whether such ideas be truly or falsely associated? And so we end where we might as well begin.

I suppose, sir, you have read Mr. *Balguy's* tracts, one of which is an answer to a gentleman, who had made some remarks on his *Foundation of moral goodness*, upon Mr. *Hutcheson's* plan, arguing for the necessity of presupposing a *moral sense*, for the support of virtue. But he there so strongly shows the sufficiency of reason or intelligence for that end, and its superior power, that I would rather suppose you had not read it, since you seem at a loss for an origin of our moral maxims, without recurring to a *sense* or a *habit*. Surely, sir, the reasonable faculties of a moral agent will account for them much better. And I was in hopes my *Remarks* on Dr. *Rutherforth* would have given you some satisfaction on the point of the fitness of other views than private happiness in a moral agent, *&c*.

As to the notion of an internal necessity, considered as the ground of the divine existence, it is no doubt a point of great depth and difficulty; perhaps incomprehensible by any finite mind: but that it destroys the very notion of a first cause, or gives any advantage to the Atheist, I can by no means see, after all I have read about it, by the assistance, for which I am obliged to you: The necessity is not external to the divine nature, nor dependent on anything distinct from it; but may rather be considered as a perfection of the Deity to exist by a necessity of his own nature; which implies existing from all eternity, and this can in no way destroy the notion of *first cause*; nor can it be of any service to the Atheist, but by consequences, which the maintainers of existing by necessity disown, and think too absurd even for an Atheist to urge. Necessity is one uniform thing: a series of necessities, carried on to infinity, will be but one and the same necessity still. But what will not the Atheist draw in to his service? Do not the *Spinozists*[1] apply the notion of existing *absolutely without any cause*, to the whole universe of beings, which they affirm has existed *without any cause* from all eternity. The friends of religion need not invent objections for them against a principle, which Dr. *Clarke* advanced solely for such metaphysical Atheists, as would not be convinced by the present phenomena of nature, much less by revelation. If it should satisfy any one of them, there is a brother gained. If not, he is but where he was. And no Theist can be lost by this principle: if he thinks it an error, he will let it alone; if a truth, he will the more profoundly adore the eternally necessary being.

---

1 Cockburn here refers to the followers of Benedict de Spinoza (1632–77), a rationalist philosopher who espoused the view that there is a rational order to the universe which can be known by the human mind. He famously asserted that God is identified with this rational order—a type of pantheism which earned him infamy, and the label of *atheist*. His works include *Tractatus Theologico-politicus* (1670) and *Ethics* (1677).

I beg pardon for entering so much into controversy, which I was far from intending, when I began, but writing to a person of Mr. [Law's] character insensibly draws one into subjects, with which he is most conversant. I wish I could come nearer to an agreement, especially on moral points, with one, of whose judgment I have so high an esteem: but we cannot make things appear to us otherwise than they do, or see with the eyes of others; and though we differ, I am not the less,
Rev. Sir, your respectful and most humble servant
C. Cockburn.

13. From Undated response to Sharp's letter of 8 August 1743, Cockburn to Dr. Thomas Sharp[1]

I am much encouraged in the design of printing my papers, by the favourable opinion of so good a judge as Dr. *Sharp*; who, no doubt, upon a thorough consideration, would be much better able than I am, to clear up the difficulties he finds in Dr. *Clarke's* scheme. But since he is so condescending to my weak attempts, I shall freely give my thoughts upon them. It is, I think, a good step towards removing them; that he is entirely against those, who would lay the foundation of moral obligation on such low principles, as *self-love* and *self-interest*; for, I believe, upon a farther reflection it will appear, that we must either lay it there, or upon the nature, relations, and fitness of things.

As to the word *foundation*, though metaphorically applied to those subjects, I do not find, that there is any ambiguity in the use of it, or that any misunderstanding has happened for want of explaining it. When it is spoken of *moral virtue*, it is commonly, I suppose, understood (at least I have always taken it) to mean the ground, on which moral virtue *solely* arises, or that, without which there could be no such thing as virtue. And such a foundation, I think, can be no other than the necessary relations and essential differences of things; for upon these even the virtue of obeying the will of God must be founded; since, on a supposition that there were no essential differences, or fitnesses resulting from them, there could be no more *goodness* in obedience, than in the contrary.

As to the second question, whether moral virtue and moral obligation must have the same foundation, and in the same

---

1 Thomas Sharp (1693–1758), a prominent theologian and biographer, who wrote primarily on questions of religious doctrine.

sense? it seems clear to me, that if the *nature and reason* of things is the foundation of *moral virtue*, it must be the foundation of *moral obligation* likewise to *reasonable* beings. Yet not in such a sense, as that there can be no other foundation of it. The *moral sense*, and the *will of God*, are both grounds of obligation to moral agents; though perhaps their being so may be ultimately resolvable into the eternal *reason and truth* of things, which I take to be the most noble of all principles, as that, to which the divine will itself is always conformed.

On the third question, whether the reason, nature, and fitness of things, when considered as *antecedent* to the divine will, do appear under *that* consideration to be obligatory to morality? I have largely expressed my sentiments in the papers, but not, it seems, to the judicious Doctor's satisfaction; who apprehends, that *rules* of action, and *obligation* to action, may be *quite distinct, &c.* For my part, I know not how to conceive *reasons* or rules of action, (I mean eternal and immutable reasons) distinct from *obligation* to action. The reasons of a law are indeed distinct from the *authority* of the law; and those laws, that are founded on *temporary and mutable* reasons, oblige solely by the authority of the legislator; but those, that are founded on the *necessary* relations and *essential differences* of things, have, from those eternal reasons, a *right* of obliging moral agents *prior* to the authority, that enforces them. The reasons and authority, though distinct, are, as I conceive, both proper foundations of obligation; for what are reasons and rules of action, if they do not oblige reasonable beings to act conformably to them?

I would ask, for what end was man endued with a faculty of perceiving the essential differences of things? It is said by Mr. *Warburton* and others, that they are the rule, which God has given his creatures to *bring them to a knowledge of his will.* Very good; it is certainly a rational deduction from those *perceptions*, that it must be the will of the author of our nature, that we should act suitably to them; and this discovery lays us under an *additional* obligation. But by what means do those perceptions bring us to this knowledge? Is it not by first showing us our duty, showing us what course of action our nature requires us to follow, and forcing us to stand self-condemned, if we counteract them? And must not then the essential differences be the *primary* foundation of moral obligation? What then can hinder them from continuing to have a *right* of obliging reasonable beings, even though such beings should stop short of considering them as a *rule, by which to know the will of God,* either from having false notions, or no notions at all of a Deity? Since, notwithstanding this, they will unavoidably *approve or condemn* their own, and other men's actions, according to the *immutable nature* of things. And that this brings them under *obligation*, I the rather insist on, because I see not otherwise, how it is possible to solve the difficulty proposed to Mr. *Warburton*.

The Doctor enquires, if there is any inconsistency in resolving morality, as considered to be in the mind of God *before creation*, into the divine *understanding*; and morality, considered in its *obligations on rational creatures*, into the *divine will?* I should think this a very proper distinction, if applied to *positive* precepts: but if by morality is understood that law, which *necessarily* results from the nature of such a system as mankind; and which God eternally saw, would be fit and right for them to practice, whenever he pleased to determine their existence; I do not apprehend, how the *obligations* to morality thus understood can, any more than the eternal reasons of them, be *ultimately* resolved into the *divine will*. It is very true, as the Doctor finely reasons, that obligation to morality could not *take place*, till God had expressed his *will* as well as his wisdom in a system of works, exhibiting those relations and fitnesses that were eternally in the divine mind. But I see not how it follows from thence, that the *foundation* of obligation to conform to those fitnesses *could not be antecedent to the divine will*; since the ratios themselves are allowed to be so, according to which the divine will determined to create such a system; for it is those *eternal ratios*, that are maintained to be the ultimate *foundation* of moral obligation. The *obligation itself* indeed, being *subsequent* to the creation, though founded on the eternal reason and nature of things, may perhaps be more properly said to be antecedent to all *consideration* of the divine will, and to any *prospect* of reward or punishment. Whether this *distinction* might, in any measure, contribute to reconcile the advocates of Dr. *Clarke* and Dr. *Waterland*,[1] I much doubt, since the last seem resolute to admit of no obligation but what arises from a superior will.

But I would ask, if the will of God is supposed to be the *only* foundation of moral obligation, upon what grounds we are obliged to obey his will? I can conceive no other, but either his

---

1 Daniel Waterland (1683–1740), a theologian and writer. In his work *A Vindication of Christ's Divinity* (1719) he attacked what he perceived to be heretical tendencies in *Clarke's* views.

absolute power to *punish and reward*; or the *fitness* of obedience from a creature to his creator. The first of these would bring us down, I fear, to those low principles the Doctor disapproves; and if that is rejected, the other returns us to that reason, nature, and essential differences of things, into which, I apprehend, all obligation must at last be resolved.

The Doctor is pleased to impute to an *undistinguishing* head, that he could never tell how to separate the essential differences of things (as they now appear to moral agents) from the will of God. But though he cannot *separate*, no doubt he does *distinguish* them. "All *created* nature (as he justly says) is an expression of the will of God in these very essential differences and fitnesses flowing from them." They are indeed expressions of his will, that all his own works, and the free actions of moral agents, should be conformable to them: But he did not *create* those necessary and eternal truths, according to which the perfect rectitude of his will determined him to act. His will may therefore be *distinguished* from those essential truths, to which it conformed, though, as they entirely *coincide*, I think they ought not to be *separated*.

I do not know, whether there is anything in these reflections, that may deserve the attention of Dr. *Sharp*; but I hope he will receive them as instances of my respect, and a desire of approving my sentiments to his judgment, being, with the greatest esteem,
His most humble servant,
C. Cockburn.

14. From 14 October 1743, Cockburn to Dr. Thomas Sharp

Rev. Sir,
1. Though I fear I am but ill qualified to continue a debate with you, who appear to have been more conversant than I with the writers on the subjects we are enquiring about; and to have gone into nicer distinctions, and more remote views of them, than I have had occasion to consider; yet I beg leave once more to lay before you my plain apprehensions, upon those *farther thoughts* you have condescended to favour me with.

2. After setting down what I apprehend the writers on the subject of moral virtue understand by the word *foundation*, *viz.* *The ground, on which virtue solely arises;* you are pleased to ask, *but are they agreed, whether this ground be any one simple principle, or compounded of more principles than one?* To which I answer, no cer-

tainly. They are far from agreeing, whether this *ground* is the reason and nature of things, the will of God, the moral sense, or all three united; for that is the very matter in dispute. But then, Sir, I do not take these to be *different senses* of the word foundation: all these writers seem to me to agree in the general idea of a foundation, and each of them to apply that word in the *very same sense* to his own principle, as the ground, upon which he thinks virtue *solely* arises. [...]

3. As to those, whom you suppose to have different conceptions of that word, because one considers it as the ground, from which virtue *immediately* arises, and another considers it as a more *remote* ground, on which it arises, by the *intervention of some mediums:* I confess I do not well apprehend the use of mediums for the production of virtue, if a sufficient ground of it is allowed, into which it must be ultimately resolved. But as I have had no occasion to consider these nice distinctions, which have not come in my way, I may be in danger of blundering about them, and therefore shall only say, that I imagine these authors may agree in their idea of foundation, as *a real ground, on which virtue arises*, though one excludes, and another admits the intervention of mediums, which do not hinder the ground from remaining immovably the same.

4. You next object to the *explanation* of my ground, *viz. that, without which there could be no such thing as virtue;* that this seems not to enter into *their* notion of foundation, who place it in self-love, and self-interest; for virtue, you say, even according to them, may be considered as *disinterested.*

5. Now here again, Sir, you are gotten among authors, that I am a stranger to; for though I have met with several, who make *self-interest* the foundation of *moral obligation*, I know of none, who make it the foundation of *virtue*. This those writers commonly deduce from the will of God. But if those you speak of, *found virtue on self-interest,* and yet allow, that it may be considered as *disinterested*; there must be such inconsistencies in their schemes, and such confusion in their ideas, both of *virtue* and *foundation*, that I will not pretend to answer for what they may mean by either.

6. But on this occasion, Sir, I am obliged to take notice of a mistake you have made in setting down as my words, that the foundation of *moral virtue*, upon farther reflection, will be found to lie, either in the essential differences, *&c* or in self-love and self-interest; upon which you remark, *but not in the same sense of foundation*. Now, sir, if you please to look once more into my last

paper, you will find, that those words were spoken of *moral obligation,* and not of *moral virtue*; for I had no notion of anyone's founding *virtue* on self-love and self-interest. And as to your remark, there was no occasion to consider, in what sense foundation might be applied to those principles, since my only intention was to engage you on the side of the essential differences, by observing, that *obligation* must either be founded on them, or on those *low principles,* which you had before agreed with me in rejecting.

7. Again, you object to my explaining the word foundation, by calling it *that, without which there could be no such thing as virtue,* that the same may be said of free will, or of reason in moral agents: supposing them away, there is an end of moral agency, an end of all virtue. And yet you conclude, I would not call these foundations, at least not the *sole* foundation, *purely because they are absolutely necessary to the very being of virtue.* Reason and free-will I acknowledge, sir, to be absolutely necessary to *moral agency:* they are qualifications, without which there could be no such thing as *the practice of virtue,* and may, if you please, be called *foundations of virtuous practice.* But that is quite another idea, than *the general abstract nature of virtue,* the foundation of which we are enquiring about; and to the constituting or production of virtue in this sense, I see not that anything can be necessary, or at all contribute, but the immutable relations and essential differences of things, from which virtue, considered in its *abstract nature,* directly and solely arises. If this idea were strictly kept to, as it ought to be in the question concerning the origin of virtue, there would perhaps have been less disagreement about it; for I apprehend there has been much ambiguity in the use of the term *virtue,* though I cannot perceive any in that of the word *foundation.*

8. But to go on with your objections, *space,* you say, *is that, without which there could be no such thing as matter:* yet you suppose I would not infer from hence, that *space was a foundation, and the sole foundation of matter.* So far from it, sir, that I cannot consider space as having anything at all to do with the *production* of matter; and therefore I should rather choose to say with respect to them, that *the existence of matter supposed,* the existence of space must be likewise admitted. But the dependence of virtue on the essential differences, *&c* is of quite another nature, since it entirely derives its being from them.

9. If your ingenious florists who dispute about the origin of a flower, or the admirers of music, whose enquiry into the true *foundation* of it you so elegantly describe, are agreed, that the

thing they seek for is, *the ground, on which the flower, or the music solely arises, or, that to which either owes its being*: then it should seem plain, that they are all agreed in the sense of the word *foundation*, and only differ about the thing, to which it may be most properly applied. And if their error lies in each man's making his beloved principle the *sole foundation* of the flower, or of the music; when various principles contribute to their respective beings; then this controversy is not to be decided by the definition of a foundation, the general idea of which will agree indifferently to one or more principles; but till they can convince each other, either that some one, or more, or all the principles together, go to the production of the flower, or the music; they may indeed *dispute to the world's end*, notwithstanding the exactest agreement in their idea of *foundation*. A company of architects might dispute forever, whether stone, or brick, or wood, or all together, were the most proper foundation for a house; and yet have all the very same idea of foundation, *as that on which a house is solely erected.* And this, sir, I apprehend to be pretty nearly a parallel case with that of the contenders about the *foundation of moral virtue*, who, I cannot but think, are generally agreed in the precise meaning of that word.

10. But now, Sir, it is not the same as to the term *virtue*, which you next consider; for I am apt to think there is a great deal of ambiguity in the use of *that*, as I hinted before. Not but I am persuaded, that most people are agreed in their general notion of the *nature* of virtue; but when writers come to contend about the foundation of it, they are apt to substitute in place of the *nature of virtue*, either our *idea* of it, or the *practice* of it by moral agents. And this perhaps may have been some occasion of their assigning different foundations to virtue; for our *idea* of virtue, or our *practice* of it, may arise from other *grounds* than that, on which the *abstract nature* of virtue is founded. And these different senses of the term *virtue* may occasion likewise various *definitions* of it, everyone defining it according to the light he has viewed it in, and to the foundation he has given it in that view. For you may be pleased to observe, that the several definitions you have instanced in, are rather *determinations of the foundation* of virtue, than *explications of its nature*. For instance, to say, that virtue is a *conformity of a reasonable creature to the will of its creator*, is the same as to say, that the will of the creator is the foundation of virtue: but this gives us no manner of light into the *nature of virtue*, till we are informed by other means what the will of the creator is, and therefore is no proper definition of it. The same may be said of

the rest, excepting only that, which considers virtue as *the conformity of a reasonable creature to the nature and reasons of things*; for that directly acquaints us with the nature of virtue. It is true, this definition determines likewise the foundation of virtue, which in this controversy is a kind of *begging the question*: but then it may be said in excuse of this, (what cannot be said of any of the others) that it is scarce possible to give a just and proper definition of virtue, without expressing its relation to the nature and essential differences of things. And this too may serve as a proof, that virtue owes its origin solely to them, since the consideration of them enters necessarily into the just idea of its essence. And give me leave to say, that even in the different views, according to which the several writers have defined virtue, the reasons and immutable nature of things might be (what you think is in vain to search for) *a common foundation to support them all*: all may easily be resolved into them, and securely rest upon them.

11. I agree with you, Sir, that the precise meaning of *obligation* is as little settled, as you suppose that of the term foundation to be: and yet I cannot think with you, that it is chiefly owing to the different notions of obligation, that we have different foundations assigned to it; for I have all along allowed, that there are several *grounds* of obligation, though I have constantly kept to one precise meaning of that term. And according to my apprehensions of this matter, there can be but *one sort of obligation*, if there were fifty different foundations of it. What you call three sorts of obligation seems to me three sorts of foundations, upon which obligation in *one and the same sense* may, and does arise. Obligation surely is, or ought to be the same idea, whatever is supposed to be the foundation of it. I acknowledge, that the precise meaning of it has not been scientifically settled, and that some have obscured, and others begged the question by defining it; but I do not find, that any misunderstandings have happened in the controversy from these defects. I believe, Sir, you will allow, that people in common discourse understand one another well enough, when they say they are *under an obligation* to do such or such a thing, though perhaps they could not define the word. And so writers on the subject may be sufficiently agreed in the general meaning of the word, to talk to the purpose about it without explaining it; which some of the best of those on Dr. *Clarke's* side of the question seem to have thought unnecessary, by their neglecting to do it. And this has been complained of by one of their adversaries, who himself defines obligation to be *such a necessity of action, as is consistent with liberty*: which I think does not

make the term more intelligible than it was. Others of them tell us, they mean by it a *necessity of action arising from a prospect of obtaining happiness, or avoiding misery.* And this I take to be begging the question in favour of their beloved principle. But the most accurate and judicious writer on Dr. *Clarke's* side, that I have met with, defines obligation to be *a state of the mind, into which it is brought by the perception of a plain reason for acting or forbearing to act, arising from the nature, circumstances, or relations of persons or things.* Yet I think this defective, as not explaining what that state of mind is, in which he places obligation; besides that it is a kind of determining the foundation he assigns to it, which is the subject of debate, and the fault I observed in their adversaries. After so many great names as have engaged in this controversy, I have not ventured upon any definition of obligation in my *Remarks*, nor did any occasion for it offer. But since we are now upon the unsettled meaning of that term, I take the liberty, Sir, to lay before you the explanation I would choose to give it, and leave to your judgment, whether it is less exceptionable than those I have objected against. By obligation then I understand, *such a perception of an inducement to act, or to forbear acting, as forces an agent to stand self-condemned, if he does not conform to it.* This I think expresses that *state of mind*, which my admired author hints at; and it determines no particular foundation, though it may suit with them all; and therefore it might be equally received by the maintainers of each. But I much doubt whether their agreement in this meaning of *obligation* would bring them all to agree on the *grounds*, from which it arises.

12. We have now come, Sir, to the last and most important question between us, whether the reason, nature, and fitness of things, considered as antecedent to the divine will, do appear under *that consideration*, to be obligatory to morality, or whether rules of action, *&c*. In my answer to this, it seems, I have not considered eternal rules in the same view, in which you took them, when you asked the question. I confess, Sir, I did not consider them in the view you have now explained them; for I did not apprehend, that you intended to enquire, whether the eternal reasons of things were *obligatory* before there were any creatures capable of obligation; or, that you meant by *antecedent to the will*, antecedent to his will *as expressed in the creation.* These are remote views, in which I had never before occasion to consider things, except with respect to the Deity himself, who is said to be eternally obliged by the eternal ratios: but in that I do not see, that the present controversy is directly concerned.

That, which Dr. *Clarke* and his followers maintain, is, that the immutable nature and truth of things have, in themselves, an obligatory power, to which all reasonable beings ought to conform; and that this right of theirs is antecedent to the divine will, that is, to any *declaration* of it, by an *explicit* command to practice moral duties; antecedent to all *consideration* of the will of God in them, or of reward and punishment annexed to the observance or neglect of them. This is plainly their meaning. But when their adversaries support the contrary doctrine, by arguing, that the relations and fitnesses of things, and the obligation to conform to them, are *consequences of the determination of the will of God in the creation*, and therefore cannot be antecedent to his will; they put a manifest fallacy upon their readers (which perhaps they themselves are not aware of) by substituting a quite different consideration of things, in the room of that, which they pretend to oppose, *viz.* particular existences, for *general abstract ideas*; and the will of God, as expressed in the creation, for the will of God *explicitly discovered* by the command of moral duties. The question surely is not, whether the eternal reasons of things were obligatory to reasonable creatures, before the will of God had brought any such into existence; for who ever supposed this? But if God created a system of beings, conformably to certain relations and fitnesses eternally perceived by the divine understanding; and if he gave them no other law but what resulted from their nature, discoverable by their natural faculties: Then the query is, whether that law of nature does not *in itself* oblige them to conform to it, before any discovery *either by reason* or revelation of the will of God concerning it? To urge, in answer to this, that *the will of God is expressed in the creation, exhibiting those relations and fitnesses, &c* is a plain fallacy (though it has passed unobserved) for the will of God, *as expressed in the creation*, is the very same with that reason and truth of things, which are said to be obligatory *as such*, without *considering* them as the will of God. They are indeed, perfectly conformable to the will of God, but not *explicitly discovered* to be so, or considered under that formality; yet have a *right in themselves* of obliging moral agents, whenever any such exist, independently of any consideration of the will of God in them: So, that, though obligation could not take place, as I observed, till God had exhibited those eternal ratios in a system of beings conformable to them; still the rule of their duty, and their obligation to conform to it, must, as I apprehend, be ultimately resolved into those eternal truths, according to which they were formed, and by which they were left to discover what course of action their nature required of them to follow. And all I think, that can be justly *inferred* from obligation's being *subsequent to the creation*, is, that the *existence* of creatures, *capable of obligation*, is solely resolvable into the divine will.

What I have said, Sir, will, I hope, set me right in your thoughts as to any mistake I may have been in of your meaning, or any misapprehension you may have had of mine; though I do not minutely go through every particular relating to them, for fear of being tedious, and giving you too much trouble. But I beg leave to take notice of a *distinction* you have supposed for me, where I intended none. You are pleased to say, that on the discussion of this last query, *it appears, that they*, viz. the reason, nature, and fitness of things, when considered as antecedent to the divine will, *are not obligatory themselves, but they are nevertheless a foundation of obligation*. Now, Sir, as I have all along maintained, that those eternal ratios are absolutely obligatory under every consideration; when I said they were *foundations of obligation*, I took that to be an equivalent expression with the other, and therefore used them indifferently, designing no distinction; and wherever I have affirmed, that any principle is a *foundation of moral obligation*, I beg to be understood, that it is *obligatory to morality*.

13. You tell me, Sir, that you will not deny, that the eternal ratios are, in *some sense*, a foundation of obligation; but if I make them the *primary* and the *ultimate* foundation, of this you must doubt. Now if they are neither the one nor the other of these, I cannot guess in *what sense* you allow them to be a foundation at all. You add, that, as you observed upon the second question, they can only be considered as a foundation of obligation in one particular sense of obligation, among three senses that it is taken in. But here the difference between us is, that what you call three *senses of obligation*, I look upon as three *distinct foundations* of it, and allow them all to be properly such. *The right, that truth has to be preferred before falsehood*, is according to my apprehension, not obligation, but *a ground from where obligation arises*; and this I must have leave to call the *ultimate foundation* of it, or that, into which all obligation must be resolved, since the moral sense, and even the will of God, can only oblige, in virtue of reason, and truth, and the fitness of things.

14. What you say of the claim the *moral sense* would have to the primacy by my argument, as the first principle, that lays men under moral obligation, I think, may admit of a doubt: It seems to depend so much on custom, education, *&c* that I apprehend it

rather to be a *consequence* of the perception, which every mind has, in some degree, of the essential difference of good and evil. However, I was only taking notice, that our knowledge of duty, by those essential differences, was previous to our discovery of *the will of God* in them, and that therefore they were a foundation of obligation prior to it.

15. And now, Sir, however we may differ about the use of terms in this controversy; and though I must still maintain, that the essential differences of things are the *sole* foundation of moral virtue (the nature of which I cannot apprehend to depend on *will*, being eternally what it is in the divine understanding) and that I must likewise consider them as the *ultimate*, though not the *sole* foundation of moral obligation: yet I entirely agree with you in your conclusion, *that the only proper ultimate foundation of moral virtue, and moral obligation, is God himself, the fountain of everything, that is perfect, true, or right, &c.* All essential truths are but the necessary perceptions of the *eternal mind*; and acting agreeably to them is acting in conformity with the most *perfect will*. So that I hope, Sir, you will allow, that virtue and obligation cannot have a more sacred or divine origin, than that, which the followers of Dr. *Clarke* assign them; and if you cannot altogether agree with them, you will at least excuse the shortsighted views of one, who would gladly see things in the same light with you, of whose judgment and candor I have the highest esteem, and am,
Sir,
Your most humble Servant,
C. Cockburn.

15. From 2 October 1747, Cockburn to Dr. Thomas Sharp

Rev. Sir,
I hope you will excuse my keeping the MS. so long, which you favoured me with. I was desirous to accompany it with some thoughts of mine upon it, which I have not been able to do sooner.

I make no doubt, Sir, that the term *foundation*, as it is figuratively used, may have different significations, when applied to different things; but you will think me very tenacious of my opinion, when I say, that I still think most writers mean by it the ground, on which that, which they apply it to, stands, or from which it arises; nor do I think, that their different applications of it is any just ground of suspicion, that they do not agree in their idea of it. For my own case in particular, I am pretty sure I have the same idea of it, and use it in the same sense, when I apply it to *virtue* and *obligation*; and though I say of one, that it arises *solely* from the nature of things, and of the other, that it may arise from *several grounds*, this I apprehend to make no difference in the sense of the term *foundation*, when applied to both; but only to express a difference in the nature of things, to which I apply it, to express my opinion, that it is of the nature of virtue in the abstract, to arise from no other foundation than that which I have assigned it; but that obligation, though arising from the same foundation, may, by the nature of it, arise likewise from several other grounds, all equally foundations in the very same sense, as *grounds on which it arises*; for I cannot see, that assigning one or more foundations to a thing makes any difference in the sense of the term.

Then, Sir, as to the difference between Mr. *Warburton* and me, you know he allows, that virtue is founded on the essential difference, nature, *&c* of things; and yet he maintains, that nothing but *will*, or the law of a superior, can constitute the morality of actions. I on the other hand assert, that acting agreeably to the essential difference, nature, and fitness of things, is *moral virtue*; and that the free choice of an agent, judging his action to be right or wrong, though without reference to any will, *properly constitutes the morality of it*. Here are, I think, included three of the logical divisions of causes, *viz. the material, the formal, and the efficient*: But how the use of those terms, or any explanation of foundation can help to adjust this difference of sentiments, I confess I do not see. [...]

Sir, Your obliged humble servant,
C. Cockburn.

Select Bibliography

Selected Primary Sources: Catharine Trotter Cockburn

Collected Works

The Works of Mrs. Catharine Cockburn, Theological, Moral, Dramatic, and Poetical. Several of them now first printed. Revised and published, with an account of the life of the author, by Thomas Birch. M.A. F.R.S. Rector of the United Parishes of St. Margaret Pattens, and St. Gabriel Fenchurch. 2 vols. London: printed for J. and P. Knapton, 1751. (Reprinted, London: Routledge/Thoemmes, 1992.)

Philosophical Works

A Defence of the Essay of Human Understanding, Written by Mr. Lock. Wherein its Principles with reference to Morality, Revealed Religion, and the Immortality of the Soul, are Consider'd and Justify'd: In answer to some Remarks on that Essay. London: Printed for Will Turner and John Nutt, 1702. (Reprinted in *The Works*, Volume I, p. 44–111.)
Remarks upon some Writers in the Controversy concerning the Foundation of Moral Virtue, and Moral Obligation; Particularly the Translator of Archbishop King's Origin of Evil, and the Author of the Divine Legation of Moses. To which are prefixed some Cursory Thoughts on the Controversies concerning necessary Existence, The Reality and Infinity of Space, The Extension and Place of Spirits, and on Dr. Watts's Notion of Substance. In *The History of the Works of the Learned.* London: Printed for T. Cooper, 1743. (Reprinted in *The Works*, Volume I, p. 380–450.)
Remarks upon the Principles and Reasonings of Dr. Rutherforth's Essay on the Nature and Obligations of Virtue: in Vindication of the contrary Principles and Reasonings, enforced in the Writings of the late Dr. Samuel Clarke. London: Printed for J. and P. Knapton, 1747. (Reprinted in *The Works*, Vol. II, p. 1–107.)

Theological Works

A discourse concerning a Guide in controversies, in two letters. Written to one of the Church of Rome, by a person lately converted

from that communion. London: printed for A. and J. Churchill, 1707. (Reprinted in *The Works,* Vol. I, p. 1–42.)
A discourse concerning a Guide in controversies, in two letters. Written to one of the Church of Rome, by a person lately converted from that communion. 2nd edn. Edinburgh: 1728.
A letter to Dr. Holdsworth, occasioned by his sermon preached before the University of Oxford: on Easter-Monday, concerning the resurrection of the same body. In which the passages that concern Mr. Lock are chiefly considered. By the author of, A defence of Mr. Lock's Essay of Humane Understanding. London: Printed for Benjamin Motte, 1726. (Reprinted in *The Works,* Vol. I, p. 113–53.)
A Vindication of Mr. Locke's Christian Principles, from the injurious Imputations of Dr. Holdsworth. Part I. Now first Printed. In *The Works of Catharine Trotter Cockburn,* Vol. I. (Reprinted in *The Works,* Vol. I, p. 155–378.)

Plays

Agnes de Castro a tragedy, as it is acted at the Theatre Royal by His Majesty's servants. London: Printed for H. Rhodes, R. Parker, and S. Briscoe, 1696.
Fatal friendship a tragedy, as it is acted at the New-Theatre in Little-Lincolns-Inn-Fields. London: Printed for Francis Saunders, 1698. (Reprinted in *The Works,* Vol. II, p. 461–553.)
Love at a Loss, or, Most Votes carry it. A comedy. As it is now Acted at the Theatre Royal in Drury Lane, by His Majesty's Servants. London: Printed for William Turner, 1701.
The Revolution of Sweden. A Tragedy. As it is Acted at the Queens Theatre In The Hay-Market. London: James Knapton and George Strahan, 1706.
The Unhappy Penitent: A Tragedy. As it is Acted, At the Theatre Royal in Drury Lane, by his Majesty's Servants. London: Printed for William Turner and John Nutt, 1701.

Selected Anthologies: Early Modern Moral Philosophers

Atherton, Margaret, ed. *Women Philosophers of the Early Modern Period.* Indianapolis: Hackett, 1994.
Raphael, D.D., ed. *British Moralists: 1650–1800.* Oxford: Clarendon, 1969.
Schneewind, J.B., ed. *Moral philosophy from Montaigne to Kant: An Anthology.* Cambridge: Cambridge UP, 1990.

Selby-Bigge, L.A. *British Moralists, Being Selections from Writers Principally of the Eighteenth Century.* Reprinted with a new introduction by Bernard H. Baumrin. Indianapolis: Bobbs-Merrill, 1964.

Warnock, Mary, ed. *Women Philosophers.* London: J.M. Dent, 1996.

Secondary Sources: Suggested Reading

Selected Works on Early Modern Women

Anderson, Bonnie and Judith Zinsser. *A History of their Own: Women in Europe from Prehistory to the Present.* 2 vols. New York: Oxford UP, 2000.

Bell, Maureen. *A Biographical Dictionary of English Women Writers, 1580–1720.* New York: Harvester Wheatsheaf, 1990.

Broad, Jacqueline. *Women Philosophers of the Seventeenth Century.* Cambridge: Cambridge UP, 2003.

Ferguson, Moira. *First Feminists: British Women Writers, 1578–1799.* Bloomington: Indiana UP, 1985.

Fraser, Antonia. *The Weaker Vessel: Woman's Lot in Seventeenth-Century England.* London: Mandarin, 1989.

Kelley, Anne. *Catharine Trotter: An Early Modern Writer in the Vanguard of Feminism.* Hampshire, England: Ashgate, 2002.

McAlister, Linda Lopez. *Hypatia's Daughters: Fifteen Hundred Years of Women Philosophers.* Bloomington: Indiana UP, 1996.

Smith, Hilda L. *Reason's Disciples: Seventeenth-Century English Feminists.* Urbana: U of Illinois P, 1982.

———. *Women Writers and the Early Modern British Political Tradition.* Cambridge: Cambridge UP, 1998.

Tougas, Cecile T. and Sara Ebenreck. *Presenting Women Philosophers.* Philadelphia: Temple UP, 2000.

Waithe, Mary Ellen, ed. *A History of Women Philosophers: Modern Women Philosophers, 1600–1900.* Volume 3. Dordrecht: Kluwer, 1991.

Selected Works on Enlightenment Philosophers

Aaron, Richard I. *John Locke.* Oxford: Clarendon, 1971.

Cassirer, Ernst. *The Philosophy of the Enlightenment.* Princeton: Princeton UP, 1951.

Chappell, Vere, ed. *The Cambridge Companion to Locke.* Cambridge: Cambridge UP, 1994.

Darwall, Stephen. *The British Moralists and the Internal "Ought": 1640–1740.* Cambridge: Cambridge UP, 1995.
Garber, Daniel and Michael Ayers, eds. *The Cambridge History of Seventeenth-Century Philosophy.* Vols. I and II. Cambridge: Cambridge UP, 1998.
Pyle, Andrew. *The Dictionary of Seventeenth-Century British Philosophers.* Bristol: Thoemmes Press, 2000.
Redwood, John. *Reason, Ridicule and Religion: The Age of Enlightenment in England 1660–1750.* London: Thames & Hudson, 1976.
Schneewind, J.B. *The Invention of Autonomy.* Cambridge: Cambridge UP, 1998.
Stephen, Sir Leslie. *History of English Thought in the Eighteenth Century.* 2 Vols. New York: Peter Smith, 1949.
Willey, Basil. *The Eighteenth-Century Background: Studies on the Idea of Nature in the Thought of the Period.* New York: Columbia UP, 1961.
———. *The English Moralists.* London: Chatto & Windus, 1964.
———. *The Seventeenth-Century Background: Studies in the Thought of the Age in Relation to Poetry and Religion.* London: Ark Paperbacks, 1986.
Wolterstorff, Nicholas. *John Locke: An Ethics of Belief.* Cambridge: Cambridge UP, 1996.
Yolton, John W. *The Dictionary of Eighteenth-Century British Philosophers.* Bristol: Thoemmes Press, 1999.

Index

abstract ideas, 50, 105, 131–35, 144, 243
Addison, Joseph, 97
"Age of Reason," 9
Agnes de Castro (Cockburn), 13
agreeable or repugnant to nature. *See* fitness
Antoniano, Silvio, *Dell'educazione cristiana dei figliuoli*, 10
Aristotle, 84, 205n1
association of ideas, 113, 123, 149, 236, 239, 243
Atheists, 137–38, 140, 142–43, 168, 180, 244

Bacon, Francis, 9
Balguy, John, 129, 150, 243
  Divine Rectitude, 228
  Essay on Redemption, 232
Baxter, Andrew, *Enquiry into the nature of the human soul*, 103
Bayle, Pierre, 96n2, 137, 148
benevolence, 22, 25, 113, 124, 236–37
  disinterested, 113, 126, 152, 159, 169, 204, 221, 239
benevolent affections. *See* benevolence; disinterested affections
Berkeley, George, 95
Birch, Thomas, 15–16
  Works of Mrs. Catharine Cockburn, The, 12n1, 31
Bolton, Martha Brandt, "Philosophical Work of Catharine Trotter Cockburn, The," 26
Bonum Utile / Bonum Honestum distinction, 47–48
Broad, Jacqueline, *Women Philosophers of the Seventeenth Century*, 26
Burnet, Elizabeth, 11n2
Burnet, Thomas, 38–39, 49, 52, 56, 58, 229
  intuitionism, 23
  Remarks upon an Essay concerning Humane Understanding, 13, 37n1, 41, 50–51, 53–54, 57, 60, 62, 66, 80
  Second Remarks upon an Essay concerning Humane Understanding, 13, 37n1, 40–43, 45–48, 51, 55, 57, 59–62, 65, 80–81
  Third Remarks upon an Essay concerning Humane Understanding, 13, 37n1, 40, 63, 70–72, 74–76, 78–84
Burnet, Thomas (of Kenmay), 13
  letters to, 14n1, 225–27
Butler, Joseph, 153n, 233, 235–37, 240

Cartesian dualism, 27
Catharine Trotter Cockburn (Kelley), 27
"Catharine Trotter Cockburn" (Waithe), 26
Characteristics of men (Shaftesbury), 218
choice. *See* freedom of choice
Christianity, 231–33, 236
Christianity as old as the Creation (Tindal), 127, 229
Cicero, 84
Clarke, Samuel, 15, 25–26, 111, 116–18, 126, 128, 143, 228, 232, 244, 247, 252–54, 256
  Demonstration of the Being and Attributes of God, 20, 91, 93, 199
  Discourse concerning the Unchangeable Obligations of Natural Religion, 20
  Rutherforth's criticism of, 147
  on space, 97, 104–05
  theory of fitness, 20–21, 23–24, 106–09, 175
  on virtue, 130, 150, 177, 193
  on will of God, 115, 121
Cockburn, Catharine Trotter, 9

PHILOSOPHICAL WRITINGS   263

Agnes de Castro, 13
anonymous publications, 13–14
biographical background, 12
chronology, 29
correspondence, 225–57
critical approaches to, 25–27
Defence of Mr. Locke's Essay of Human Understanding, 13, 22, 26, 226
Fatal Friendship, 13
Letter to Dr. Holdsworth, A, 15
marriage, 14–15
plays, 11, 13–14
Remarks upon Dr. Rutherforth's Essay, 25, 87n3, 230n1, 234, 236–38, 243–44, 253
Remarks upon some Writers, 15, 24
Revolution of Sweden, The, 14
social and intellectual climate, 11, 16, 225
Vindication of Mr. Locke's Principles (unpublished), 15
Cockburn, Patrick, 14–15
common sense, 151, 209
conscience. *See* moral sense; natural conscience
consciousness, 55–56
Cudworth, Ralph, 131

Defence of Mr. Locke's Essay of Human Understanding (Cockburn), 13, 22, 26, 226
Deism, 80–82, 84, 87n3, 126–27, 147n1, 230
Dell'educazione cristiana dei figliuoli (Antoniano), 10
Demonstration of the Being and Attributes of God (Clarke), 20, 91, 93
Descartes, René, 9
Dictionary of National Biography (Stephen), 26
difference, moral, 131, 138–39. *See also* essential differences
difference of persons (in divine nature), 91
Discourse concerning the Unchangeable Obligations of Natural Religion (Clarke), 20
disinterested affections, 113–14, 117, 124–25, 158, 162–63, 204
appearance of, 123

gratitude as, 164–65
parental, 124–25, 159, 236
disinterested attachment, 168
disinterested benevolence, 113, 126, 152, 159, 169, 204, 221, 239
disinterestedness, 166–67, 236
divine immensity, 105
Divine Legation of Moses (Warburton), 87n3, 137–43, 147, 230
divine natural law. *See* natural law
Divine Rectitude (Balguy), 228
divine will, 24, 69, 134, 246–47. *See also* will of God
Du Chatelet, Marie, 10
duty. *See also* moral obligation; obligation
ignorance of, 18
positive, 138
self-duties, 155, 237

early modern period, 9, 18
empiricism, 173n1, 241n1
Enlightenment, 9, 17
Enquiry into the Nature of the Human Soul (Baxter), 103
Epicurism, 134
error of the Stoics, 130
Essay Concerning Human Understanding (Locke), 13, 19, 35–85, 101, 103, 236
Essay on Moral Obligation (Johnson), 116–31
Essay on Redemption (Balguy), 232
Essay on the Nature and Conduct of the Passions and Affections (Hutcheson), 21
Essay on the Nature and Obligations of Virtue (Rutherforth), 15, 147n1–223
Essay on the Origin of Evil (King), 87n2, 91–95, 104, 106, 110–15, 123, 230, 232
Essays on the Law of Nature (Locke), 19
essence, 105
essential differences, 47n, 112, 120, 133, 135, 137–39, 142, 170, 172–203, 209, 236, 246, 248–50, 256. *See also* fitness; nature of things
eternal mind, 131

Eternal Obligation of Natural Religion, The (Johnston), 131–36
evil. *See* good and evil
example of God. *See* God's example
extension and place. *See under* soul
external motives, 179, 219

Fable of the Bees (Mandeville), 156
faith (as virtue), 233
The Fall, 220
Farquhar, George, *Love in a Bottle*, 13
Fatal Friendship (Cockburn), 13
feminism, 26
final good, 207
fitness, 47n, 106–21, 127–29, 139, 147, 180, 182, 197, 199, 248, 253, 255
   Clarke's theory of, 20, 22, 147n1
   consciousness of, 220–21
   disinterested benevolence and, 152, 154
   of harmony, 129
   to honour and obey benevolent creator, 142, 194–95
   moral fitness, 23–25, 106, 130, 237n1
   obligation arising from, 141, 150, 177
   and relation of things, 184, 187, 189, 191–92, 197, 199, 211–12, 234
foundation, 249–52, 256–57
   of moral obligation, 106–15, 137, 157, 169–70, 235, 246, 249–50, 255
   of moral virtue, 246, 248, 251
free agents, 85, 135, 138–39, 141, 143, 171, 248
free will, 250
freedom of choice, 92, 140, 173, 175
friendship (disinterested), 166
future state, 52, 68, 176–77, 179. *See also* rewards and punishments
happiness in, 219

Gassendi, Pierre, 96n2, 97
Gentiles, 207–08
God, 145, 147, 256

chief design of, 217
as free agent, 240
goodness, 198, 201–03, 211–12, 218 (*See also* perfection)
imitation of (See God's example)
natural attributes of, 199
nature of, 241
necessity of existence, 89, 91–95
promises, 222
role in morality, 19
unity of, 91
God's example, 192–93, 197–203, 218, 222
God's laws. *See* laws; sanctions
God's veracity, 23, 48–52
God's will. *See* will of God
good and evil, 40, 70–72
   essential difference, 111–12, 120, 133
   final good, 207
   greatest good, 208
   natural good and evil, 24, 42–48, 108, 120
goodness of God, 198, 201–03, 211–12, 218
gratitude, 164–66, 189–92
Grotius, Hugo, 44n1
ground. *See* foundation

happiness, 24, 44, 48, 108, 118–19, 145–46, 162, 181–82, 206–08, 214
   from disinterested benevolence, 159
   perfection and, 131, 136
   private happiness, 112–13, 115, 125, 149, 179, 203–05, 216
   promise of, 219
   from reverence to creator, 106
Hartley, David, 243
Heathens, 112, 214, 222–23
hedonism, 147n1
Hepburn, Anne
   letters to, 228–42
History of the Works of the Learned, The, 15, 232
History of Western Philosophy (Russel), 9
Hobbes, Thomas, 80n, 173, 186, 217, 241
   Leviathan, 18
Holdsworth, Winch, 15

Hubert, Marie, *World Unmasked*, 231
human nature, 24–25, 43–46, 241. *See also* nature
human reason. *See* reason
Hutcheson, Francis, 22, 113, 157n2, 158, 238, 243
  Essay on the Nature and Conduct of the Passions and Affections, 21
  Inquiry into the Original of our Ideas of Beauty and Virtue, 21
  "moral sense" theory, 21
  rejection of rationalism in morality, 22

ideas, 97
  abstract, 50, 131–35, 144, 243
  association of, 113, 123, 149, 236, 239, 243
  Locke's view of, 20
  of substance, 102–03
  of virtue, 251
identity and diversity, 55, 82–84
imitation of God. *See* God's example
immateriality of the soul, 63–64, 66–67, 69, 80, 83, 103
immortality of the soul, 23, 38, 53–69, 81, 84, 103
immutable nature of things, 89, 91, 117, 133, 136, 246–47, 250, 252, 254. *See also* essential differences
infinitude of space, 24n1, 104
innatism, 18, 59, 70–79, 116–18
Inquiry Concerning Virtue, An (Shaftesbury), 167
Inquiry into the Original of our Ideas of Beauty and Virtue (Hutcheson), 21
instinct, 109, 113, 116–17, 147, 157, 169–70, 184, 213, 234, 236, 238–39
interested scheme (hedonism), 183, 186–87, 217, 240
  private interest, 158
  self-interest, 117, 126, 144, 245, 249
internal principles (*vs.* external motives), 179, 221–22
"internal sense." *See* moral sense
intuitionism, 23

Johnson, Thomas, *Essay on Moral Obligation*, 116–31
Johnston, George, *Eternal Obligation of Natural Religion*, 131–36

Kelley, Anne, *Catharine Trotter Cockburn*, 27
King, William, 100, 105
  Essay on the Origin of Evil, 87n2, 89, 91–95, 104, 106, 110–15, 123, 230, 232

Law, Edmund, 89, 91–94, 105, 123, 242n1
  on foundation of moral virtue, 106–15, 121
  Locke's philosophy and, 87n1
  on moral obligation, 118, 121
  on space, 95–97, 100, 104
laws, 47n, 114, 127–28, 210, 216, 246, 254
  law of Moses, 219
  law of virtue, 210
  natural law, 17–20, 43–45
    as product of God's will, 24, 87n1, 170
  of a superior, 139
Leibniz, G. W., 110, 226
Letter to Dr. Holdsworth (Cockburn), 15
Leviathan (Hobbes), 18, 217
liberalism, 9, 18
"Life of Mrs. Cockburn, The" (Birch), 12n1
Locke, John, 9, 21–23, 26, 97, 99, 102, 104–05, 123, 226, 233, 240–42
  death, 227
  Essay Concerning Human Understanding, 13, 19, 35–85, 101, 103, 236
  Essays on the Law of Nature, 19
  Ideas, 20
  "mixed modes," 20
  moral philosophy, 19–20
  on reality of space, 95
  Reply to the Bishop of Worcester, 65, 81n
  response to Catharine Trotter, 14
  Two Treatises on Government, 18
Love in a Bottle (Farquhar), 13

Mandeville, Bernard, *Fable of the Bees*, 156n1
Manicheism, 80n, 134, 194–95
Masham, Damarais, Lady, 227
Materialists, 80
mathematics, 18–19, 42, 104
matter, 95–96, 101–03, 250
"mixed modes," 20
Mole, Thomas, 131n1
moral agents, 145, 216, 248, 250. *See also* free agents
moral beliefs (universality of), 17
moral choice, 140. *See also* free agents; freedom of choice
moral difference, 131, 138–39. *See also* essential differences
moral epistemology, 23
moral fitness, 24, 106, 237n1. *See also* fitness
    Cockburn's account of, 23, 25
moral good, 43, 108
moral goodness, 156, 158
moral knowledge, 18–19, 24
moral laws. *See* laws
moral obligation, 24–25, 46n, 89, 115
    Essay on Moral Obligation (Johnson), 116–31
    foundation of, 106–15, 137, 157, 169–70, 235, 246, 249–50, 255
    from reason and nature of things, 136, 175, 219
    solely on will of God, 143–44, 147
moral reasoning. *See* reason
moral rules. *See* laws; rules of action
moral sense, 21–23, 109, 113–14, 116–17, 122, 137, 147, 157, 169, 171, 234–36, 243, 246, 255
    as blind instinct, 238
"moral sense" or "sentimentalist" school of thought, 232n3
moral truths, 64
    as innate, 18
moral virtue, 89, 122, 146–47, 156, 234, 245
    foundation of, 106–15, 121, 246, 251
morality
    foundation of, 38, 40, 137
    metaphysical theories of, 21
    science of, 18

Mosaic history of the fall, 220–21

natural and essential differences. *See* essential differences
natural conscience, 62, 69–79. *See also* moral sense
    Burnet's understanding of, 70
natural disinterested benevolence. *See* disinterested benevolence
natural fitness. *See* fitness
natural good and evil, 24, 43–44, 108, 120
natural instinct. *See* instinct
natural law, 17–19, 43–45
natural religion, 75, 77, 79, 91, 209
    Locke's account of, 70
natural and revealed religion, 52
nature of God, 241
nature of man. *See* human nature
nature of things, 18, 34, 47n, 92, 137, 146, 148, 169, 187, 199, 215, 236
    immutable, 89, 91, 117, 133, 136, 246–47, 250, 252, 254
    necessary relation of things, 107, 115, 121–22, 133, 246
necessity, 24n1
necessity of existence, 89, 91–95
negative infinity, 104–05
Newton, Isaac, 9
Norris, John, 131
    Reason and Religion, 49n

obedience to God's will. *See* will of God
objectivity, 9
obligation, 109, 126, 135, 139–41, 246, 253. *See also* moral obligation
    meaning of term, 252
    subsequent to creation, 255
outcomes (utilitarian), 22

pain, 24–25, 145n1, 147n1, 180–82, 185–87
perfection, 17, 43, 45, 49–52, 79, 91–94, 104, 135, 146, 181, 196–97, 200, 206, 221, 244
    happiness and, 131, 136
Peripatetics, 205, 208
permanent substance. *See under* substance

personal identity. *See* identity and diversity
Phil-orthos. *See* Johnston, George
Philosophical Essays on Various Subjects (Watts), 87n4
"Philosophical Work of Catharine Trotter Cockburn, The" (Bolton), 26
piety and virtue, 155–56
false notions of, 168–69
place, 60–61, 89, 99
pleasure, 25, 147n1. *See also* happiness; outcomes
Pope, Alexander, 146n1, 166
positive duties, 138
positive infinity to space, 104
practical morality, 147–48
private happiness, 112, 115, 125, 149, 203–05, 216. *See also* self-interest
private interest, 158

Quinta Essentia, 84

rational agents, 130, 184, 188–89, 246
reason, 246
Clarke's theory of, 21–22
ideals of, 9
in moral agents, 250
and nature of things, 219, 253, 255
as route to moral knowledge, 18–20
Reason and Religion (Norris), 49n
reasonable beings. *See* rational agents
reflection, 41, 50, 52
Locke's view of, 23
Remarks upon an Essay concerning Humane Understanding (Burnet), 13, 37n1, 41, 50–51, 53–54, 57, 60, 62, 66, 80
Remarks upon Dr. Rutherforth's Essay (Cockburn), 25, 87n3, 230n1, 234, 236–38, 243–44, 253
Remarks upon some Writers (Cockburn), 15, 24
resurrection, 82, 84
revelation, 19, 65, 128, 149–50, 209, 219, 230

reverence, 106–07
Revolution of Sweden, The (Cockburn), 14
rewards and punishments, 24, 46–47, 62, 68–69, 80, 108, 131, 142, 170, 177–78, 201, 217, 221, 235, 254. *See also* sanctions; self-interest
obligation from, 87n2, 114, 122, 135–36, 144–45, 170, 180, 235
Rousseau, Jean-Jacques, 9
on intellectual women, 10
rules of action, 70, 127, 148, 198, 246. *See also* laws
Russell, Bertrand, *History of Western Philosophy*, 9
Rutherforth, Thomas
definition of virtue, 237
Essay on the Nature and Obligations of Virtue, 15, 147n1–223
view of moral obligation, 25

sanctions, 21, 25, 109, 117, 142, 170–71, 178, 180, 219, 230, 235. *See also* laws; rewards and punishments; will of God
scientific method, 9
Scientific Revolution, 9, 16
Second Remarks upon an Essay concerning Humane Understanding (Burnet), 13, 37n1, 40–43, 45–48, 51, 55, 57, 59–62, 65, 80–81
self-duties, 155, 237
self-interest, 117, 126, 144, 245, 249. *See also* private happiness
self-love, 117, 158–60, 236–37, 239, 245, 249
selfishness, 158
sensation, 23, 40, 71
and reflection, 41, 50, 52
sensible being, 119–20, 130, 181–82, 188, 205, 211, 213, 217
sensory appreciation of moral phenomenon. *See* moral sense
sensualist, 152–53
Shaftesbury, Anthony Ashley Cooper, Earl of, 232, 235–36, 240–41
Characteristics of men, 218
Inquiry Concerning Virtue, An, 167

Sharp, Thomas, 156
  letters to, 245–57
Smith, Adam, 11
social and intellectual climate, 11, 16, 225
soul, 98. *See also* spirits
  as distinct permanent substance, 81, 83–85, 100 (*See also* substance)
  Enquiry into the Nature of the Human Soul (Baxter), 103
  extension and place, 60–61, 89, 99
  immateriality of the, 63–64, 66–67, 69, 80, 83, 103
  immortality of the, 23, 38, 53–69, 81, 84, 103
sovereign good, 208
space, 104–05, 250
  reality of, 89, 95–98, 100
Spinoza, Benedictus de, 92, 244n1
spirits. *See also* soul
  nature and existence of, 24n1
spiritual causation, 17
Stephen, Leslie, *Dictionary of National Biography*, 26
Stoicism, 130n1, 220
  error of the Stoics, 130
substance, 24n1, 55–56, 81, 83–85, 95, 98–103
  Cartesian theory of, 27
  nature of, 89
  permanent, 57, 60–61
suffering virtue, 215
superior will, 135

thinking, power of, 103
Third Remarks upon an Essay concerning Humane Understanding (Burnet), 13, 37n1, 40, 63, 70–72, 74–76, 78–84
Tindal, Matthew, *Christianity as old as the Creation*, 127, 229
Toland, John, 226
toleration, 9
truth (moral truths), 42
Turner, Daniel, 109
Two Treatises on Government (Locke), 18

unbelief (as vice), 233

unity of God, 91
universal, 103
universal natures, 131
universality of moral beliefs, 17

vices, 40, 43, 191, 217, 241
  as prosperous, 215
Vindication of Mr. Locke's Principles (Cockburn), 15
virtue, 25, 40, 43, 113–14, 130–31, 137, 143, 228–29
  abstract nature of, 250–51
  Cockburn's definition, 252
  disinterested, 166
  and duty, 193, 208
  Essay of the Nature and Obligations of Virtue (Rutherforth), 147–223
  eternal and unalterable nature of, 241
  foundations of, 106, 117, 157, 234, 236, 249–51
  greatest good, 205, 208
  natural duty of mankind, 177
  necessary to happiness, 218
  of obeying the will of God, 211, 245
  obligation to, 112, 115–16, 150, 171, 189
  and will of God, 121, 127, 143

Waithe, Mary Ellen, "Catharine Trotter Cockburn," 26
Warburton, William, 109, 147n1, 174n1, 209, 246–47, 257
  Divine Legation of Moses, 230
Warburton, William, *Divine Legation of Moses Demonstrated*, 87n3, 137–43, 147
Waterland, Daniel, 107, 247
Watts, Isaac, 95–96, 98–102
  Philosophical Essays on Various Subjects, 87n4
will of God, 43–44, 46–47, 127, 245–49
  as eternal rules of justice, 196–98
  as foundation of moral obligation, 142–44, 146–48
  as foundation of moral virtue, 107, 109–15, 117, 120–22, 127
  infinite wisdom of, 199
  laws expressing, 24

moral laws as, 87n1
obedience to, 47, 70, 114, 145, 180, 195–96, 202, 217, 219–22, 245, 248
sanctions and, 176, 178–80, 209–10, 214, 217, 230
as sole foundation of morality, 148, 230
women, 225–26
education, 10

Women Philosophers of the Seventeenth Century (Broad), 26
women's education, 11, 227
Works of Mrs. Catharine Cockburn, The (Birch), 31
World Unmasked (Hubert), 231
Wright, Samuel S., *Remarks on a sermon*, 131

Yolton, John, 87n4